W9-BGD-914

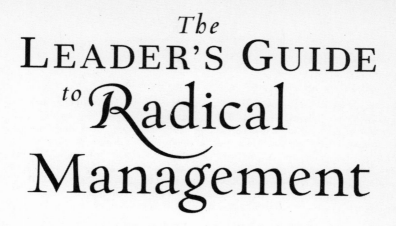

The LEADER'S GUIDE *to* Radical Management

REINVENTING *the* WORKPLACE *for the* 21ST CENTURY

STEPHEN DENNING

JOSSEY-BASS
A Wiley Imprint
www.josseybass.com

Published by Jossey-Bass
A Wiley Imprint
989 Market Street, San Francisco, CA 94103-1741 www.josseybass.com

Jossey-Bass books and products are available through most bookstores. To contact Jossey-Bass directly call our Customer Care Department within the U.S. at 800-956-7739, outside the U.S. at 317-572-3986, or fax 317-572-4002.

Jossey-Bass also publishes its books in a variety of electronic formats. Some content that appears in print may not be available in electronic books.

Library of Congress Cataloging-in-Publication Data

Denning, Stephen.
The leader's guide to radical management : reinventing the workplace for the 21st century / Stephen Denning.
p. cm.
Includes bibliographical references and index.
ISBN 978-0-470-54868-4 (cloth); ISBN 978-0-470-65102-5 (ebk); ISBN 978-0-470-65135-3 (ebk); ISBN 978-0-470-65136-0 (ebk)
1. Organizational change. 2. Creative ability in business. 3. Management. I. Title.
HD58.8.D457 2010
658.4—dc22

2010021298

Printed in the United States of America
FIRST EDITION
HB Printing 10 9 8 7 6 5 4 3

CONTENTS

PREFACE

> "Remarkably, the return on assets for U.S. firms has steadily fallen to almost one quarter of 1965 levels . . . very few [workers] (20 percent) are passionate about their jobs . . . executive turnover is increasing. Consumers are becoming less loyal to brands . . . the rate at which big companies lose their leadership positions is increasing."
>
> **Deloitte Center for the Edge[1]**

Total Attorneys is a rapidly growing Chicago-based company that provides services and software to small law firms. As a start-up in 2002, it was highly energized: work was done on the fly, new products were developed, new markets opened, and new customers were identified. But as the firm grew, so did bureaucracy. Departments were formed, processes and structures were put in place, work slowed down, and the staff morale deteriorated. In some cases, Total Attorneys moved so slowly that by the time its software was completed, the client wanted something different. By 2008, with around 160 employees, Total Attorneys was still making money, but it had gone from being an exciting place to work to a bureaucratic logjam.

Up to this point, Total Attorneys was a depressingly familiar story. But Total Attorney's CEO, Ed Scanlan, began asking himself: "Why were we able to get more done in forty-five days with three guys than I had just accomplished in the last six months with several departments? Why are our tires stuck in the mud?"

So Scanlan decided to change the story and recapture some of the start-up energy and excitement. He replaced departmental silos with small cross-functional teams that themselves decided how to do the work and even how much work to do. The teams began working in cycles, implementing a prioritized series of tasks that reflected what clients wanted to see developed. At the end of each cycle, the work was demonstrated to clients, and their feedback was incorporated in the next cycle. In this way, the work was always focused on tasks of high priority to clients.

Scanlan started the approach with the software developers, but it was so successful there that he soon extended it to the call centers. For instance, the eighty-five call center employees were divided into fifteen teams and colocated on the same floor as the software developers to enhance direct communication.

More recently, the approach has spread spontaneously to sales, marketing, accounting and the general counsel's office. Now the whole firm is buzzing with energy and excitement and laughter again.

"This way of managing appeals particularly to the new generation," says Scanlan. "They want autonomy. They want ownership. They want purpose. It makes sense to them. But it also resonates with older workers."

Many firms are now discovering what Total Attorneys discovered: that a revolutionary way of organizing and managing work is emerging that can generate continuous innovation, deep job satisfaction, and client delight. It is very different from the practices of traditional management: hierarchy, command and control, tightly planned work, competition through economies of scale and cost reduction, and impersonal communications.

Traditional management practices, which continue to be taught in business schools and described in management textbooks, worked well enough for much of the twentieth century but are a poor fit for today's economic context.

The signs of the misfit are widespread. The rate of return on assets keeps on its decades-long decline. Innovation continues to falter. Workers are disgruntled. Customers are frustrated. Brands are unraveling. Reorganizations, downsizings, and outsourcings proliferate. Executive turnover is accelerating. Institutional life expectancies are less than two decades. In the past twenty-five years, start-ups created 40 million jobs in the United States, while established firms created almost none.[2]

Early in 2008, I set out to understand the source of these problems and to discover what could be done about them. This book tells the story of that journey.

There must be workplaces, I thought, where work is highly productive, new ideas are embraced, and jobs are deeply satisfying. Could the conditions that had enabled that to happen be identified? Could those conditions be reverse-engineered? Is it possible to create an environment that was congenial to ideas that are vibrant, exciting, or different, in a sustained way, not just in isolated cases?

I began by asking people if they knew about any such workplaces. My expectation was that finding them would be difficult—like searching for a needle in a haystack. Few people would know about them, I thought, let alone have personal experience of them.

My first surprise was that I had no difficulty at all in finding them. In fact, almost everyone I talked to could tell me about an experience that they had, although typically it wasn't in their current workplace.

The second surprise came when I noticed that an unusually high proportion of these extraordinary experiences had been in software development. Initially I didn't pay this any attention. After all, these were geeks, and they talked with a strange vocabulary. What could I possibly learn about management from people who had, I imagined, gone into computing because they preferred machines to people?

My third surprise was what was going on in these companies. When I checked it out, I discovered a way of managing that was much more productive than traditional management and where the people doing the work were having serious fun.[3]

The fourth surprise was that it wasn't limited to software development. Once this different way of managing got under way in one part of the company, it tended to spread to other parts of the company, even the entire firm. It was also widespread in some parts of auto manufacture and in successful start-ups. In fact, once I understood the principles, I started to see signs of it in many different sectors.

The final big surprise was that when I joined the dots and fully understood the elements, I realized that what I had stumbled on was more than a management technique. The idea was larger, with far-reaching economic, social, and ethical implications.

Overall, this was very different from the way most companies are currently run. As Mikkel Harbo, director of business development and operations at the Danish company Systematic Software told me, "Once you introduce this, it affects everything in the organization—the way you plan, the way you manage, the way you work. Everything is different. It changes the game fundamentally."

It is for this reason that I call it *radical management.*[4] It goes to the root of what makes things happen in the world. The workplaces that it creates are drastically different from traditional management. It implies fundamental shifts in how we think, speak, and act at work.

In this book, I am inviting you to take the journey that I have taken and learn what I have learned. It will mean spending time to think about what we are doing in organizations today and why. It will entail considering what kinds of organizations we want to create, as well as imagining why and how they could be very different from most organizations today—providing work that is much more productive and much more satisfying.

This book doesn't offer a quick fix, because the nature and scale of the issues that we are dealing with in today's workplaces are not susceptible to a quick fix.

Nor is this a book about what's new, even though that is an eternally intriguing topic. When pursued exclusively, it results in a preoccupation with fads and trivia.

In this book, I am concerned with the questions: What is good? and Whom is it good for? Is it good for the organization? Is it good for those doing the work? Is it good for those for whom the work is done? Is it good for society at large? These are questions that cut deeply. They involve examining: What is true productivity for an organization? What is its source? What is needed to sustain it? What is responsibility? What does it mean to be genuinely authentic? What lifts up the human spirit and makes it sing?

The principles I describe in this book constitute a radical change from the way most organizations are currently managed. Standard managerial practices today systematically lead to organizational underperformance, disgruntled workers, and frustrated customers. Most proposals for reforming management advance one of those elements at the expense of the other two. The principles set out in this book magnify human capacity and simultaneously inspire high productivity, continuous innovation, deep job satisfaction, and client delight.

August 2010
Washington, D.C.

Stephen Denning

INTRODUCTION

> If a factory is torn down but the rationality which produced it is left standing, then that rationality will simply produce another factory.
>
> **Robert Pirsig**[1]

This is a book about a radically different way of managing. It's about pulling apart the black box of traditional management and putting the pieces together in a way that creates continuous innovation and client delight. It involves a wholly different way of thinking, speaking, and acting at work. It leads to workplaces that are more productive and more fun. These workplaces *feel* different.

Given the deep change that has taken place in both the marketplace and the workplace, should we be surprised that we need different management today?

THE MARKETPLACE HAS CHANGED

In the marketplace, what worked yesterday—satisfying customers by offering average products or services with zero defects—is no longer good enough. Absence of defects is expected and lacks luster. Unless clients are delighted, they can—and will—go elsewhere. The bar has been raised.

To ensure long-term growth, firms must forge relationships with their customers and turn them into long-term supporters and advocates of the firm's goods and services. They must continually find new and economical ways to provide goods or services that are differentiated, noteworthy, surprising, or remarkable. They need constant innovation.[2]

Delighting clients goes beyond reconfiguring the marketing department.[3] It means committing the entire organization, and everyone in it, to delighting clients as the firm's principal goal *and* putting in place the management principles and practices needed to accomplish that goal.

THE WORKPLACE HAS ALSO CHANGED

"Management was originally invented," management theorist Gary Hamel has noted, "to solve two problems: the first—getting semiskilled employees to perform repetitive activities competently, diligently, and efficiently; the second—coordinating those efforts in ways that enabled complex goods and services to be produced in large quantities. In a nutshell, the problems were efficiency and scale, and the solution was bureaucracy, with its hierarchical structure, cascading goals, precise role definitions, and elaborate rules and procedures."[4]

With the continuing shift from semiskilled work to what economists call knowledge work, hierarchical bureaucracy is no longer a good solution. Its consequences are well known. It results in the talents, ingenuity, and inspiration of the workforce not being fully tapped. Only one in five workers is fully engaged in his or her work.[5] For the organization, this means that the energies and insights of four out of five people in the workplace are being needlessly squandered. When the firm's future depends on what knowledge workers can contribute, leaving talent unused becomes a serious productivity problem.

For the customers of these organizations, the situation is similarly grim: a firm full of people who are not fully engaged in their work is not much fun to deal with. Although firms talk about customer service and responsiveness, they are more often engaged in one-way communications. The recorded message might say, "Your call is important to us," but customers know that it isn't.

THE SYSTEM IS THE PROBLEM

I argue in this book that the problems of today's workplace are not the personal fault of the individual managers. They are largely the fault of the system they are implementing, which relentlessly constrains the capacity of people to contribute, limits the firm's productivity, and practically guarantees that clients will be dissatisfied. The mental model of management that these companies are pursuing, with interlocking attitudes and practices, methodically prevents any individual management fix from permanently taking hold.

In the chapters ahead, I introduce a very different way of managing. I offer one extraordinary example after another: software developers, car manufacturers, house builders, staff in a call center, and songwriters, among others. And I will show people having serious fun in their work and becoming steadily better at doing it.

The emerging approach to managing is proving to be not only more productive than traditional management. It also liberates the energies, insights, and passions of people. It creates workplaces that enable the human spirit. It delights clients and creates shining eyes among the people doing the work.

This is not about firms becoming more productive by having people work longer hours or by downsizing or outsourcing. It's about deploying energies differently. In some areas, managers have to do more. In other areas, they need to do less. Overall they will have to act on the basis of principles that are quite different from those of today's traditional managers.

THE SEVEN PRINCIPLES OF RADICAL MANAGEMENT

The seven principles I describe form a self-reinforcing sequence (Figure I.1). Radical management begins by getting the goal right: the purpose of work is to delight clients, not merely to produce goods or services or make money for shareholders (Principle #1).

FIGURE I.1 Radical Management: The Seven Basic Principles of Continuous Innovation

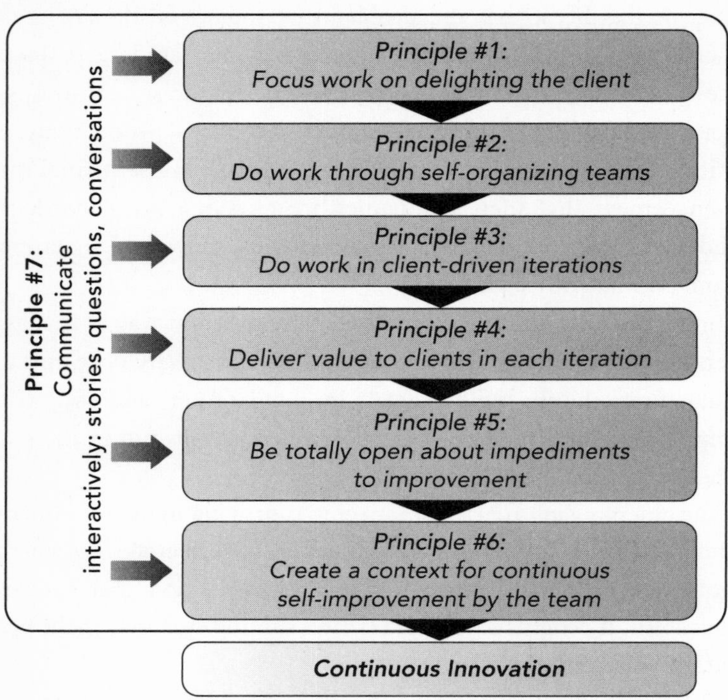

Focusing on client delight leads to self-organizing teams, because client delight requires continuous innovation, and a self-organizing team is the management arrangement most likely to generate continuous innovation (Principle #2).

This leads to working in client-driven iterations, because delighting clients can be approached only by successive approximations. And self-organizing teams, being life forms that live on the edge of chaos, need checkpoints to see whether they are evolving positively or slipping over the edge into chaos (Principle #3).

Similarly, client-driven iterations focus on delivering value to clients by the end of each iteration. They force closure and enable frequent client feedback (Principle #4).

Self-organizing teams that are working in an iterative fashion both enable and require radical transparency (Principle #5) so that the teams go on improving of their own accord (Principle #6).

An underlying requirement of all of these principles is interactive communication (Principle #7). Unless managers and workers are communicating interactively, using authentic narratives, open-ended questions, and deep listening, rather than treating people as things to be manipulated, none of the other principles work.

When self-organizing teams are set up and supported by implementing these principles, they naturally evolve into high-performance teams that are significantly more productive than the norm and deeply satisfying to workers.

Together the principles constitute a radical shift in the practice of management and an approach that is well adapted to meet the challenges of the twenty-first-century organization.

PRINCIPLES AND PRACTICES

These principles comprise the seven most important elements of radical management. At the end of each chapter, I describe a large number of practices—more than seventy of them in total—that offer some of the ways to go about implementing the principles. Some practices support more than one principle.

The principles are more fundamental than the practices. If you think about the principles enough, you should be able to deduce the practices from them. If you keep the seven principles steadily in mind, you shouldn't go too far wrong.

Thus, in implementation, it's important to focus on the spirit of radical management and not get lost in the fine print. Even if you're not doing all of the seventy-plus practices yet are living the seven principles, that's still radical management. However, if you are doing lots of the practices but not living some of the principles, then you should probably ask yourself whether you still have at least one foot in the land of traditional management.

This is not a book about praising famous firms or the current media darlings. Instead I discuss how ordinary people become extraordinary and how every firm can continuously reinvent itself. Rather than talking about prodigies or celebrities, I describe a way of working that is broadly available to all.

The organizations that I cite in the book have embarked on journeys. They are all at different stages of the journey, and none of them has in any permanent sense "arrived." We will see more than one company that implemented the principles for a period and then lost its way. Implementing the principles requires constant energy and attention.

I rarely use Japanese terms like *kanban* or *kaizan,* although Japanese firms have made an enormous contribution to management thinking and practice. My goal is to communicate certain truths that transcend any particular country or culture.

I also make sparing use of the terminology that is widespread in software development, under the labels of "Agile" and "Scrum," with terms like *scrum-masters, product owners, burndown charts,* and *sprints.* Software developers deserve credit for advancing some of the thinking described in this book to its fullest extent. Their terminologies were deliberately chosen to differentiate this way of developing software from the roles and practices of traditional management.[6] The terminology has been helpful in software development. My goal here is to explain in plain language how the underlying managerial principles and practices have roots in many different fields and apply to all sectors of the economy.

Some critics will say that the principles and practices I describe are not possible, that they embody an unbelievable utopia, or that they have already been tried and shown not to work. They will give a thousand reasons that we have no choice but to keep on managing the way we always have, with stunted productivity, dispirited workers, and frustrated customers.

It would be easier to accept that version of events if scores of organizations were not already practicing the principles of radical management and achieving extraordinary performance.

WHO THIS BOOK IS FOR

This book is intended for:

- Leaders and managers who want to reinvent the workplace and inspire extraordinary productivity, continuous innovation, deep job satisfaction, and client delight—all simultaneously
- Leaders and managers who want to lift their game and create organizations that buzz with extraordinary energy, excitement, innovation, and genuine high performance
- Leaders and managers who want to run established organizations with the energy and innovativeness of a start-up
- Anyone trying to understand how software developers practicing Scrum and Agile or manufacturers implementing lean production achieve extraordinary gains in productivity, and how to apply what they do to general management
- Anyone who wants to make leadership storytelling an integral part of the culture of an organization.

In short, this book is intended for those who wish to enjoy a life filled with passion, excitement, and productivity and create that for others. This is about taking charge of your life and experiencing the spirit and the exhilaration of extraordinary performance.

THE DIFFERENCES BETWEEN TRADITIONAL AND RADICAL MANAGEMENT

The differences between traditional management and radical management are stark. They flow from different goals. They involve different modalities. They have different consequences, as this table shows:

	Traditional Management	**Radical Management**
Goal	The purpose of work is to produce goods or services.	Focus work on delighting the client.
How work is organized	Work is done by individuals reporting to bosses.	Do work through self-organizing teams.
Plan	Work is done in accordance with a comprehensive plan.	Do work in client-driven iterations aimed at continuous innovation.
Measuring progress	As work proceeds, provide progress reports of what is under way.	Deliver value to clients each iteration.
What is communicated	Communications cover what people need to know.	Be totally open about impediments to improvement.
Improvement	Bosses are responsible for productivity.	Create a context for continuous self-improvement by the team itself.
How it is communicated	One-way communication: send people messages, and tell them what to do.	Communicate interactively through stories, questions, and conversations.
Principal focus of competition	Cost reduction: economies of scale, downsizing, outsourcing.	Time: deliver more value to the client sooner.
Consequence	Rates of return on assets steadily decline. Innovation is stunted. Four in five workers are not fully engaged in their jobs. Customers receive average products and services.	Continuous innovation: self-organizing teams normally evolve into high-performance teams, focused on delighting clients, with above-average productivity and deep job satisfaction.

1

MANAGEMENT TODAY

> "Tomorrow's business imperatives lie outside the performance envelope of today's bureaucracy-infused management practices."
>
> **Gary Hamel[1]**

"Can you think of a time in your life when you were in a group where everyone was pulling together and the group was vibrantly alive and extraordinarily productive, when it was all for one and one for all? And after it ended—even long after it ended—you went on having reunions with the other people in the group because the experience had been so meaningful? Can you think of a time like that?" I have asked hundreds of people in many countries and all walks of life these questions, and almost all of them could recall at least one such experience.

It might have been in the workplace, at school, in a community, or in a network. The duration may have been long or brief. Generally the groups they mentioned were small. Sometimes the experience was recent, sometimes a long time ago. Sometimes it was listening to the experiences of others that jogged their own memory. But in the end, almost no one said that they didn't know what I was talking about.

Then I would ask another question: "Are you in such a group right now in your workplace?" The answer to this question was usually very different. Few of them said that they were having such an experience in the workplace at this time.

Why is that? Why is the modern workplace dispiriting for so many of the people who work there?

Why do we see symptoms of management malfunction everywhere? Why is innovation slowing? Why are knowledge workers so disgruntled? Why do most of the so-called reforms of work make things worse, not better? Why is service to customers deteriorating? Why are some firms addicted to "bad profits," that is, profits that are made at the expense of customer satisfaction? Why do repeated crises seem to come from nowhere without warning from those who should have known better?[2]

Why are so many smart people working so hard yet producing results that no one really wants?

To answer these questions, we have to go beyond thinking about management in abstract terms and see what's really going on in today's workplace. When it comes to a subject as vast and controversial as this, I cannot hope to present a comprehensive picture. What I can do is show a couple of narrative snapshots that reveal why I have reached the verdict that I have.

The following five accounts are inspired by actual events, though they do not depict any actual person or firm. It is for you, the reader, to discern to what extent they depict the reality of today's workplaces.

THE ABSTRACT WRITER

When Paul took a job as an editorial assistant for an online publisher, his role was to prepare summaries of business books that executives were too busy to read. The publisher sold the summaries to subscribers, who could view them online.[3]

Paul had recently graduated from college and was happy to have a job after an extended period of job hunting. He saw it as an opportunity to understand publishing and gain an in-depth view of the world of books.

On that first day when he was shown to his cubicle, Paul was optimistic. He now had a place in the world where he could think and make a contribution to the corpus of human knowledge in a real company with actual employees. Despite his skepticism about organizations, Paul went out and bought a suit.

His feelings toward the job changed as he actually experienced the work, which entailed reading each book and completing a table that analyzed the book on seven dimensions. His initial quota was three books per day. After the first six months, his quota was accelerated to four books per day and then, after a year, to five. The pace demanded total concentration yet precluded reflecting on the meaning of what he was reading.

He was not allowed to duplicate the careful summary of the book that the author and the publisher had included on the book's back cover. The fees that his firm was charging required his summary to be different.

Meeting his quota meant suppressing his inclination to think and ignoring any sense of responsibility to the book's author or to eventual subscribers who might be deluded into thinking that his summary reflected the content of the book.

He received no indication that subscribers ever read his summaries. He suspected that they were too busy to read them, just as they were too busy to read the books themselves. But purchasing a subscription for a hefty fee relieved their conscience of the need to read anything. He came to see that keeping his job required setting aside any personal concerns about the value of his work.

Paul worked alone. His only respite from the daily grind consisted of lunches with his fellow workers, who were equally dispirited by the working conditions. They confessed on occasion to committing sabotage or taking drugs to relieve the tedium.

He noted that there was no quality control of the work in the sense of anyone reviewing whether his summary accurately reflected the content of the books he reviewed. His supervisor, Anne, approved his work according to generic standards of grammar and formatting without, as far as he could detect, ever having actually verified the content.

Anne seemed to be a decent person. Yet his efforts to turn her decency into meaning for his own work proved fruitless. Her advice was to keep his head down and get on with the summaries.

Paul had taken the job expecting that he would learn a lot. But learning was incompatible with the pace of work that was imposed.

The firm continued to increase the number of subscribers through sales pitches that made harried executives feel guilty for failing to keep up in their reading. The pitches implied that by subscribing to the service, they would be automatically up to date, in the same way that commercials for exercise machines imply that buying the machine will make you fit. The firm had calibrated the workload and the quality of his output to a level that was just good enough to keep subscribers from abandoning their subscriptions.

It was not that the firm or the executives who ran it were being in any sense greedy or immoral by pushing Paul's production goal to the limit. They were simply playing their role in a system that practically guaranteed that any subscribers who ever tried to get value from the service would be exasperated.

THE AUDITOR

When Alan completed his tenth year with one of the world's top global audit firms, he was relieved to see that he still had job security even if the work was inherently dull.[4]

When he looked back on the ten years of audits he had completed, one job merged into another in his memory. He could recall nothing remarkable—nothing that he could look back on and say that he had made a difference.

He had done his job competently. It was a solid job, which he was at no risk of losing provided that he kept playing the game. He could see his life at the firm stretching ahead for a couple of decades. He would have the chance of advancing up the managerial ladder several rungs. He could write the biography of his entire life right now.

He was conscious of the steadily increasing pressure to get the audits done faster. He wasn't sure where this would lead. He was experienced, and so more was expected of him. He recalled his early days when he had taken pride in spotting problems that needed to be resolved. Now the pressure was to get the job done on schedule or, preferably, ahead of schedule. A good audit was a smooth audit with no complications.

Maintaining consensus and preventing any conflict that might slow the work down was a constant preoccupation. He sometimes felt as though he was walking on eggshells, a feeling accentuated by the sessions on political correctness that he was required to attend.

The work itself was carried out in work groups called teams, but essentially all members of the team handled their part of the work alone. At the team meetings, everyone demonstrated a kind of complaisant affability with fellow team members: keeping off their turf and making sure that they kept off his.

He listened to the CEO talk about the audit function as a critical pillar of the financial system, although this kind of talk had become less frequent since the financial meltdown. He was aware that if he left the firm, someone else would step in and take his place. No one would notice the difference.

The firm purported to take an interest in his mental well-being. He had access to a help hotline, as well as to karaoke competitions to stimulate creativity. He could also compete in an employee-of-the-month program that treated winners with harbor cruises and dinners with the CEO.

He had no difficulty in maintaining the mask of shallow cheerfulness that kept the office running smoothly. He participated in the retreats and played along with the team-building exercises that took place there. It passed the time, and occasionally it was fun. But in the end, it was a game. When he got back to the workplace, there was no discernible change.

When he thought about it, he was puzzled as to why so much time was spent on these efforts at contrived conviviality and so little time on real work.

At the end of a day, Alan was back in his apartment, at a loss. The interactions of the office had kept him on his toes throughout the day.

Now he was drained, but also impatient and restless. He was in no state to do anything as heavy as reading a book. The usual solution was a couple of quick drinks, followed by a police procedural on television.

THE SOFTWARE DEVELOPER

Nathalie, a software developer, is the head of corporate Internet solutions for a major insurance company.[5] When she inherited the software development team, it was facing a typical set of problems—software was late, over budget, and full of bugs. So she set about fixing the problems by introducing practices known as Scrum and Agile. She placed confidence in self-organizing teams that performed work in an iterative fashion, and the team rapidly became more responsive, efficient, and effective. After six months, the team had proved itself increasingly capable of delivering whatever software management wanted.

It gradually became apparent that the real problem wasn't in the team at all. Rather, the organization could not make up its mind what it wanted.

The firm provided a full range of financial services. As a large conglomerate, the varied product lines and distribution channels would have presented a challenge for any team charged with improving customer experience across the board. For many years, the operating model had been a loose federation that provided each company with a great deal of autonomy. At one time, scores of Web sites were associated with the firm.

Nathalie's team was charged with consolidating and improving the user experience of the firm's Web site. Although things began well, she could see problems. Under the Agile and Scrum methodologies, management was supposed to specify what software it wanted developed in the next monthly work period. But the various departments found it difficult to agree on what should be done. The implementation period would often start without the organization having reached agreement on what precisely should be developed. As a result, the software development team would begin working on something, only to find that the signals changed when it was halfway along with the work.

The group responsible for setting priorities was composed of representatives of interested departments. But the individuals in the group had no mandate to make decisions on behalf of their departments, and if they did, they were likely to be second-guessed. Time-consuming checking back with their constituencies slowed decision making to a crawl, and often a halt.

Compounding the problem was the fact that a duo of senior managers affectionately known within the firm as the Gruesome Twosome weren't happy. The Gruesome Twosome insisted on signing off at certain critical decision points, and during their reviews, they would often second-guess the instructions that had been given to the team of software developers. As their interventions became more frequent and disruptive, the group charged with setting priorities became less willing to make decisions for fear of being reversed upstairs.

Nor were the Gruesome Twosome's decisions entirely clear: the group setting priorities had no way of getting clarification from them and was unwilling to substitute its own judgment. So like the oracle at Delphi, the group deployed an ambiguous dialect that enabled them to be on the right side of the winning decision whatever it turned out to be.

Nathalie came to see that no one was held to what they had said in a previous meeting because everyone knew that decisions were provisional. The only constant was deniability. The more troublesome a problem was, the vaguer the language became.

Nathalie knew that her team of software developers was working well, but it wasn't productive because the firm couldn't make up its mind what it wanted.

THE BANKER

Ben had entered banking with a romantic notion of the profession.[6] He had in his mind an image of bankers as pillars of the community. He imagined that he would be adding value to society by contributing his skills and judgment to the complex issue of which borrowers could be entrusted with money.

As it turned out, Ben's role as a banker was different. Since the mortgage he arranged would be sold by his bank to some other financial institution, the creditworthiness of the applicant was essentially irrelevant. His bank had little interest in whether the loan would ever be repaid. Its focus was on the fees it got from originating the loan. The mortgages would be bundled together and sold to investors somewhere else in the world.

In his imagined role as a banker, his job would have depended on his judgment as to who could be trusted. But as his job evolved, his bank was pressed by both Wall Street and Washington to pursue new kinds of loans in which the borrowers didn't even need to pretend that they had any income or assets, let alone present evidence of their existence. Trust simply didn't enter into the picture.

If Ben had paused to ask himself what he was doing writing loans that had little hope of being repaid, he might have replied that he was assisting citizens buy their own home. He was helping unprecedented quantities of capital find a safe resting place. He was doing his part in relieving the enormous worldwide hunger for mortgage-backed securities among investors. The fees associated with the transactions were making money for everyone. The process of lending had to go on. Even better, in some cases, the banks were able to make financial bets against the shaky instruments that they themselves had created and thus make another handsome profit when those instruments went bad.

Remarkably, little changed in Ben's world after the meltdown of 2008. Within months, he was again being pressed to lend to buyers who put no more than 5 percent of their own money in the deal. Everyone could see that most of those who had caused the meltdown had walked away immensely rich from the bonuses they had earned in the good years, even though their high-risk strategies had devastated their companies as well as a large part of the financial system. Bank executives continued to be lavishly rewarded when they delivered juicy short-term profits. They were still in no jeopardy if their firms incurred losses later.

Why should Ben question the system in which he worked when he was helping make so much money? Raising questions about the system wasn't in his job description.

THE CONSULTANT

When Connie made partner in the prestigious global consulting firm where she worked, it was a happy, but not unexpected, day. She had been first in her class at prep school and at the Ivy League college she attended.[7] She wasn't surprised to be recruited into the Firm, as it was known, which thought of itself as first in its field. She had made steady progress climbing the managerial ladder.

On becoming partner, she had been on top of the world. The perks; the first-class travel; the corner office; the respect of her juniors, her fellow partners, and her bosses: these were everything that she had wanted. Nevertheless, the pressure of work was phenomenal. She was working close to seventy hours a week. Everyone else at the Firm did too. It was the way things were.

Her field was business strategy, and she was now a global practice leader. Because she was following so many projects, it took her quite some time to catch up to where she was on any piece of work.

She derived satisfaction from being a partner, someone whom CEOs listened to with respect, and at such moments, she felt like the queen of the universe. At other moments, she realized that she had no real life outside work. Nevertheless, she welcomed her role as someone who embodied the corporate culture, having mastered its intricacies.

She exhibited a high level of buy-in to the firm's mission and did so willingly. Any division between private life and work life had disappeared long ago. The Firm was the controlling unit of her personality. It gave purpose to her life.

On many occasions, she had shown herself ready to put the team objectives ahead of her personal interests, while at the same time making sure that her turf was not significantly at risk and that her career concerns were also taken care of. She believed that the Firm had a higher purpose in terms of making the world a better place, even if the specific content of what that meant was ambiguous.

Some years ago, cross-functional teams had been introduced, and at first, everyone had wondered what that might mean. It soon became apparent that despite talk of teams and teamwork, cross-functional teams were simply another way to divide and conquer.

In the Firm, everything was, on the surface, very collegial. In fact, everyone was exquisitely sensitive to the pecking order in the hierarchy and the consequent division of labor. The thought that anyone should help someone outside their own territory or make suggestions about her work would have been seen as bizarre. The possibility that everyone on a team would pitch in so that the team got the most important task done first would have been a real sea change.

When the team spent time together, the talk was rarely about the work. In fact, they would talk about anything except the work, and then go off and do their own thing.

Whether anyone advanced up the hierarchy and made partner or beyond was determined as much by an ability to fit in as it was by actual performance on the job. It had been this way at school, where her role as chair of the senior fund and champion money raiser for the school's annual charity drive had been at least as important as her stellar grade point average. It had shown that she was a joiner, a team player, a rounded package. Her self-assessment as a successful young woman had been reinforced by the rewards dispensed by the gatekeeping institutions. This had resulted in a smooth, frictionless path of scholarships, internships, a job at a prestigious consulting firm, and now partner at the Firm. She had accomplished this—happily—without ever having to assert independence, demonstrate intellectual adventurousness, or take a stand against authority.

Connie did the same work as her subordinates, only she was better at it than they were. She knew precisely how the Firm liked to have strategy analyzed, the way the analysis should be laid out, which points to emphasize and which to slide over. It was a Firm-specific expertise that had taken her years to acquire. The fact that the finer points of this particular expertise were sometimes lost on her clients was irrelevant. Satisfying the internal quality requirements was ultimately more important to her career than delighting the client: the client might be gone tomorrow, but the Firm would still be there, glorious in its unchangeability, its rocklike permanence, its prestige, its power to set the agenda. If the job took longer in order to satisfy the Firm's internal requirements, that was what was involved in working with the Firm; that's how clients got the Firm's legendary quality, the basis of its global reputation.

Within the Firm, the best proposals were those that resolved every issue down to the last detail. Curiously, the more detailed the Firm's proposal, the less the client seemed to understand or own it, let alone persuade its own staff to implement it.

The bottom line of her performance was none of those things: it was whether the work that she did or supervised met the requirements of the Firm. She had seen cases where managers had cut corners in terms of the Firm's requirements to meet the perceived need of a client. The consequence for the managers in question had been a permanent blot on their record that no amount of client delight could remove.

She was vaguely aware that this way of working was not very productive. Far too much time was spent politicking. She could see that her career, which was currently flourishing, depended on a network of personal relationships up and down the hierarchy. Because the criteria of evaluation were nebulous, she spent a good deal of her time managing what other people thought of her. Despite her success, she had never gotten over the sense of being on perpetual probation, acutely aware that at any moment, a rearrangement of the players might result in a different clan having control of the levers of power in a way that could cripple her career. The specter of arbitrary disaster was never far away.

When she sat back and reflected on her situation, late at night, hard at work on a client proposal, she was not unwilling to admit that her quality of life was appalling. She had more than enough money, but she saw little of her family, who understood that she was doing it all for them.

Despite these issues, she was pleased to see that the Firm's recommendations were always accepted by the client's top people, even if implementation down the line was a problem. Down the line, the people weren't committed to it. They didn't see it as *their* solution, even though the Firm's report showed that it was the right thing to do. Nevertheless, when a company was in trouble, it was reassuring to know that they would always come back to the Firm, which remained the gold standard, a legend in its own time.

No one was ever faulted for hiring the Firm. It was the ideal insurance policy for any CEO.

THE PARADOX OF MANAGERIAL SUCCESS

Thirty years ago, these job situations might have been considered good enough. People are getting paid. Managers are getting the job done. The firms are making money. To be sure, the work isn't particularly fulfilling. It could even be seen as dispiriting and demeaning. But whoever promised fulfillment in work? A salary, yes. But fulfillment? Whoever said that was part of the package?

Even today, some might see nothing anomalous or disturbing in such unproductive working conditions, the lack of personal responsibility for what is being done, the systematic inattention to the outcome of work, or the lack of centrality of the client. Yet viewed through the lens of the twenty-first century, these situations are unsustainable. The work is not as productive as it could be. Innovation is stifled. Managers are trapped. Customers are dissatisfied. Brand liabilities that accrue from pursuing "bad profits" are accumulating in the background. Any kind of moral compass is absent.

The performance of these workplaces is suboptimal, but not because workers are unwilling or because managers are lackadaisical. Everyone is working hard. Yet the workers feel used. The managers feel just as much victims as the workers. And the customers end up getting the short end of the stick. Whether the participants realize it or not, these workplaces are quietly dying.

Paradoxically, the traditional system of management depicted here has been extraordinarily successful economically. Over the twentieth century, it resulted in a fifty-fold increase in the productivity of workers and a massive increase in the standard of living in the developed countries.[8] This way of managing was considered a model for businesses and public sector organizations throughout the twentieth century. In many ways, the modern corporation is a stunning economic accomplishment.

That this way of working is no longer perceived to be performing well enough is not due to some failure of implementation or some personal delinquency of the individuals involved. Rather, the world has shifted beyond the limits of the system to adjust and evolve. This way of working was good enough for the conditions that existed for much of the previous century. It's not good enough today because the world has changed. We have changed.

As change has accelerated, the malfunctions have become fundamental. The system is no longer a good fit for today's conditions. Patches and fixes and new bells and whistles don't help. We need radically different management.

2

A BRIEF HISTORY OF MANAGEMENT

> "The goals and motives that guide human action must be looked at in the light of all that we know and understand; their roots and growth, their essence, and above all their validity, must be critically examined with every intellectual resource that we have."
>
> **Isaiah Berlin**[1]

A peculiar feature of traditional managerial discourse is the unspoken assumption of its inevitability. It is as though the practices of traditional management—hierarchy, command and control, tightly planned work, competition through economies of scale and cost reduction, impersonal communications—reflect timeless truths of the universe, so obvious that there is scarcely any need to articulate them, let alone reexamine them. In reality, these managerial practices arose as a response to a specific set of social and economic conditions. When those conditions change, the validity of the principles can become an issue.

WHY TRADITIONAL MANAGEMENT IS STRUGGLING

Four major changes have occurred that help explain why traditional management, which performed so well in economic terms in the twentieth century, is no longer a good fit for today's social and economic conditions. Understanding these changes is fundamental to understanding where management has come from, why individual fixes didn't take hold, and where it is heading.

Work Has Shifted from Semiskilled to Knowledge Work

The first change is the continuing shift from semiskilled work to what economists call knowledge work. When modern management was being invented almost a century ago, most employees were semiskilled workers, such as laborers and production line workers. Doing their work required little training and practically no brainpower. They were expected to do what they were told. How they felt about it was irrelevant.

Traditional management was developed principally to get these semiskilled employees to perform repetitive activities competently, diligently, and efficiently. As their work has been steadily replaced by machines and computers, meeting that challenge has become steadily less relevant in today's workplace.

Work today increasingly requires the application of brainpower and knowledge. Workers include lawyers, doctors, accountants, marketers, administrators, software developers, and researchers with Ph.D.s. These workers—knowledge workers—are expected to identify issues, think through problems, and come up with new solutions. The shift from semiskilled work to knowledge work has changed the relationship between those in charge and those doing the work.

As management sage Peter Drucker noted, "Workers throughout history could be 'supervised.' They could be told what to do, how to do it, how fast to do it and so on. Knowledge workers cannot, in effect, be supervised."[2]

The Organization Needs the Commitment of the Workforce

Second, the engagement of the workforce has become a serious productivity issue. As social critic Alain de Botton points out, "Once it became evident that someone who was expected to remove brain tumors, draw up binding legal documents or sell condominiums with convincing energy could not be profitably sullen or resentful, morose or angry, the mental welfare of employees commenced to be an object of supreme concern."[3] Yet although the mental welfare of employees is recognized as a supreme concern, that concern hasn't led to supreme success: only one in five of the global workforce is fully engaged.[4]

For much of the previous century, people were happy enough to have a job—any job—that provided a good salary. That's no longer enough. As work has shifted from semiskilled labor to knowledge work, workers want not just jobs, but meaningful jobs—jobs where they can contribute and make a difference. They want these jobs today, not five or ten years from now, and they will give preference to employers who can provide them.

From the firm's point of view, unused talent is a serious productivity problem. And it's not merely suboptimizing for the firm. Since the workers themselves are aware that they are not being allowed to give their best and are spending their time unproductively, both managers and workers become disgruntled. Internal processes grind away, and the customers become more and more an afterthought. The fact that current management practices prevent a full human flourishing is in itself an economic, management, social, and moral problem of the first order.

The Customer Takes Charge

Third, customers are no longer willing to be treated as an afterthought. The twentieth-century firm wasn't sharply focused on pleasing customers. That was because, by and large, it wasn't necessary. Demand was soaring, and firms could sell whatever product or services they generated. Oligopolies had control of the marketplace.

For much of the previous century, oligopolies could interrupt whomever they wanted with any message they cared to transmit. And the buyers were forced to watch it because there were only three television channels. The system was spamming people over and over again with impersonal, irritating, irrelevant TV commercials that people didn't want to see about stuff they weren't interested in.

This worked as long as there were only a few channels of communication and a few sellers and a few products, and buyers had limited information and little choice. But the situation changed. A few channels of communication turned into multiple channels of communication. A few sellers turned into many sellers. A few products turned into the clutter of multiple products. Once buyers had instant access to reliable information and became fed up with being spammed, the old model fell apart. The result was a fundamental shift in the balance of power from sellers to buyers. Now, unless clients are delighted, they can—and will—go elsewhere. So businesses have to change their focus from producing goods and services to an explicit goal of delighting clients.

Some organizations might feel that the word *delight* is implausible as a serious business proposition. Yet any firm that aspires to create enduring customer loyalty must find a way to turn passively satisfied customers into active advocates and promoters of its goods and services. That usually means doing something noteworthy—something sufficiently different that customers take notice and talk about it to others.

It's no longer enough merely to remove defects. Customers expect zero defects. If the customer's experience fits a predictable pattern, it will be boring to the customer, who will therefore ignore it. The bar has been raised. To turn customers into advocates and promoters of the firm's goods and services, organizations must not only minimize errors: they must innovate. They must break out of the pattern that their customers have come to expect. They must find new and economical ways to provide goods or services that are differentiated, noteworthy, surprising, or remarkable.[5]

Delighting clients is the primary goal—a means to competitive advantage and profitability. It takes precedence over profits, turnover, and market share. That's because unless the firm is delighting clients and turning its customers into enthusiastic advocates and promoters of its products and services, those financial indicators are emblems of temporary success that won't endure.[6] Following several decades in which many firms aimed at maximizing shareholder value, we are now entering the era of customer capitalism, in which the purpose of the firm is to serve clients.[7] (See Chapter Four.)

Delighting clients becomes the primary goal of work. One of management's key functions is to give everyone a clear line of sight as to how their work is—or isn't—leading to client delight.

The System Has Stopped Delivering

The unhappiness of workers and the dissatisfaction of customers are big problems in themselves. Yet the root cause of today's troubles—the fourth big change in the world of work—is something more serious and less obvious. The root cause is that the gains in productivity that came from conceiving of work as a system of things that can be manipulated to produce goods and services have largely run their course.

The productivity gains accomplished in the twentieth century using that mental model of management were amazing—indeed unprecedented in the history of the human race. However, the expectation that those gains would continue uninterrupted into the new century has not materialized. The reasons are corollaries of the other shifts.

Once a firm sets out to maximize the full talents, ingenuity, and inspiration of its workforce, it discovers that it is interacting with people, not inanimate things that can be manipulated. Any hint of manipulation is dispiriting and counterproductive. Managers have to be able to inspire genuine enthusiasm for worthwhile goals. Even more important, once a firm goes beyond the relatively simple task of producing goods and services and sets its sights on the complex goal of delighting clients, it finds that it is dealing with a radically more difficult challenge.

Producing a certain quantity of goods or services is a task that can be accomplished in its entirety. Management can set up a hermetically sealed system and be confident of 100 percent "success" every time. Success is finite, linear, and under management's control.

Delighting clients is different: it can only be approached by increasingly close approximations; it is never fully attained or assured. Client delight is mercurial. What was good enough yesterday might not be good enough tomorrow. Continuously delighting the client requires continuous innovation.

Moreover, in the twentieth century where the workplace consisted of a system of things to be manipulated, a firm could get away with sending messages to customers and telling workers what to do. Now the firm suddenly finds that these communication behaviors no longer work. They not only rub people the wrong way; they often have the opposite effect of what was intended.

Today managers have to recognize that they cannot delight clients or draw on the full talents of the workforce merely by sending messages and telling people what to do. Instead, they need to be having interactive conversations, using authentic narratives and open-ended questions, and engaging in deep listening. They need to be communicating with people as responsible, thinking, feeling adults, so that communications leave them energized and clients positively excited rather than dispirited and used. Managers have to stop doing things *to* people and start doing things *with* people. What business once saw as a utopian moral ideal has now become an inexorable economic necessity.

The reality is that most established firms—no matter which business they are in, no matter how sophisticated their products or services, or what the country of origin—are still operating on the assumption that the workplace can and should be built around the central idea of a system of things to produce goods and services.

Today's manufacturers, financial institutions, pharmaceuticals, and oil companies have been built on the notion that the workplace is a system of things that is more important than the particular individuals within the system. "The system" is what enabled the formation of large organizations that exceeded the management span of control of a single manager. It is what enabled the huge gains in productivity of the twentieth century. From the outset, the United States led the world in the application of "systems of things."

HOW THE WORKPLACE HAS EVOLVED

To figure out why and how this old system needs to change, it helps to see where today's workplace has come from. The workplace of today is intelligible only when we see how it has evolved from the past.

Work as a System of Things

According to Peter Drucker, the first—and best—traditional manager was the man who designed and built the first Egyptian pyramid four thousand years ago: it still stands.[8]

Other theorists date the emergence of traditional management to the period when large organizations began to appear in the early nineteenth century—particularly the railroads. As the population grew in the United States, the railroads were laying rails across the vast territory and sending trains down a one-way track in both directions. Inevitably there was a collision. The first major accident happened on October 5, 1841, when a couple of trains on the Western Railroad had a head-on collision. A conductor and a passenger were killed, and seventeen others were injured.[9]

Following a public outcry, the directors of the Western Railroad appointed a committee headed by an army man, Major George W. Whistler, to determine what sort of organization should be in place to prevent this kind of thing from happening. The committee could have looked at two very different approaches for running large organizations.

One approach was the army, which at the time was predominantly a steep hierarchy with detailed control from the center. Its focus was on order and certainty. The practices were centralization, coercion, formality, tight rein, imposed discipline, obedience, and compliance. The practices were founded on distrust: unless people were tightly controlled, they might do the wrong thing. The goal was to reach optimal decisions, even if they were not the most rapid. The linchpin of the approach was the brilliant general at the top who would study the situation, make the right decisions, give orders, and win the battle. This had proved to be a successful model of military organization down the centuries. The more disciplined the army, the more successful it was. The communications were top down, explicit, and linear. It was a hierarchy in which the management style was directive and transactional. The assumption was that the world was knowable and predictable. People at the top were best placed to know what was going on and to run the organization.[10]

By contrast, a variety of other large organizations had relatively flat organizational structures. The Roman Catholic church, the Hanse, the East India Company, the British Empire, and the Hudson Bay Company had all prospered by establishing at the center the values and principles to be followed, but allowing the application of the values and principles to particular situations to be handled at lower levels; self-discipline and individual initiative were highly valued. The approach placed a great deal of trust in the person on the spot to adjust actions to the local context. Overall, despite strong centralist tendencies, the leadership style implied a remarkable level of delegation: an ability to lead at the lowest levels was valued.

These were the two very different historical approaches to large-scale organization. As the committee was headed by a military man, it is hardly surprising which model Major Whistler chose: central offices to be run by "managers."[11] It established a chain of command with clear lines of authority and clear descriptions of responsibilities at every level. The strengths of the approach were obvious. Out of chaos and confusion, it created order, workability, and predictability.

The system was founded on defining responsibilities in writing and detecting derelictions of duty so that the offending individuals could be punished. At the time, the risk that such a system might limit individual initiative, flexibility, and innovation seemed less important than the goal of establishing order.

Workers were instructed to act in accordance with rules that enabled the system to be predictable and safe. Instructing people to conform to established procedures remains the essence of traditional management even today.

In modern management parlance, workers are turned into "human resources": things, not people. Harold Geneen, the CEO of ITT, expressed the idea pithily in 1965: "The goal of management is to make individuals as predictable and controllable as the capital assets for which they are responsible."[12]

In this way, the system enabled companies to become big. But could the system enable companies to become better?

Frederick Taylor: The System Ahead of People

The man who answered the question about how the system could help companies be better was Frederick Winslow Taylor, author of *The Principles of Scientific Management* and, by some accounts, the father of twentieth-century management.

In 1899, Taylor became fascinated by a simple question: How many tons of pig iron bars can a worker load onto a railcar in the course of a working day? Management theorist Paul Stewart depicts the situation:

> Taylor was forty-three years old and on contract with the Bethlehem Steel Company when he began thinking about pig iron. Staring out over an industrial yard that covered several square miles of the Pennsylvania landscape, he watched as laborers loaded ninety-two-pound bars onto rail cars. There were 80,000 tons' worth of iron bars, which were to be carted off as fast as possible to meet new demand sparked by the Spanish-American War. Taylor narrowed his eyes: there was waste there, he was certain. After hastily reviewing the books at company headquarters, he estimated that the men were currently loading iron at the rate of twelve and a half tons per man per day.
>
> Taylor stormed down to the yard with his assistants ("college men," he called them) and . . . found a "high-priced man," a lean Pennsylvania Dutchman whose intelligence he compared to that of an ox. Lured

by the promise of a 60 percent increase in wages, from $1.15 to a whopping $1.85 a day, Taylor's high-priced man loaded forty-five and three-quarters tons over the course of a grueling day—close enough, in Taylor's mind, to count as the first victory for the methods of modern management.[13]

After Taylor was let go from Bethlehem Steel in 1901, he went around the United States regaling audiences with stories about the Pennsylvania Dutchman he called "Schmidt" and the improvements in productivity that were achieved through "scientific management." In due course, his thinking was adopted by an emerging breed of management experts. In 1909, Taylor's principles of scientific management were introduced into the curriculum of the newly opened Harvard Business School.

In 1911, in *The Principles of Scientific Management,* Taylor issued his ominous, prescient declaration: "In the past, Man has been first. In future, the system must be first."[14] Although at times Taylor occasionally professed an interest in improving the lot of workers, he was well aware that "the system" was ultimately about making more money for the company. As he wrote in *Shop Management,* "The full possibilities of this system will not have been realized until almost all of the machines in the shop are run by men who are of smaller capabilities and attainments, and who are therefore cheaper than those required under the old system."[15] And so the practice of dumbing down the workplace and outsourcing jobs was born.

The Assembly Line

Next came Henry Ford's assembly line. Here, the activity of self-directed labor conducted by the worker was sliced into tiny parts and then reconstituted as a process controlled by management and delivered to the worker. Initially there was revulsion from the workers, and Ford had to hire many men to add one to his production line.[16] Eventually the workers either got used to it or were required to adopt it, as Ford was able to eliminate the other companies that did not adopt his assembly line methods. Ford prospered even if the jobs were monotonous.

Applying Taylorism to Management Itself

Ford's system was more productive for the company but not agile enough for the customer. It was constantly producing too many, or not enough, cars. So the next step was to apply Taylor's methods to management itself.

This time it was General Motors that showed the way. Alfred Sloan created decentralized divisions that managers could oversee from corporate headquarters simply by monitoring production and financial numbers. He created one division for each car model: Chevrolet, Pontiac, Buick, Oldsmobile, and Cadillac. Corporate executives were experts not in making cars but in finance. Engineering and manufacturing specialists were assigned to oversee those functional areas. Operations were not seen as a top management responsibility.

Executives managed by the numbers: output, inventory, sales, margins, market share, profit, and loss. They reviewed whether each division was performing in accordance with the plan; if it was not, adjustments were made. In this way, managerial work was sliced into smaller pieces just as manual work had been.

Applying Taylorism to Marketing

With the introduction of radio, mass marketing gave companies the chance to reach a wide variety of potential customers. The goal was to induce a broad audience with different needs to buy the same product. By mass-marketing and mass-producing the same product in roughly the same way to all consumers, companies could reach the largest potential market at the lowest cost. The result was average products that sold well.

Planning, Programming, and Budgeting

The lack of management involvement in the work created a risk that its decisions would not correspond with the realities of the workplace or the marketplace.

In the 1950s and 1960s, the risk wasn't significant given the heavy and growing demand for goods and services and the difficulty of new entry into the market. Customers, deprived of material goods for two previous decades of depression and then war, didn't insist on high quality or service. They were happy just to get any television or refrigerator.[17]

The regime of Robert McNamara at Ford, the Defense Department, and the World Bank epitomized the management of the era. Through elaborate planning exercises, McNamara, with his teams of the best and brightest, decided which sectors to be in, how much capital to allocate to each, and what returns they would expect the operating managers to deliver to the company.

Staffs of corporate programmers and budgeters assembled data about divisional performance and intervened to adjust plans and activities. The arrangement was scalable: when a company needed to grow, it added more workers at the bottom and then more managers in the layers above. Now both managers and workers could be manipulated like things.

These arrangements were appropriate to a world where paying customers could be taken for granted, the entry of aggressive new competitors was rare, and the supply of compliant managers and workers was not something to worry about.

THE SITUATION REACHES A CRISIS POINT

By the 1990s, the situation had changed. Accelerating economic and social change in the global economy, the consequent imperative for ever faster innovation, the emergence of global networks of partners, the increasing ownership of the means of production by knowledge workers, the escalating power of customers in the marketplace, the multiplication of media channels, and burgeoning diversity in both the workplace and marketplace: all of these forces caused traditional management to become dysfunctional.

The diagnosis at the time was grim: American companies had become "bloated, clumsy, rigid, sluggish, non-competitive, uncreative, inefficient, disdainful of customer need and losing money."[18] It was clear that the system needed to be replaced by something different.

But what?

Business Process Reengineering

In 1993, traditional management jumped on the bandwagon known as business process reengineering. The initial idea was sensible: to reengineer processes, essentially a new fix to the system—particularly processes that took advantage of technology to minimize handoffs and enable smaller teams to work on tasks from start to finish.[19] Such process improvements could lead to modest gains in productivity, although the change was hardly the kind of reform needed to deal with the profound structural problems of the traditional workplace. Nevertheless, Michael Hammer and James Champy were able to hype this modest proposal into something they called "radically new," "a fresh start," "something entirely different."[20]

The claim was attractive to traditional managers for several reasons. For one thing, it was a technology fix: managers didn't need to change their behavior. They could sit back while technology solved the problem. For another, the reengineering could be done by experts—even by reengineering "czars."[21] The fact that managers could hire others to do the hard work of reshaping the organization fit the prevailing Taylorist culture.

It offered CEOs an attractive image of immaculate top-down power, since the "almost perfect model" for the reengineered organization was the National Football League (NFL) team: the head coach called in every play, and the players flawlessly executed his will.[22] It also happily provided management consultants with "the next new thing" and opportunities to market newly minted prowess in process reengineering.

The downsides of the approach were mirror images of the advantages. Because the management problems organizations faced were not inherently problems of technology, the introduction of technology did little to address root causes. Being designed by "experts" who didn't always understand the requirements of the work, the solution often didn't fit the specific workplace. Because the process changes were introduced without basic change in the behaviors of the managers or the workers, the problems caused by those behaviors continued.

Business process reengineering was something done to the workforce. For most workers, it made jobs worse. Because business process reengineering didn't affect the goals of business, which continued to focus on improved efficiency through downsizing and outsourcing, often using fewer, less educated, and cheaper people, the social problems of the workplace were aggravated. Nor was thought given to the strategic implications of the wholesale shipping of expertise overseas to countries where workers could be more easily manipulated.[23]

The metaphor of the firm as an NFL football team, with the head coach calling in every play, revealed how little Hammer had grasped the need for greater agility and innovation in a rapidly changing environment. It was assumed that the world was knowable and predictable. The guy at the top could figure out what was going on and make all the key decisions.[24]

In fact, a principal attraction of business process engineering was precisely that under the guise of being something entirely different, it was more of the same. It was another superficial fix to a system that was suffering from rot from within. It was a bandage on a cancer.

The Crisis Worsens

By 2009, the problems facing management were formidable. A study by the Deloitte Center for the Edge catalogued the long-term performance trends. The return on assets of U.S. companies continued its steep decline. With economies of scale evaporating, resort to downsizing and outsourcing weakened firms' future ability to compete. Meanwhile, as barriers to entry eroded and competition intensified, modest gains in labor productivity were mainly captured by customers and creative talent. "Winning" companies barely held on to their success, and market "losers" destroyed value more rapidly than ever before. Customers were increasingly disloyal to brands. Executive turnover accelerated.[25] In the past twenty-five years, start-ups created 40 million jobs in the United States, while established firms created almost none.[26]

In effect, organizations today face a crisis. It's not a crisis involving a single catastrophic event, like the financial meltdown of 2008, although that too is a symptom of the trouble that is afoot. The crisis is more insidious and more serious.

A crisis of this scale and age is not something that can be resolved with a single management fix, such as instilling a sense of urgency[27] or putting more emphasis on intrinsic motivation.[28] Individual fixes are impotent to deal with a crisis of this size and complexity. They don't stick.

The System Is the Problem

What the champions of business process reengineering failed to see was that the fundamental problem of the workplace wasn't this or that particular system or process. The deeper problem lay precisely in thinking about work primarily as an internally driven set of processes, using people who could be manipulated, rather than viewing the workplace as an interaction of thinking, feeling, laughing, caring human beings whose talents, energies, and ingenuities are fully engaged in finding ways to delight clients.

When process engineers started talking about work as an improved system of processes, they were already well on the way to aggravating the problems they were trying to solve. They had lost sight of what work should be about—what it takes to make a truly productive and vibrant organization.

And where was the client? As long as the purpose of business process reengineering was conceived as the more efficient production of goods and services, it was likely that the client would also end up getting the short end of the stick and have to spend vast amounts of time waiting on the phone to have a confused conversation with some call center on the other side of the planet.

The champions of business process reengineering failed to see that the activity was Taylorism under a different label.

A NEW START

What's exciting now is that in some organizations, the workplace is being reinvented from first principles. They have made a genuinely fresh start.

This is not because the past is something to be discarded. Indeed we can understand the workplace of today only if we also understand how we got to where we are. We have come to a point in the evolution of management where the past needs to be corrected and transcended. This doesn't mean that the principles described here are in any sense a permanent solution: the principles correct and transcend the past in a way that leaves the present also open to future improvement. They represent a step in our ongoing journey to understand and implement ways to manage work that meet the needs of all interested parties.

These firms are focused on making work radically more productive, and productivity is fundamental. To get accountants' hearts beating faster, leaps in productivity are needed, not just marginal improvements. Just as Frederick Taylor got attention by offering two- to four-times improvements in productivity, so radical management must deliver similar jumps in productivity.

But becoming radically more productive by itself is not enough. The change must be brought about in a way that makes things better for customers, managers, and those doing the work. This means not just finding new managerial gadgets or tricks, or manipulating people by contriving a sense of urgency with respect to the firm's "mission" to increase shareholder value, or inducing employees to wear masks of shallow cheerfulness and ignore what they intuitively know is really going on.

A workplace filled with dispirited, cynical managers and workers isn't going to be the cutting-edge organization of the future. It will never be the engine of growth, a hub of greater productivity, the inventor of winning new ideas, or the generator of creativity. A workplace that cuts costs but frustrates customers has no sustainable future.

Breaking the Iron Triangle

The new way of managing means busting the iron triangle of constraints in which firms have for too long been imprisoned. All too often, gains in organizational productivity have made things worse for workers and

FIGURE 2.1 The Iron Triangle

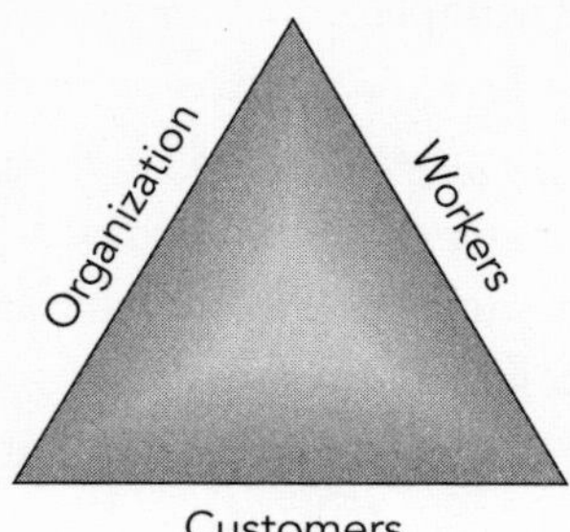

lowered quality of service to customers. Improvements in the workplace for workers have increased costs and undermined productivity. Upgrading service to customers has also been at odds with improving productivity. Enhancing one dimension has led to setbacks on one or both of the other two.

Reform of the workplace means rethinking work from first principles and seeing how the productivity of the organization, the life of workers, and the experience of customers can be simultaneously upgraded. It means breaking the iron triangle (Figure 2.1).

Reinventing the Workplace from First Principles

Equipping organizations to break the iron triangle requires a fundamental shift in management thinking and practice. In effect, the underlying sources of productivity are being rethought while simultaneously making things better for the workforce and becoming more responsive to customers.

The inquiry is not about what sort of personality is needed to tolerate a blizzard of half-truths that managers must transmit and employees have to swallow in some new "system." It's not about offering workers health spas, gourmet cafeterias, or karaoke competitions at lunchtime while leaving jobs unchanged.

It's about fundamentally restructuring work and generating a true partnership. It's about draining the swamp of nontransparency in which most managers and employees currently swim and exposing the rocks for what they are, so that firms can get rid of them and become more productive. It's about what it takes to continuously deliver client delight.

It speaks to the goals, behaviors, economics, and ethical principles that must govern the workplace for this century.

3

WHAT RADICAL MANAGEMENT MEANS

> "Equipping organizations to tackle the future would require a management revolution no less momentous than the one that spawned modern industry."
>
> **Gary Hamel**[1]

Radical management entails a journey—one that will never end. The journey needs to be conducted not through detached contemplation, but from immersion in the nitty-gritty of work, the kind that sings when clients are delighted and kicks back when they're not. It's about creating a workplace based on agency and responsibility.

It means exploring what's involved in replacing the daily grind with discovery and surprise. It's about becoming more productive by working smarter.

It involves examining what choice-worthy work looks like and understanding what kind of activity enlivens the human spirit. It builds on intuitions that many people have had for a long time but have rarely been pursued to their conclusion in business forums.

Ultimately it's about generating work that involves doing things with people who share a common passion for the activity and for being excellent at it, in service of other people whose ever-increasing delight we can see and experience.

It means implementing seven basic principles of continuous innovation.

SEVEN BASIC PRINCIPLES OF CONTINUOUS INNOVATION

Principle #1: Focus Work on Delighting the Client

Radical management begins by clarifying the goal of work. In the twentieth century, the traditional view of an organization was an entity principally aimed at the production of goods and services or making money for the company. These goals don't get anyone's juices flowing. That's because goods, services, and money are means, not ends.

In today's world of global competition and continuous change, a firm that isn't delighting its clients and turning them into active promoters of its goods and services is unlikely to endure. If the firm is making profits while leaving customers disgruntled, then the profits are "bad profits" and are generating brand liabilities that will have to be repaid one day. The true bottom line of any organization is whether and to what extent it is delighting clients and stakeholders.[2]

A firm that adopts client delight as its goal is also making inroads on improving job satisfaction. Improving the lives of others is something worth believing in and fighting for.

Principle #2: Do Work Through Self-Organizing Teams

Adopting the goal of client delight leads to the self-organizing team. That's because inspiring client delight requires continuous innovation, and a self-organizing team is the management arrangement most likely to generate innovation. Self-organizing teams are well suited to accomplish this complex task; when they are properly executed, they draw on all the talents, energies, and passion of the workforce.

Self-organizing teams also speak to the economics of work: self-organizing teams have the potential to be radically more productive because when they are properly supported, they tend to evolve into high-performance teams.

Principle #3: Do Work in Client-Driven Iterations

Principle #2 leads to working in an iterative fashion, with teams completing work in relatively short time slices aimed at delivering value to clients. In part, this is because delighting clients can be approached only with successive approximations as to what might succeed or fail. Continuous feedback from the clients or their proxy is needed as to whether they are in fact being delighted by the direction in which the work is heading.

In part, it is because delegating work to self-organizing teams is a risky undertaking that requires constant vigilance to ensure that teams are focused on delighting the client and evolving toward high performance. And in part, it is because doing work in short iterations is generally more economical overall than long production runs.[3]

Principle #4: Deliver Value to Clients Each Iteration

Iterative work patterns necessitate a focus on getting things done by the end of each iteration of work.

Rather than issuing progress reports about where the project stands, the teams produce finished work each iteration so that clients or their proxies can touch, feel, use, and experience it and find out whether this is something that delights them.[4] Whereas traditional management focuses principally on reducing costs, radical management focuses principally on reducing time to market and delivering more value to clients sooner. It turns out that being more responsive in terms of time also tends to be more efficient.

The origins of this principle lie partly in lean manufacturing: inventory is a problem because it ties up money and, even more important, tends to delay the discovery and resolution of quality problems. A focus on delivering value to clients each iteration also tends to lower costs.

Similarly, in knowledge work, having a lot of work in process is damaging to productivity. Hence, efficiency also requires that once work is started, it should be completed as soon as possible so that work in progress is kept to a minimum.

Principle #5: Be Totally Open About Impediments to Improvement

Working in an iterative fashion both enables and requires the workplace to be radically transparent so that the team goes on improving. Firms cannot accomplish the complex task of delighting clients or establish genuine responsibility for work if people are telling each other what they want to hear or limiting their communications to what they think listeners need to know.

The openness is multidirectional: the team members with each other, the team with management, and management with the team. This multidimensionality is accomplished not simply by urging people to be more open, but by implementing a set of management practices that systematically catalyzes transparency aimed at removing impediments.

Principle #6: Create a Context for Continuous Self-Improvement by the Team Itself

Once the arrangements promoted by Principles #1 to #5 are in place, the team can accept responsibility for getting work done and enjoy the freedom to proceed without interruption or second-guessing while impediments are being identified and removed. Teams know their velocity and trajectory. In such a setting, they typically want to get better and generally do improve.

This is not about the management imposing a pace of work that undermines quality or pressing for unreasonably long working hours. Rather it creates conditions under which teams enjoy what they are doing and want to become more productive.

Principle #7: Communicate Through Interactive Conversations

Implementing Principles #1 to #6 requires communication that is different from traditional management. Instead of telling people what to do, radical managers have interactive conversations, using authentic narratives, posing open-ended questions, and engaging in deep listening, as well as encouraging horizontal communications to enhance learning. It entails a willingness to see what is really happening in the workplace and to have the open-mindedness to learn. It involves getting things done *with* people, not doing things *to* people.

Interactive communication flows from the purpose of work: inspiring workers to find ways to delight clients. To achieve these goals, communication practices need to be people-centric inside and outside the firm.

An Inexorable Sequence

These seven principles form an inexorable, mutually reinforcing sequence. They begin by identifying the goal that is appropriate to the twenty-first century: client delight. This becomes the basis for everything—the guiding light to which all work should aspire.

Focusing on client delight leads inevitably to self-organizing teams, the management arrangement most likely to generate the continuous innovation that delights clients. Doing work through self-organizing teams leads to working in client-driven iterations, because delighting clients can be approached only by successive approximations. And self-organizing teams, being a life form that lives on the edge of chaos, need checkpoints to see whether they are evolving positively or decaying into chaos.

Client-driven iterations require a focus on delivering value to clients each iteration. This forces closure and enables the productivity gains that flow from delivering value to clients sooner rather than later. Self-organizing teams working in client-driven iterations both enable and require radical transparency, so they continue to improve of their own accord and evolve naturally into high-performance teams.

An underlying requirement of all of these steps is interactive communication. Unless managers and workers are dealing with people as people, with respect and dignity, rather than as things to be manipulated, none of the other six principles are likely to work.

AN INTEGRATED SET OF MEASURES

Individually none of these seven principles is new. Each principle has been implemented by some organizations for many years:

- Finding ways to measure client delight and the consequent impact on firm growth has been systematically studied by Fred Reichheld and his colleagues at the consulting firm Bain & Company for over twenty-five years.[5]
- Self-organizing teams have been the staple of new product development for several decades.[6]
- Iterative work practices have been promoted since the 1930s by Walter Shewhart, a quality expert at Bell Labs.[7]
- Reducing inventory and delivering value to clients each iteration lie at the heart of lean manufacturing, which was invented by Toyota some fifty years ago.[8]
- Radical transparency has been a guiding principle of software development practices known as Scrum and Agile for several decades.
- Continuous self-improvement is a legacy from the total quality movement for more than half a century.[9]
- Interactive communication—storytelling, questions, conversations—has a rapidly growing literature and practice in the past decade.[10]

Individually, then, none of the seven principles is new. What is new is for organizations to break free from the interlocking assumptions of traditional management and put all the principles of radical management together as an integrated, mutually supporting whole. It's the integrated implementation of all the pieces that gives the approach its full power. Each of the components adds an increment: when they are combined, the increment becomes exponential.

When the principles are linked, we can see the sequence and the causal connections. We can see why the principles fit together and reinforce each other. We can see how any one of these seven principles will lead to some benefit. We begin to grasp the extraordinary benefits that accrue by implementing all of the principles together.

The practices work consistently, efficiently, and with minimal risk for a number of reasons. For one thing, they are aligned with the true purpose of work: delighting clients. For another, they pay careful attention to the intrinsic value of and satisfaction inherent in performing excellent work within the limitations of pace arising from the nature of the work itself. And finally, they lead to a radically more productive way of doing work.

THE IDEA IN ACTION: EASEL CORPORATION

Let's look at an example of a firm that explicitly implemented this approach. It occurred in Boston in 1993 at the very moment when traditional management was jumping on the bandwagon of business process reengineering.

In 1993, Jeff Sutherland joined a Boston-based software development firm called the Easel Corporation. Today Sutherland is a vigorous man in his sixties with silver hair and sharp, sparkling eyes. He dresses neatly in a black shirt with a button-down collar, black pants, and sneakers. A devotee of tai chi and Buddhist thinking, he was a fighter pilot in the U.S. Air Force and flew scores of combat missions over North Vietnam, achieving Top Gun status in 1967. He still has the military bearing of a man who has been through many battles, which have given him a keen sense of the ironies of life.

In 1983, Sutherland began working as a systems architect and chief technical officer in a series of companies, trying to figure out what could be done about the software developers whose work was always late, over budget, and plagued by quality problems. Clients were upset, and firms lost money. The developers were seen as culprits and were punished. They worked harder and harder. They labored evenings and weekends. They got divorced. It made no difference. The software was still late, over budget, and full of bugs. They were fired, but their replacements did no better. Something was amiss in this picture, and Sutherland set out to fix it.

By the early 1990s, he was working for a firm that was shipping software to big customers like the Ford Motor Company, which had around a thousand developers using its products. Ford's developers were fairly ordinary performers, and Sutherland wondered: Is there some way I could transform these developers from ordinary to extraordinary?

The conventional wisdom said no. But Sutherland was not the kind of person to accept the conventional wisdom. He knew the value of persistence. When studying at West Point, he had trained as a gymnast on the parallel bars under a man who was also the coach for the Olympic team. Sutherland recalls coming to the gym every afternoon and getting up on the parallel bars. When he did a flip, the coach would say, "That's not quite right. Get up and do it again." For three hours every day for three years, including some weekends, it was never right. And every once in a while, just to show him that it wasn't right, the coach would get up on the parallel bars and do a perfect flip just to rub it in. But at the end of those three years, Sutherland could do the flip better than most of the people that he was competing with. From that experience, he learned about constantly failing and retrying in order to reach for a higher level where he had never been before.

The Surgical Team

The first thing Sutherland did was to review thirty years of IBM's system journals. IBM had done research on the best way to develop software, and its conclusion was the surgical team: a team where one brilliant person had all the architecture, all the designs, in his or her head, and wrote every single line of code. It was like the surgeon in the operating room. The surgeon was the only one who cut the patient. Everyone else passed the scalpel or monitored the vital signs.

That was the level of performance that Sutherland was looking for. But there was a problem: companies like Ford weren't staffed with "surgeons." And even if they had been, the project would fail if the surgeon were run over by a bus, so it was a high-risk way to develop software. It was also inefficient because it didn't draw on the full talents of the team. Moreover, it didn't scale. There was only so much that one mind, even a brilliant mind, could master. In really big projects, with millions of lines of code, it didn't work. The projects were just too big. There had to be another way.

The High-Performance Product Development Team

Sutherland's challenge was how to get surgical performance from a team of fairly ordinary developers. So he began researching the computer science literature and talking to everybody, looking for high-performance teams.

He found that the best-performing teams for handling innovation were self-organizing teams.[11] The model had generally been used to deal with one-time crises. But why wait for the crisis? Why not get this kind of performance on a daily basis?

The elements were clear. The teams would need to see the goal as something that was important, something special, and to see it as a challenge. They would need to have a deadline so that projects didn't go on forever. They would need to have the space—mental and physical—in which they were free to get work done, as opposed to talking about the work or doing rework due to second-guessing. They would need to be cross-functional teams and have the leeway to organize themselves, including the responsibility for figuring out how to do the work. The teams would be small, with no more than eight or nine people—preferably smaller, but still with cross-functionality. And the team would be expected to produce something that was completely done by the deadline.

The role of management was not to manipulate the people doing the work; it was to set direction, eliminate anything that was preventing the team from performing at an extraordinary level, and then get out of the way.

Putting the Pieces Together

By 1993 Sutherland could see how to put the pieces together, and a financial crisis at the Easel Corporation gave him the opportunity to try out his ideas in practice. The traditional way of producing software had just failed miserably, and the firm was on the brink of being put out of business. Unless new software could be developed within six months, it would be history.

Sutherland went to the CEO and asked him how long he had been overseeing software development.

"Twenty-five years."

Sutherland asked him whether, in all that time, the plans that were supported by Gantt charts and looked good on paper had ever led to software being delivered on time.

The CEO said, "Never." Worse, slippage was rarely discovered until it was too late to do anything about it.

Now the situation was desperate, and Sutherland proposed doing something different. Instead of trying to manage the team more tightly, with detailed plans and Gantt charts, Sutherland proposed standing back and asking the team to manage itself.

The CEO was skeptical of putting the future of the firm in the hands of a team when he had never seen a team deliver on time and within budget even once during the previous twenty-five years. Sutherland then pointed out the definition of a fool: someone who keeps doing the same thing and expects a different result. They had to do something different.

So Sutherland got his mandate to set up the team according to the principles he had developed. He created a container in which the team could operate: the team itself was given the responsibility of figuring out how long each piece of work would take and how to do the work.

Within the team, he introduced the communication practices that he had observed in the best self-organizing teams. It was an iterative process with frank daily communication among the team members, with the manager serving as a coach to remove impediments and help the team improve. This radically altered the nature of the work going on within the team. It allowed sharing of information about the state of software components so that development tasks that had been expected to take days could be accomplished in hours using someone else's code as a starting point. By having every member of the team see every day what every other team member was doing, they began to get suggestions: one developer would see that if he changed a few lines of code, he could eliminate days of work for another developer.

A process was put in place for setting priorities on a monthly basis. It could be adjusted as the work evolved, so that the team worked only on issues of the highest priority. During the monthly increment of work, the team was not to be interrupted. The team was under the gun to produce the solution by the six-month deadline, or the firm would fail.

Sutherland also took steps to bring in outside ideas. He held demonstrations, usually on a Friday, and brought in development experts from other companies to look at the evolving product. As a result, the developers had to show their work to their peers. This was a powerful accelerator. The outside experts would say, "That sucks. Look at product X to see how it should be done." Or, "How could you possibly have a dumb bug like that?"

And the next week, everything would be fixed! The developers refused to be embarrassed again in front of their peers. Sutherland also sought feedback from software developers in MIT and companies along Route 128.

At the end of each month, the CEO got his demo. He could use the software himself and see how it was evolving. Sutherland also gave the software to the firm's consulting staff to use in prototyping consulting projects. This generated ideas to incorporate into the list of features that were desirable to have. At the beginning of each month's work, the list of features to be worked on was reprioritized before transformation into development tasks. This allowed the CEO to steer product development.

And in that very first team that Sutherland set up at Easel Corporation in 1993, the team went into a hyperproductive state. This effect was so dramatic that the project accelerated to the point that it began to overwhelm the documentation staff and testing engineers. The team was delivering so much software that management said it was too much. "Slow down!" they cried.

The CEO saw significant step-by-step progress in each monthly increment and agreed the software was ready to ship in the fifth increment, one month ahead of schedule. The firm offered a money-back guarantee that this new software would double developer productivity in the first month of use. It sold well, and the company had won a reprieve.

Although Sutherland's team had saved Easel from bankruptcy, the company didn't go on to become another Microsoft. The market hole into which it had already dug itself was too deep. In the topsy-turvy world of software development, Easel prospered for a while and then was swallowed by another firm. It no longer exists as a separate entity.

Nevertheless, something important had happened. Sutherland had shown that a high-performance team could be deliberately seeded. He had shown that the conventional wisdom was wrong: high-performance teams are not matters of luck or chemistry. Once the teams were set up right, it was possible to generate hyperproductivity.

Sutherland was interested in changing more than just a single team in a single organization. His goal was to change the whole software industry.

In the early 1990s, Ken Schwaber had used an approach similar to what was done at the Easel Corporation at his company, Advanced Development Methods. In 1995, Sutherland and Schwaber jointly presented a paper entitled the "SCRUM Development Process" at a software conference in Austin, Texas, its first public appearance. They collaborated during the following years to merge their writings, their experiences, and industry practices into what is now known in software development as Scrum.[12]

Six years later, in 2001, Sutherland, Schwaber, and fifteen colleagues got together in Snowbird, Colorado, and drafted the Agile Manifesto, which became a clarion call to software developers around the globe to pursue this radically different type of management.[13] Since then, Sutherland, Schwaber, and their colleagues have gone on to generate thousands of high-performance teams in hundreds of companies all around the world under the labels of *Scrum* and *Agile*.

Teams using the practices that Sutherland and his colleagues had pioneered have been unexpectedly productive. These were not just improvements where the teams were just slightly better than the norm. The best teams routinely obtain productivity increases of 200 to 400 percent, changes that are potentially industry-disruptive improvements.[14]

WHERE IS IT HAPPENING?

What happened in software development was similar in some ways to what was occurring in lean manufacturing (particularly at Toyota and Honda) and in new product development. Self-organizing teams have also been used for decades as an exception to hierarchical bureaucracy in the form of task forces that have been set up to solve a crisis and then typically disbanded. What is now happening is that this way of managing is now being to used get almost any work done more productively.

A further incentive for management to move in this direction is that the best talent will seek out firms that can provide this kind of a workplace. As managers start to see the benefits in one area, the approach tends to expand to every other aspect of firm activity. As a result, a radical new way of managing work is emerging. It involves a different way of thinking about work, managing work, and participating in work. It isn't a quick fix or an incremental change or shift at the periphery. When fully implemented, it affects everything in the organization. It is radically new management.

In the end, the productivity numbers—two- to four-times gains in productivity—by themselves make the change persuasive. When combined with client delight and deep job satisfaction, the wider adoption of radical management becomes inevitable.

That said, however, radical management isn't a panacea. It isn't applicable, for instance, in these situations:

- *Where the work is best done alone.* Most significant activities in the modern organization require collaboration. However, some individuals prefer to work alone, and some work is best done alone, such as writing novels or composing symphonies.

- *Where the work has a small knowledge component.* Firms with mainly unskilled labor may decide to organize the work in a traditional fashion as a hierarchical bureaucracy. They may, however, be at risk from competitors who figure out a way to draw on the knowledge and ingenuity of their workers, get on a steadily improving team approach, and provide more value to customers. As some firms have shown, there is really no such thing as unskilled labor: "unskilled labor" simply means that no one has yet taken the time and applied the intelligence to figure out how to do the job at a higher level.[15]
- *Where a public sector organization must be neutral.* The dispensation of justice, for instance, is required to be neutral for all parties. In the end, society as a whole may be delighted by the performance when this impartial implementation of justice is achieved. But that is a possible outcome rather than the goal sought after.

HOW WILL IT HAPPEN MORE WIDELY?

For most organizations, radical management is a fundamental change, even a wrenching shift in culture.

How will it happen?

The riskiest way is for top management to try to impose it. This will usually backfire, because that would be a continuation of traditional management practices.[16]

Among the mistakes of business process reengineering was to imagine that a bunch of experts in a back room could dream up a better process, design it in great detail, and then impose it on people doing the work. Not surprisingly, this exercise didn't take into account the realities of the work itself. It wasn't based on interactive communication with people so that they could participate in the cocreation of a new kind of workplace. It led to more of the same.

Radical management is about mobilizing the energies, spirit, and ingenuities of workers and focusing them on delighting clients and to go on doing it time after time in a sustainable way. To accomplish that, managers have to abandon their faith in backroom reengineering and enlist the workers in taking responsibility for cocreating a new, more productive, and more fulfilling future.

It means exploring the possibility that working together with other human beings responds to some permanent requirement of our nature—some ancient and deep-seated need to do things together with people to delight others.[17] It means breathing fresh life into timeless ideas like authenticity, truth, and team, even though these terms have been misused and abused and have fallen into contempt in some quarters. It speaks to both the economics and the ethics of respect. It means exploring what's involved in creating occasions for the kind of spiritedness that is called forth when people take things in hand for themselves.

It is ultimately about what it means to live a good life: working on something we love, together with people who share our enjoyment, to the delight of others, and getting steadily better at doing it.

Part 1

THE SEVEN PRINCIPLES OF CONTINUOUS INNOVATION

4

PRINCIPLE #1: DELIGHTING CLIENTS

> Delighting your customers is the only path to true growth.
>
> **Fred Reichheld**[1]

It is six-thirty in the morning in Golfe-Juan, a little village in the south of France. We are just a few kilometers from the big modern city of Cannes, but the scene I am looking at is as different from a big city as it is possible to be.

On this pleasantly crisp June morning, the sky is blue. I am sitting at an outdoor table of a café, Le Corsaire, sipping an espresso coffee. As I linger, the rich, irresistible smell of fresh warm bread is wafting across the one-lane street from the boulangerie, Mille Epis (literally, "a thousand ears of corn"), and tantalizing my nostrils. The bread is baked on the premises by people who are masters of their craft. Even at this hour, customers are coming to pick up their freshly baked baguettes. They usually buy two. It is no use buying one baguette. The bread is so tasty and aromatic that just about everyone who buys it will eat one on the way home.

I spend several months a year in France and the rest of the year in the United States. Each time I am away from France, I begin to think: Maybe

I was mistaken? Maybe I have exaggerated? Maybe I am romanticizing the quality of the baguettes? After all, French bread is French bread, available in countries outside France. Then I arrive in Golfe-Juan, and I bite into a freshly baked baguette. At once, all doubts vanish. There is no need to die. I am already in heaven.

Does Mille Epis make the best bread in Golfe-Juan? The debate is endless among the residents. Despite its tiny size, Golfe-Juan boasts three boulangeries in the center of the village, along with several others just a few hundred yards away. Some residents believe firmly in the bread made by Banette. Mille Epis also has its vocal supporters. A neighbor swears by the Boulangerie Artisanal, although even he concedes that his judgment could be clouded by the *décolleté* of the young woman who works there. Who is right? By any international standard, all of these boulangeries are making bread that is delectable.

Just a few steps away, in the two *boucheries,* the butchers are preparing veal steaks and lamb chops as carefully as pieces of jewelry. And just around the corner, in the three fish shops, or *poissonneries,* of Golfe-Juan, where the fish are laid out as carefully as fine clothing, the fishmonger can tell you when and where each fish was caught, what its merits are, and how to cook it. If you have the time and the inclination, she will also deploy her talents as a part-time philosopher and help you solve any personal problem you might be having.

The scene is somewhat reminiscent of a 1950s movie set. As I sit in the café, I would not be surprised to see Maurice Chevalier strolling merrily down the narrow street, with baguettes and a copy of the local newspaper, *Nice-Matin,* under his arm, gaily tipping his hat to the people he met.

By some idiosyncratic miracle, Golfe-Juan has been spared the ravages of commercial development. Everything is on a small scale. The commercial part of the village has only a couple of short streets.

It is not that everyone knows everyone else here; there are quite a few summer visitors like our family. But people in business here know who their customers are. They have direct and immediate contact with them daily. The customers care deeply about what they are buying. The people doing the work know in the most direct way on a daily basis whether they are delighting them.

THE MEANING OF WORK

Once upon a time, all work was like this. All work was local. The people for whom work was being performed were others in the area. The people doing the work could immediately see the results of it and understand how what they did related to the people they were doing it for. It wasn't that everyone was necessarily happy, but everyone knew the meaning of their work.

With the growth of giant corporations and the atomization and specialization of work, that clear line of sight of the people doing the work to the people for whom they were ultimately doing it was lost.

How did this happen?

One aspect of it is physical. As the scale of commerce and enterprises grew, the distance between the place where the work was done and whom it was being done for became steadily greater. Now it is just as likely that the things that we buy are made on the other side of the planet as that they are made down the road. When the client is ten thousand miles away, it's difficult to know whether he or she is being delighted.

But the other aspect of the loss had its source in a conceptual error going back to that author of twentieth-century management, Frederick Taylor, and his 1911 classic, *The Principles of Scientific Management.* When Taylor set out to induce the workman he called Schmidt to quadruple the amount of pig iron that he was able and willing to load in a day, he didn't bother to tell Schmidt why the pig iron was being loaded, what it would be used for, or who would be the eventual user.

The purpose of Schmidt's activities was decided in some other place. Schmidt had no line of sight as to the purpose of his work, clear or otherwise. He was engaged in a purely financial transaction. Schmidt's labor was being bought. If Taylor paid him more and taught him better work methods, Schmidt could be induced to work harder and produce more. Taylor treated Schmidt as a dull oaf whose job was to do what the boss wanted and not ask questions.

If we peruse the rest of Taylor's book and ask ourselves about the "other place" that was addressing the questions as to why Schmidt was being asked to load all that pig iron and whom it was for, the answers are not explicit. There is an unspoken assumption that whatever amount of pig iron the company was producing, somehow or other the company's sales department would be able to sell it.

From this way of looking at the world, we get to the viewpoint that the purpose of a firm, a project, or even work itself is to produce goods and services. This principle is laid down in management textbooks even today.[2]

Producing goods and services.

Things.

From this way of looking at the world, we can easily slide into thinking—mistakenly—that the purpose of work is to please the boss, who has decided what things are to be produced, or earn a salary, or advance up some managerial ladder. This way of thinking and acting is deadening, dispiriting, soul destroying—and pervasive.

In Golfe-Juan, the businesspeople in the boulangeries, the boucheries, and the poissonnerie, face-to-face with their ultimate customers daily, are not likely to be deluded into thinking that the purpose of work is to produce things, please the boss, or advance up some managerial ladder. These are people who do what they are doing because it delights their customers. Whether they can articulate it or not, these boulangers, bouchers, and poissonnières in Golfe-Juan are living in a world where the delight of customers is what the business is about.

When the delight of the client is kept continuously and rigorously in mind, many of the problems of the workplace disappear, and the possibilities of a different kind of work—more productive and more satisfying—become possible. When that principle is ignored, all sorts of workplace problems become insoluble. And we end up with the current situation where only one of five people is fully engaged in his or her work, and customers are being systematically frustrated.

THE NEW LOCALISM

A number of books have been written about the possibility of returning to a more local approach to work in order to combat the malfunctions of the modern workplace. In *The Craftsman,* Richard Sennett suggested that craftsmanship was a solution to the horrors of corporate bureaucracy.[3] In *Deep Economy,* Bill McKibben preached the value of localism and urged readers to live the kind of life that I see at 6:30 A.M. in my café in Golfe-Juan.[4] In *In Defense of Food,* Michael Pollan sang the praises of small farms and local produce.[5] In *Shop Class as Soulcraft,*[6] Matthew Crawford urged "a return to real work," by which he meant a return to tangible activities like repairing motorcycles. For Crawford, the solution to big business is small business. He extols the scrappy spirit of small business against "the softly despotic tendencies" of "outsized corporations."

These calls for a return to a local approach to work are romantic but unrealistic. They imply not just stopping the clock, but turning it back a few hundred years. The idea that we could solve the woes of the modern economy by abandoning globalization and returning to a world of local economies is more than a little nutty. There is no way that a set of local economies could possibly generate the prodigious array and attractive prices of the products and services that the global economy generates and consumers demand. Localism is possible today only because it piggybacks on the global economy.

The boulanger, or the boucher, and the poissonnière in Golfe-Juan can spend their days delighting clients by making gourmet bread or selling jeweled beef or the freshest fish. They can then make a short trip to the supermarket and buy an iPod, a computer, a flat-screen TV, or whatever else takes their fancy from around the world at reasonable prices. They have the best of both worlds. So globalization and big corporations are here to stay, at least for the foreseeable future.

As a general economic theory, the new localism may be nutty, but there is nevertheless some truth in it: the importance of a clear line of sight from those doing the work to those for whom the work is intended, and the possibility of focusing work on delighting those people as a way of relieving the threat to the human spirit posed by boring, meaningless labor. This is what the shopkeepers in Golfe-Juan, Sennett's craftsmen, Pollan's local farmers, and Crawford's motorcycle repairmen all have in common. They know who their clients are and can, if they so choose, focus their attentions on delighting them and ascertain almost immediately whether they are succeeding. It's not that their work is inherently more interesting than work in a large corporation. The difference is that their work has more meaning. It has a point. People can understand the story in which they are involved and can see immediately the results of their labors.

The fact that clients are more likely to be delighted, businesses are more likely to be profitable, and workers are more likely to be fulfilled in their work constitutes a triple win for all involved. The same principle was illustrated in 1911 when F. W. Taussig wrote in *The Principles of Economics*: "The actor, even though his occupation involves the monotonous and long continued repetition of the most trifling details, never fails to get a thrill of pleasure from the breathless silence or stirring applause of the audience. Were he compelled to go through his part as often and as rigorously under the cold supervision of an indifferent supervisor, and under that only, how flat and stale it would become!"[7]

Creating a clear line of sight from workers to clients is relatively easy when the business is local. But what about when the business is huge and global and the markets are vast, with tens of millions of customers? Is it possible to set up the same line of sight between workers and their clients?

At first glance, this seems to be impossible. But I discovered that it isn't so difficult after all. Before I get to that, let me first explain how the concept of client delight is used in practice.

THE ORGANIZATION'S PRIMARY GOAL: THINGS VERSUS PEOPLE

Management writers are unanimous that a key management function is to articulate a compelling purpose. Jim Collins calls it "big, hairy, audacious goal."[8] John Kotter says that the goal should be "desirable, feasible, focused, flexible and communicable."[9]

A firm needs a compelling purpose because, as Gary Hamel notes, "initiative, creativity and passion are gifts. They are benefactions the employees choose, day by day, and moment by moment, to give or withhold. They can't be commanded."[10] Exhortations to work harder or ordering workers to love their customers or kill their competitors won't induce people to give their very best. Managers need to articulate a purpose that is inherently self-motivating.

To see how to do that, let's put ourselves in the shoes of an organizational strategist and examine the possible options for crafting a compelling purpose for an organization. One obvious wrong turning would be to propose, as Frederick Taylor implied, that the purpose of a firm, a project, or even work itself is to produce goods and services. As a goal, producing goods and services doesn't get anyone's juices flowing. It's about mundane things and therefore deadening as a goal.

Another angle of attack would be to articulate the goal in terms of bigger things. Some firms have done this in the hope that if the thing is big enough, it will inspire enthusiasm. Thus, Google may offer to give people a chance to "change the world,"[11] and GM may say that it is "reinventing the automobile."[12] The problem with this approach is that it may be difficult for people doing the work to see how such grandiose goals relate to what they do on a day-to-day basis.

Yet another approach would be to draw on the language of sports and aim to be "a winner." Jack Welch did this famously in his goal to make GE number one or two in every sector it was involved in. However, when every firm is trying to be a winner, the ability of such a goal to inspire people on a long-term basis is questionable.

Nor would aiming to maximize shareholder value be likely to get people jumping out of bed in the morning with a spring in their step. Once the goal becomes making money for the company, then people start thinking about making money for themselves, and collaboration and creativity tend to fall by the wayside.[13]

Or we could go in the opposite direction and formulate the organizational goal in terms of lofty, big-hearted ideals like beauty, truth, or love.[14] These moral imperatives have aroused human beings to extraordinary accomplishments throughout the millennia. The problem with articulating a business goal in terms of such moral imperatives is that they usually have little to do with what the business is about. Cynicism sets in when the organization's real goals turn out to be very different from the stated ideals.[15]

Still another approach would be to point to the firm's activities as a good corporate citizen ("Yes, the principal function of our firm is to make money, but we also care for the environment, make charitable contributions, and undertake other worthwhile social activities"). The difficulty with this approach is that as long as the primary goal is to make money, these acts of corporate citizenship are likely to be seen both internally and externally as window dressing. And window dressing is unlikely to bring out the very best in people.

Strategists faced with these issues may despair of ever being able to articulate a goal that is simultaneously compelling, realistic, and unlikely to breed cynicism. Yet the problem is not as insoluble as it looks. In fact, the answer is so obvious that it is actually staring us in the face. Once we begin to think of articulating the organizational goals in terms of customers and stakeholders, the solution is simple.

In 1973, Peter Drucker provided a clue as to where to look: "There is only one valid definition of business purpose: to create a customer. . . . It is the customer who determines what a business is. It is the customer alone whose willingness to pay for a good or for a service converts economic resources into wealth, things into goods. . . . The customer is the foundation of a business and keeps it in existence."[16]

The shift in focus from things to people is a first step, but by itself, it's not enough to constitute a compelling goal today. In 1973, it might have been enough for an organization to *have* a customer—someone who is willing to pay for the good or service. In today's more intensively competitive world, merely having a customer who is willing to pay for the good or service is a precarious existence for any firm. The key to an enduring future is to have a customer who is willing to buy goods and services both today and tomorrow. It's not about a transaction; it's about forging a relationship. For this to happen, it isn't enough that the customer be passively satisfied. The customer must be delighted.

Delighting customers is not only a requirement of business survival; it also offers a solution to the dilemma of how to articulate a morally worthwhile and inspiring goal that is closely related to what the organization does. That's because delighting other people is inherently motivating. It leads to an understanding of the meaning of work, which relates to people, not things.

The meaning of work isn't in the bread that we're baking: it's in the enjoyment the customers get from eating the bread.

The meaning of work isn't in the words the actor is reciting; it's in the response of the audience to those words.

The meaning of work isn't in the toy that we're putting together; it's in the smile on the face of the child.

The meaning of work isn't in the bricks and mortar of the house we're building; it's in the happiness we generate in a family with a house that precisely meets their needs.

The meaning of work isn't in the words or the musical notes of the song that we're writing; it's in the feeling of yearning we generate in the heart of the listener.

The meaning of work isn't in the paper and print of the insurance policy we've issued; it's in the security that we're providing to the spouse and the children.

The meaning of the boutique hotel that we're running isn't in the rooms and the physical facilities; it's in the feeling of being at home away from home that we generate in people who stay there.

The meaning of the software we're coding doesn't lie in bits and bytes; it's in the cool things that users can do with the software.

The meaning that we see in work resides in the responses of the people for whom we are doing the work.

A key reason that traditional management is so dispiriting and often devoid of meaning is its focus on things and systems ahead of people. In such a world, workers find it difficult to see the point of what they are doing. By contrast, once the focus is on providing a clear line of sight—and continuously updated information—as to whether and to what extent clients are being delighted by what is being done, the meaning of work becomes obvious.

Articulating the goal of an organization as one of delighting customers changes the relationship from one of commercial manipulation to human interaction. It means a shift from thinking about how to manipulate customers into spending money on the organization's goods and services toward considering how we could do something that these people would genuinely enjoy, as a result of which, incidentally, money might change hands. The adjustment is subtle but fundamental. Customers appreciate their needs being attended to.

Even better, delighting clients as a goal also makes dramatic inroads on the problem of worker disgruntlement: delighting clients is an inherently inspirational goal for people doing the work, because delighting other people intrinsically appeals to our hearts. Thinking about and helping other people is central to ethics.

To top it off, delighting clients also makes hard-headed business sense. By focusing activity on what delights clients and jettisoning anything that is irrelevant to that goal, work is tightly linked to accelerating innovation and attaining higher productivity.

THE CASE OF THE PUBLIC SECTOR ORGANIZATION

In 1973, Peter Drucker was careful to limit his articulation of an organization's purpose to businesses in the private sector, which were driven by marketing: "Marketing is the distinguishing, unique function of the business. A business is set apart from all other human organizations by the fact that it markets a product or a service. Neither church, nor army, nor school, nor state does that. Any organization that fulfills itself through marketing a product or a service is a business. Any organization in which marketing is either absent or incidental is not a business and should never be managed as if it were one."[17]

True, public sector organizations face certain constraints that make it more difficult for them to generate delight. First, these organizations tend to have stakeholders rather than paying customers. It can be more difficult to identify the stakeholders whom the organization should focus on delighting, particularly if there are multiple groups of stakeholders with differing interests. Second, private sector firms have more latitude in choosing their clients. Often the key to delighting clients in the private sector is to focus on one set of clients over another. But the stakeholders of public sector organizations are often determined by law. Thus, an organization charged by law with collecting garbage in a city must pick up everyone's garbage, not just the garbage in certain neighborhoods. Third, some public sector organizations are deliberately designed to be neutral among different stakeholders. For instance, by definition, the system of justice not only cannot choose who seeks its services, it must also be even-handed among parties, not favoring one group over another.

Nevertheless, public organizations that provide services to the public can usefully address the question of who their stakeholders are, whether and to what extent priorities can be established among their needs, and whether and to what extent the organization is meeting those needs. The underlying principle is the same: the purpose of public sector organizations is to delight their principal stakeholders, although the constraints under which they operate sometimes make it more difficult for them to achieve that goal.[18]

DEVELOPMENT VERSUS PRODUCTION

The goal of client delight is most obvious where the work is explicitly related to innovation, that is, a new product or service that is being developed or enhanced. Where work is being done in a production setting and the product or service is already defined, client delight will come from process improvements rather than transformation of the product or service itself; the product or service remains the same. The question then becomes: How can we deliver it faster, cheaper, safer, or with higher quality?

BASIS OF CLIENT DELIGHT

Production

Nature of the work: Produce a standard product or service

Source of client delight: Finding ways to deliver the product or service sooner or more cheaply or more safely or in a more environmentally friendly way

Development

Nature of the work: Produce a new product or service

Source of client delight: Finding ways to produce something new, remarkable, different, or unexpected, in a way that meets real needs and creates pleasant surprise

In effect, where production work is being done in a mindful, intelligent fashion, the team explores hypotheses for learning. Flight attendants can consider how to make a flight more enjoyable or memorable for this group of passengers. Factory workers can explore whether there is some way they can handle this production shift more efficiently, more safely, or with higher quality. The clerk on the hotel reception desk can investigate whether there are better ways to deal with customers who arrive with a lot of emotional baggage. The parent preparing a meal can review how to make this meal more enjoyable for the family.

In a production setting, the worker might make an explicit decision not to do work in an intelligent, mindful fashion and treat it as a chore. This person's mind-set becomes, "How do I get through this shift, meet my contractual obligations with the least possible effort, get my pay, and get out of here?" That is one option: work as a transaction, a deadening grind. But it's not the only option. Truly living in the present and having a meaningful life implies the opposite decision: treating everything one does in life as an opportunity to delight others.

I show in Chapter Nine how Toyota, despite recent stumbles, has made continuous improvement an integral part of both the way that it designs new cars and the way that it produces cars that have already been designed. Toyota implements more than 1 million new ideas each year—a dramatic difference from traditional management.[19] Many of the ideas come from the most routine parts of the production process. Innovation isn't limited to new product development; continuous innovation is part of the way the whole company runs.

Let's look at a couple of harder examples.

The Supermarket Checkout Clerk

A colleague challenged me recently: Could the job of checkout clerk at a Safeway supermarket checkout counter ever be transformed into a job that would delight clients?

At the outset, I am willing to concede that this job, as traditionally designed, has low knowledge content. Hence the difference between the best and the worst performance is likely to be quite small. The potential gains from radical management of that particular job will be constrained by this fact.

Yet a moment's reflection will show that the traditional role of a checkout clerk is one to which intelligence has yet to be applied. In some supermarkets, this position is becoming increasingly unnecessary as the task of holding products in front of a scanner is something that the customers themselves do. The job of the checkout clerk then becomes one of helping customers master the task, resolving any problems, gathering intelligence about what customers would really like from the supermarket, and finding new ways to delight clients—including not bothering those who prefer to shop in silence.

The Chinese Quilt Maker

In a similar vein, philosopher cum motorcycle mechanic Matthew Crawford asks: "Can a Chinese factory worker stitching together a vernacular rural American quilt understand the culturally specific significance to the person using it?"[20] Crawford argues that the geographical and cultural estrangement of the Chinese quilt maker precludes this kind of experience.

This is not necessarily a fatal objection if we distinguish between the team deciding what to make and the team actually making it. The quilt maker in the Chinese factory is not likely to be part of the team deciding what to make and may lack the cultural background and understanding to contribute significantly to quilt design for another country.

But that is not the only option. In a production setting where the product is already defined, the potential for client delight comes from applying knowledge to improving the process. Can we make this product better or more cheaply or quickly or safely or in a more environmentally friendly way?

Let us suppose that the quilt maker is a member of a team of quilt makers. Let us further suppose that there are potential satisfactions that come from developing better techniques for making quilts; that workers derive satisfaction from having their ideas for improvement taken seriously; and that the workers also get feedback on how quilts are received when their improvements are implemented. Is it too far-fetched to imagine intelligent management creating relatively stimulating quilt-making jobs?

Even if it were true that nothing could be done to redefine routine jobs like the Safeway supermarket clerk or the quilt maker in China, why not refocus jobs with high knowledge content that can easily be refocused on delighting clients? The hard cases of jobs with low knowledge content should not prevent us from tackling the knowledge-rich jobs where the gains from radical management will be major.

DO WE HAVE THE RIGHT GOAL?

The concept of client delight can help us get our arms around the thorny question of whether we are on the right track. The first step is to think through several questions. Who are the clients we are trying to delight with this idea? Are they, or could they be, delighted by what we are proposing? Is there something that would delight them more, or sooner?

This process is iterative. The goal can be fine-tuned during implementation. For instance, when knowledge management was introduced at the World Bank in 1996, our initial thinking about how we would share knowledge was that it would be mainly electronic. We would be using the Web as the knowledge-sharing highway and building knowledge collections. As we got into implementation, we found for a variety of reasons that electronic transfer wasn't delighting users nearly as much as connecting people who needed to know something with people who already knew about it. Connections turned out to be more of a delighter than collections. So we shifted direction to put much more emphasis on connection over collection.

By contrast, some of the top managers at the World Bank were focused on a thing: they thought that the goal was to build an information technology system. This admittedly was something that we had mentioned at the outset, and it was still part of our plan. But whereas they were looking for a system and focused on a thing, my principal focus was on people. So I would respond to them that building a system was a means, not an end. Our goal was to share knowledge in whatever way best met people's needs. It turns out that connecting people together is delighting more people than building a system, so I was focused principally on connecting people, which is more important than building a system.

Some senior managers didn't agree and even had me recruit an outside panel to review what was going on and tell us how and why we had gone wrong. We assembled a blue-ribbon panel of the world's top knowledge management experts. And they effectively told top management that the problem with knowledge management in the World Bank was top management itself: they didn't understand that knowledge management isn't about building a thing; it is about doing something for people.

When we are thinking of the goal as a thing, we tend to get stuck with the thing we started with. The thing might have been a good idea at the time, but maybe not the best idea. When we are thinking about how to delight people, a lot of options open up, both at the outset and along the way. It's not a one-time examination but an ongoing iterative process of continuously asking: How am I intending to delight the clients and stakeholders? Are they being delighted? If not, why not? How can I change that? How can I create more opportunities to delight them? How can I delight them faster?

From a productivity viewpoint, the wonderful thing is that often the customer wants less. If we can get them the one thing that they really need sooner, they will be more excited than they would be getting the whole shebang at a later date. (See Practices #3 and #4.)

From a marketing viewpoint, the tricky part is that clients don't know what they want until they experience it, and then they discover that what they thought they wanted is close to, but not exactly, what they really want. They don't realize the implications of what they asked for, and in any event, the situation has changed, so now they want something different. Simply taking direction from what people say they want is going to lead to some mistakes. The only sure way to find out is to try the idea and see what the reaction is.

WHO DECIDES?

Making clear and timely decisions on the priorities for each iteration of work is central to radical management. It should be clear to everyone who is making those decisions.

In the case of software development at the Easel Corporation in 1993, management set the general direction in terms of the type of software product to be developed. Then the software development team was responsible for setting priorities within each iteration and building the software.

Because of the difficulty of performing both functions—setting priorities and doing the work—it has become more typical (and, in some software methodology, obligatory) to separate responsibility for the two functions of setting priorities and doing the work. A product manager, product owner, or vision holder is the person who has enough knowledge of the client, knowledge of the substance of the work, and authority within the organization to be able to set priorities for each iteration of the work of the team doing the work.[21] In large projects, the product manager or vision holder might be leading a substantial team in order to accomplish the function. In some cases, the clients themselves perform the function.

However the function is performed, it is vital that it gets done in a clear and timely fashion, in collaboration with the team doing the work. The point needs to be emphasized. As in the case of Nathalie, the software developer we met in Chapter One, a frequent cause of the breakdown of self-organizing teams is the failure to set priorities in a timely fashion and make a clear decision on what work is to be done.

THE THREE AGES OF CAPITALISM

Writing in *Harvard Business Review*, Roger Martin suggests that modern capitalism can be broken down into three major eras.[22]

The first era, *managerial capitalism*, stretched from 1932 to 1965, and was characterized by the view that firms should be run by professional managers, with ownership divorced from management.[23]

The second era, *shareholder capitalism*, began around 1976 and continues today.[24] It reflects the view that the purpose of every firm should be to maximize shareholders' value.

The third era, which Martin says is now emerging, is that of *customer capitalism*. The purpose of a firm is to serve clients. If firms do that well, Martin argues, benefits for shareholders will follow.

Maximizing Shareholder Value as a Goal

Martin notes that pursuing the maximization of shareholder value as a goal suffers from inherent internal contradictions. The harder the CEO is pushed to increase shareholder value, the more likely the CEO will make moves that actually hurt the shareholders.

Since the stock price is largely driven by shareholders' future expectations, the CEO is driven to focus on those things that boost shareholders' future expectations, often at the expense of doing the things that will actually improve long-term value to shareholders.

Only One Variable Can Be Maximized

Martin's article is also helpful in eliminating an apparent escape hatch. Why not aim to maximize both shareholder value and client delight?

The mathematics of optimization shows that only one variable can be maximized. Two variables cannot be simultaneously maximized unless one variable comprises the other. It is thus possible to maximize both satisfied clients and delighted clients because satisfied clients include delighted clients. It is not possible to maximize both client delight and shareholder value. You have to choose one or the other.

MEASURING CLIENT DELIGHT

A mantra of traditional managers is that you can't manage anything unless you can measure it. How, they ask, could you possibly measure something as ethereal and mercurial as client delight?

To answer that question, let's meet Fred Reichheld. Reichheld grew up in Parma, Ohio. With a B.A. from Harvard University and an M.B.A. from Harvard Business School, he made his career as a management consultant at Bain & Company in Boston.

He and some colleagues at Bain spent twenty-five years trying to understand how firms create relationships of trust and loyalty and the business impact that they get from that. Now he devotes much of his time to writing books and lecturing on loyalty. He is an idealist and a perfectionist. He believes that people spend their lives in search of people and institutions worthy of their loyalty and commitment. "People yearn for that," he said.[25]

When Reichheld began his investigation into customer loyalty, its importance was not widely accepted; in fact, most business executives presumed that loyalty was dead. But he was unwilling to live in a world where loyalty was presumed irrelevant to how the business was run. He worked hard to quantify the importance and economic leverage of loyal customer relationships. Studies showed that most companies could double profits by increasing customer retention by just 5 to 10 percent per year.[26]

Yet even with these data in hand, he still found that few firms acted on them. One set of reasons concerned the data: customer satisfaction surveys were long and complicated, and few people filled them in. In fact, trying to get them completed tended to annoy the very customers whose satisfaction was being measured. They were useful for research but not for driving operational decisions. Another reason was that the data were slow to reach the people responsible. And even with the data in hand, managers didn't know how to interpret or act on the information. They didn't see the bearing of the satisfaction scores on the way they ran the business on a day-to-day basis. Moreover, the data were easily gamed or manipulated.

As a practical matter, customer loyalty remained a mysterious black box—an attractive mantra, but not leading to anything very practical.

So Reichheld realized that he had to do something different. He needed an instrument that companies could use to track the quality of their client relationships. It would need to be so simple that people could understand it easily. It had to be plausible and credible so that people would use it. The survey should tie in to the actual behavior being surveyed. And the survey results ought to relate to actual business results. If he could do all this with a single survey instrument, he would enable managers to focus on the real sources of long-term growth. But given all the noise in organizations, was it possible to devise such a single instrument?

One trigger came from the experience of Enterprise Rent-A-Car. Enterprise had made startling inroads into a highly competitive market previously dominated by entrenched companies like Hertz and Avis. It had done this by keeping a tight focus on increasing the proportion of enthusiastic customers. They wanted evangelists—people who loved their company and would sing its praises to friends and colleagues. And they found a way to measure that: a very simple set of questions focusing on whether customers were enthusiastic about Enterprise's services. They used this as a tool to run the business, tracking the performance of managers and units. It led to remarkable success in the marketplace.

This experience got Reichheld thinking. Maybe he had focused too much on the entire range of customers, from the most satisfied to the least, with a large body of customers falling into the undifferentiated middle. This led to a focus on glacier-like shifts in average scores, which concealed what was going on at the extremes, where the real engines of growth lay. What was more important were the outliers—the enthusiasts who loved the firm and talked it up to their friends and colleagues. Those customers became in effect the unpaid marketing department of the firm. Reichheld realized that he needed to give more attention to client delight.

Based on the Enterprise model, Reichheld set out to devise a universal process to measure client delight that linked to a firm's relative growth: a survey that would work across multiple firms and industries. The idea was to focus on one question that connected most closely to customer repurchase rates and referrals.

It took Reichheld and his colleagues several years of research to figure out which question worked best. Eventually he did find a single survey question that held out promise. That question wasn't directly about customer enthusiasm or loyalty. Rather, it was about customers' willingness to recommend a product or service to someone else. In fact, in most of the industries that he studied, the percentage of customers who were enthusiastic enough to refer a friend or colleague—perhaps the strongest sign of customer loyalty—correlated directly with whether they actually recommended the firm. He called this new process the net promoter score—and it is being used by a growing number of firms, including American Express, Apple, GE, Intuit, Philips, and Zappos.[27]

THE ADDICTION TO BAD PROFITS

One of the issues that the net promoter methodology highlighted was the addiction that many firms had to abusive practices that boosted short-term earnings at the expense of customer loyalty. When customers are delighted, they tend to tell other people about their happy experiences. Equally, when they are unhappy about their experiences, they share that too.

In 2006, Reichheld wrote: "In the past, the accepted maxim was that every unhappy customer told ten friends. Now an unhappy customer can tell ten thousand 'friends' through the Internet."[28] Today the number of people a single individual could tell could be very much larger. Thus, Comcast, the largest cable provider in the United States, trumpets on its Web site, "Comcast will deliver a superior experience to our customers every day." However, when a disgruntled customer called Comcast to have a serviceman come and repair his cable connection and then found the serviceman asleep on his sofa, he made a video of it and posted it on YouTube. The video has been seen by more than 1 million viewers.[29]

Similarly, when baggage handlers at United Airlines broke the guitar of Canadian singer David Carroll in 2009 and then refused to pay for the twelve hundred dollar repair, Carroll created a music video, "United Breaks Guitars," which has been viewed more than 6 million times. United executives met with him and promised to do better. When United lost his bag again a few months later, the story made the front page of the *International Herald Tribune.*[30]

How much does it cost for Comcast or United Airlines to fix the damage caused by those videos? In fact, *no* amount of money can fix it. Comcast and United have been caught in the act of making "bad profits": money made at the expense of a customer relationship. The only way to recover their reputations is through earning it afresh by delivering consistently superior experience.

The phenomenon of bad profits isn't new. What is new is that customers can fight back, and with a vengeance, making it difficult for any customers to believe that Comcast will really "deliver a superior experience to our customers every day" or that United is really "flying the friendly skies." The positive things that other managers and workers have done for clients can be wiped out by a single disastrous piece of publicity.

"Whenever a customer feels misled, mistreated, ignored or coerced," Reichheld writes, "then profits from that customer are bad. Bad profits come from unfair or misleading pricing. Bad profits arise when companies save money by delivering a lousy customer experience. Bad profits are about extracting value from customers, not creating value. When sales reps push overpriced or inappropriate products onto trusting customers, the reps are generating bad profits. When complex pricing schemes dupe customers into paying more than necessary to meet their needs, those pricing schemes are contributing to bad profits."[31]

Merely looking at financial results can thus conceal how the profits were made. If the profits are made in these unscrupulous ways, then the pure financial number is misleading. The company is building hidden brand liabilities that will have to be repaid in the future. This helps explain why some companies that appear to be financially flourishing suddenly run into trouble: they have been mining their long-term customer relationships with bad profits to prop up the bottom line. It hardly matters whether a firm is bringing in delighted new customers through the front door if even larger numbers of disillusioned detractors are departing through the back door.

To get a sense of whether it is making any headway in the marketplace, a firm has to take into account not only the total amount of delight it has created, but also the level of frustration and disappointment among those who were likely to become active detractors.

For those who see business as the unvarnished pursuit of profit, the very notion of bad profits is an oxymoron. For these people, a dollar is a dollar, and they should all look the same on an income statement. But Reichheld says no: bad profits are a trap. They hide brand liabilities that are accumulating behind the scenes and eventually have to be repaid in hard cash. Distinguishing between good and bad profits is thus critical to determining the true financial health of a firm.

In fact, once Reichheld brought detractors into the mix, along with promoters, he saw a strong correlation between survey responses and relative growth rate across competitors. Client delight is thus measured with this equation:

% Promoters – % Detractors = % Net promoters

Clumping customers into three groups—the promoters, the passively satisfied, and the detractors—turned out not only to provide the simplest, most intuitive, and best predictor of customer behavior; it also made sense to frontline managers. They could grasp intuitively what it meant to be increasing the number of promoters and reducing the number of detractors. This made more sense than trying to increase the mean of their satisfaction index by one standard deviation.

THE DESIGN OF THE INSTRUMENT

After much experimentation, Reichheld found that the survey question that generally worked best was an eleven-point scale from 0 to 10: 10 meant "extremely likely" to recommend; 5 meant "neutral"; and 0 meant "not at all likely." (See Figure 4.1.)

When he looked at customer referral and repurchase behaviors along this scale, he divided responders into three groups. "Promoters," the customers with the highest rates of repurchase and referral, gave ratings of 9 or 10 to the question. The "passively satisfied" logged a 7 or an 8, and "detractors" scored from 0 to 6.

FIGURE 4.1 Reichheld's Ultimate Question

"How likely is it that you will recommend this firm or service or product to a colleague or friend?"

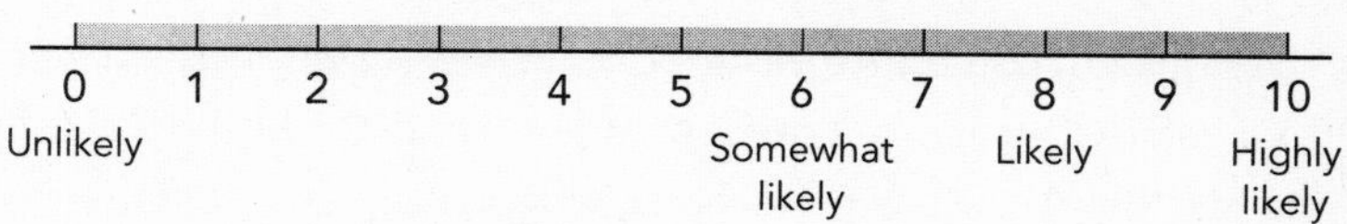

By focusing on only the most enthusiastic and the most negative customers, he sidestepped the grade inflation that often undermines traditional customer satisfaction assessments, in which someone even a tad above average is considered "satisfied."

Reichheld's work has been questioned by competitors in the survey business, particularly those who make a living by selling complex customer surveys. Some academics are not happy with it because of the loss of data that occurs by lumping customers into three main categories: the promoters, the passively satisfied, and the detractors.

Reichheld himself is careful not to overstate the reliability or validity of the method. It's not intended as a tool for academic study, he notes, and it doesn't work in some settings—in a sector where a firm has a monopoly, or in some business-to-business sectors, where a question about repeat purchases is likely to be more relevant. And the survey results need to be continuously audited against actual experience to make sure that gaming or other noise is not entering the system.

Reichheld's net promoter score thus has its limitations. The categorization of customers into three categories based on their response to one question is certainly not perfect. Nevertheless, it is practical and intuitive, and, most important, it drives rapid learning and action across the organization.

In time, better measures may be developed. But for now, the net promoter score is the best measure available for determining client delight. Many organizations have found that it is adequate for practical purposes to move ahead.

WHY ARE WE NOT BEING DELIGHTED?

One final point puzzled me about client delight. I could see that delighting clients had become a requirement for business survival, and I could see how client delight could be measured. So why was I not being delighted? As I looked back over my experiences and tried to think of a time in the past six months when I had been delighted by an encounter in the marketplace with a large organization, I found it difficult to think of more than one or two such experiences.

This led me to inquire: Are these companies even trying to delight me? So I visited the Web sites of the Fortune 20 in April 2010 and looked at what they say they are trying to do. In some cases, I found it relatively easy to determine the firm's principal goal, because there was an explicit mission statement. In other cases, I had to deduce the firm's principal mission from a page called "our values" or "who we are." These are the principal goals I identified:

- ExxonMobil: Achieve superior financial and operating results while simultaneously adhering to high ethical standards.[32]
- Walmart: Save people money to help them live better lives.[33]
- Chevron: To be the global energy company most admired for its people, partnership, and performance.[34]
- ConocoPhilips: Use its pioneering spirit to responsibly deliver energy to the world.[35]
- GE: Make money, make it ethically, make a difference.[36]
- GM: Exceed every expectation you've set for us.[37]
- Ford: Be an exciting viable Ford delivering profitable growth for all.[38]
- AT&T: Connect people with their world, everywhere they live and work, and do it better than anyone else.[39]
- HP: Explore how technology and services can help people and companies address their problems and challenges, and realize their possibilities, aspirations and dreams.[40]
- Valero: Supply fuel and other products that improve people's lives.[41]
- Bank of America: Fulfill our responsibility to the financial health of families, businesses, and communities.[42]
- Citibank: Provide financial services needed by communities in over 140 countries.[43]

- Berkshire Hathaway: Make money for shareholders.[44]
- IBM: Be a values-based enterprise of individuals who create and apply technology to make the world better.[45]
- McKesson: Deliver the vital medicines, supplies and information technologies that enable the health care industry to provide patients better, safer care.[46]
- JP Morgan Chase: Build the best financial services company in the world.[47]
- Verizon: Put customers first by providing excellent service and great communications experiences.[48]
- Cardinal Health: Make health care safer and more productive by applying customer-driven innovation and customer-focused execution to deliver the tangible results that matter most to health care organizations.[49]
- CVS Caremark: Provide prescriptions and related health services with an unmatched breadth of capabilities.[50]
- Procter & Gamble: Provide branded products and services of superior quality and value that improve the lives of the world's consumers.[51]

What the Web Sites Revealed

The summary results of my informal survey of the principal mission of the companies are as follows:

Principal Mission	Number of Companies
"Public relations" goals	4
Make money	4
Produce goods and services	9
Satisfy clients	3
Delight clients	0

Public Relations Goals

Four firms—Bank of America, GM, JPMorgan Chase, and Chevron—indicated a principal mission that is best classified as a public relations goal. In these cases, they are saying things that sound good and constitute convenient things to say rather than truly reflecting what the firm is principally trying to accomplish.

Making Money or Producing Goods and Services

ExxonMobil, GE, Ford, and Berkshire Hathaway indicated that their principal goal is to make money. GE softens the formulation by saying that its goal is to "make money for shareholders, make it ethically, and make a difference." But at least GE is frank: its principal goal is to make a buck.

Given the widespread preoccupation over the past few decades with increasing shareholder value, it seems probable that more than four of twenty firms were focused principally on enhancing shareholder value. At least some of these firms have made a public relations decision that it would be impolitic to state such a goal on their Web site.

Instead, nine of the twenty firms indicate on their Web sites that their principal goal is to provide goods and services of various kinds. They are Walmart, ConocoPhilips, HP, Valero, Citibank, IBM, McKesson, CVS Caremark, and Procter & Gamble.

Client Delight

Only three firms have a principal goal that is explicitly client centered: AT&T, Verizon, and Cardinal Health.

None of the top twenty firms in the Fortune 500 have a principal mission of "delighting clients" or anything analogous. To find this kind of mission, you have to go to a firm like Starbucks, whose mission is, "To inspire and nurture the human spirit—one person, one cup, and one neighborhood at a time," or to Southwest Airlines: "dedication to the highest quality of Customer Service delivered with a sense of warmth, friendliness, individual pride, and Company Spirit."

Implications

Now I had the answer to the puzzle as to why the largest companies are not frequently delighting me: they aren't even trying. Instead they have simpler, less ambitious goals, with significant negative consequences.

The majority of the firms see themselves as "making money for shareholders" or "producing goods and services." This leads to a characteristic way of managing: top-down bureaucracy. Once the firm sees itself in the business of producing things, a command-and-control bureaucracy becomes the logical way to structure and manage it.[52] Work is carried out by following a plan devised by management, communications are conducted on a need-to-know basis, and productivity gains are made by downsizing and outsourcing. The workplace that ensues from this way of organizing is less productive than it could be, dispiriting to the people doing the work, and dissatisfying the customers they are supposedly doing it for.

If instead a firm starts from the goal of delighting clients, then bureaucracy ceases to be a viable organizational option. Instead the firm will, like Southwest Airlines or Starbucks, naturally gravitate toward some variation of self-organizing teams as the default model for organizing work. That's because it is only through mobilizing the full energy and ingenuity of the workforce that the firm is likely to have any chance of success at generating the continuous innovation needed to delight clients.

Once the firm adopts self-organizing teams aimed at delighting clients, downsizing and outsourcing are seen in their true light as counterproductive to everything the firm is trying to accomplish.[53] Instead, doing work in an iterative fashion and providing value in each iteration are the norm. Radical transparency between managers and workers becomes a necessary principle for achieving the goal. Happily, when firms get into this mode, the risk of needing to downsize or outsource its core business is reduced: continuous self-improvement is a normal and natural way in which self-organizing teams evolve toward high performance.

These are two radically different ways of organizing and managing. One is a downward spiral with negative economic, moral, and social consequences. The other is a virtuous circle with happy consequences for firm productivity, job satisfaction, and client delight.

Bureaucracy and the supremacy of an internally driven system to produce goods and services represent the past. High-performance teams focused on igniting client delight are the future. It is to this way of organizing that we now turn.

PRACTICES FOR DELIGHTING CLIENTS

Practice #1: *Identify Your Primary Clients*

Radical management focuses tightly on its core market of primary clients: if it can delight this group, it will have a resilient client base.[54] Trying to satisfy everyone practically guarantees average products and services that will not delight anyone.

With some exceptions, analogous arguments apply in the public sector. Typically public sector organizations have multiple categories of stakeholders, each wanting different things from the organization. Establishing priorities among stakeholders can be a key step toward establishing any kind of organizational focus.[55]

Practice #2: *Delight Primary Clients by Meeting Their Unrecognized Desires*

Satisfying customers can be accomplished by meeting the explicit needs and desires that customers feel and can express if they are asked. Obviously one needs to take care of the basics: putting a lot of fancy gadgets on a car won't help if the car doesn't start.[56]

But meeting explicit needs and desires doesn't turn clients into enthusiastic promoters of the organization. To accomplish that, a firm needs to identify and meet unrecognized desires.

The world wasn't asking Apple to make cool-looking mp3 players or arrange an easy, cheap way for people to download music online. People didn't know they wanted iPods or easy music download services until Apple invented them. As Chip Conley says in *Peak*, "Apple did a bit of mind reading with respect to what their customers (or potential customers) would truly love but didn't know could be available to them." In the process, Apple "went from being an also-ran in the computer hardware wars to being at the front of the pack for how the world purchases and listens to music in the 21st Century."[57]

The boutique hotel chain Joie de Vivre isn't merely providing comfortable hotel rooms at a reasonable price. It aims to provide an environment where customers feel at one with themselves and truly in their ideal habitat. Until Joie de Vivre provided it, people didn't know they could have that.[58]

BMW isn't merely building cars that get you from A to B. It is aiming to build "the ultimate driving machine" that delights you every time you sit behind the wheel.

Harley-Davidson isn't merely building reliable motorcycles. It aims to fulfill the dreams of its customers through the motorcycle experience. If that means going beyond the signature full-throated roar of their Harley and enabling the Harley owners to embellish their vehicles with grassroots folk art, the company will help them do it.[59]

By identifying and meeting the unrecognized desires of the core clients, an organization moves beyond average to outstanding.

Practice #3: *Aim for the Simplest Possible Thing That Will Delight*

One way of delighting customers is to aim for the simplest possible thing that will delight them and subsequently enhance quality in an iterative fashion over time. The organization creates the one thing that the customer really wants and adds other elements later in the light of experience.

The iPod and the iPhone were successful initially not because they were superior as an mp3 player or as a phone, but because they met the needs of a particular set of clients: young people who wanted cool devices. The refinements came later.

By contrast, the remote control for the DVD player in my house does not delight me. It has scores of functions. I am sure all of them function perfectly—if I were to spend enough time studying the manual and learn how to use them. The few simple functions that I usually perform have become buried in a morass of possible functions that I might possibly need but probably never will. I am not delighted.

Practice #4: *Explore the Possibility of Delighting More by Offering Less*

Listening to clients is necessary. Yet it can also lead to a client-driven death spiral. As more and more customer requests are met and features are added, the product can become unlovable or even unusable.

Subjective quality is thus different from objective quality. Objectively, my DVD remote may be better: it has more functions than a simpler version that met my needs more precisely. But subjectively it's not better, and in the marketplace, it's subjective quality that counts.

Practice #5: *Explore More Alternatives*

There are generally many more ways to delight clients than are currently being exploited by the organization. As we shall see in Chapter Five, one way of doing this is to develop user stories. Put yourself inside the mind of a client and ask, "What could delight this client more or sooner?"

Practice #6: *Defer Decisions Until the Last Responsible Moment*

There are usually multiple ways of achieving what the client would like to accomplish. Rather than jumping to the first obvious thing, it can be better to wait until more is known about the client and the economics, and only then make the best decision.

Practice #7: *Avoid Mechanistic Approaches*

Companies are exhorted to "know the customer," which often translates into a compilation of detailed records of individual likes and dislikes. But customers are human beings with moods and desires that change, sometimes by the minute. For instance, hotels that keep computerized records of what clients order so that they can surprise them on later visits by anticipating their requests may well find that the client wants something different.[60]

Practice #8: *Focus on People, Not Things*

The Agile software movement has contributed greatly to our understanding of radical management. One area, however, where the thinking is less developed is determining what the goal is.

The Agile Manifesto of 2001 declares that producing "working software" or "potentially shippable software" is the primary measure of progress. Reports and charts are given less importance than the real thing: working software. This approach has contributed to greater transparency as to whether progress is really being made. However, the focus on "working software" puts emphasis on things, not the people for whom the software is being produced. Since hierarchical bureaucracy is the logical organizational arrangement for producing things, a focus on producing things increases the risk of sliding back into the world of hierarchical bureaucracy.

Practice #9: *Give the People Doing the Work a Clear Line of Sight to the People for Whom the Work Is Being Done*

The team is able to see whether and to what extent the client is delighted by its work. Management ensures that the client or a client proxy is available to give feedback on whatever is delivered at the end of each iteration.

5

PRINCIPLE #2: SELF-ORGANIZING TEAMS

> I think it's hard for those who have never been on a high performance team to understand just how cool it is.
>
> **Kristin Arnold[1]**

"Osama bin Laden's whereabouts are a puzzle," wrote Malcolm Gladwell in the *New Yorker.* "We can't find him because we don't have enough information. The key to the puzzle will probably come from someone close to bin Laden, and until we can find that source bin Laden will remain at large."[2] A puzzle may be difficult to solve, but if you have enough analytical skill and enough information, you can find the right answer.

By contrast, a mystery doesn't have a single right answer. Thus, the problem of what would happen in Iraq after the toppling of Saddam Hussein was a mystery. "It wasn't a question that had a simple, factual answer," Gladwell continued. "Mysteries require judgments and the assessment of uncertainty.... The C.I.A. had a position on what a post-invasion Iraq would look like, and so did the Pentagon and the State Department and Colin Powell and Dick Cheney and any number of political scientists and journalists and think-tank fellows. For that matter, so did every cabdriver in Baghdad."[3]

With a mystery, we could go on endlessly analyzing the problem, searching for a better solution, and never be sure that we had arrived at a "right answer" until after we had seen what actually happened. A mystery is essentially unique. It doesn't repeat.

In the twentieth century, traditional management got very good at solving puzzles. In business, the puzzle involved finding the most efficient way to deliver goods and services to eventual customers. Information could be gathered. Marketing could determine what goods and services should be supplied. Systems could be set up. Mathematical optimization techniques could be applied. As a result, productivity increased, and money was made, so management had good reason to believe that it had the right answer. But it didn't always keep in mind that in dealing with the world in this way, it was solving tame problems, namely, puzzles.

Today management is facing a more complex challenge: the mystery of how to delight clients. The question of how to do this doesn't have a single right answer. Typically we don't even understand what will or will not delight clients until after we have seen how they react. The techniques of social science, such as asking people what they want in interviews or focus groups, have turned out to be of limited help. That's because the people themselves often don't know what will delight them until they have the actual experience. Today management is confronted with trying to figure out a mystery—a wicked problem, a problem where we don't know in advance what the right answer is.

How do you solve a problem when you don't know the right answer? One of the first people to make a systemic contribution to this issue was a man called Henry FitzEmpress.

THE CASE OF HENRY FITZEMPRESS

At the age of twenty-one, Henry FitzEmpress became the head of a large and troubled organization. He was a stocky man with a round head like a lion, a fiery freckled face, and red hair. When he was angry, his gray eyes glowed fiercely and grew bloodshot. His voice was rough, supposedly because he spent so much time out of doors.

He had obtained control of the organization partly through inheritance from his mother and partly because he had seized it by his own initiative. The organization in question was the government of a bunch of squabbling tribes that occupied an island off the coast of France.

At the ceremony marking his taking control in Westminster Abbey on December 19, 1154, in the presence of two archbishops, fourteen bishops, counts and barons from overseas, and a vast multitude of the common people, Henry dared to crown himself the "king of England."[4] By contrast, his predecessors had aspired to be only "the king of the English." Henry's aspiration from the beginning was nothing less than to create a nation.

At the time, England was far from being a unified country run by something called a government. The country was still recovering from a disastrous civil war between the prior king, Stephen, and Henry's mother, Matilda. The civil war had ended with Stephen's death and the crown going to Henry. Although the war was over, the mercenary soldiers hired by both sides were still around and had taken up robbery as a profession. Local authority had broken down, as communities were still divided between the factions. Both groups had rewarded their supporters with the lands of the local opponents. Chaos ruled.

At the time, the expeditions to Jerusalem known as the Crusades were in full swing. Landowners had been away from their castles for years at a time, and squatters had been taking over unoccupied and unclaimed property.

Being crowned king of England didn't mean that Henry had any administrative apparatus that could do things like prevent crime or administer justice. Apart from a hodgepodge of local courts, the one real judicial system in the land was run by Henry's competitor for power, the Roman Catholic church, which answered not to Henry but to the pope in Rome. It acted like an empire unto itself. Being a large landowner, its judicial system was hardly considered impartial.[5]

Henry saw that if being king was to mean anything at all, he would have to establish a judicial system. It would need to solve the legal chaos that people were facing, while at the same time establishing his own power as the source of justice in the land.

The biggest disputes concerned land: no one knew who owned what. There was no central recording office for real property, and sorting things out depended on human memory and conflicting wills and deeds. Cases often arose when landowners returned from the Crusades or died thousands of miles from home. Moreover, most of the available expertise resided in Henry's competitor for power: the Church. These were the people who had access to books and learned treatises and could read and write. How could Henry's justice compete with the Church when he had no trained legal people to rely on?

Henry, a young man, was clever. He spoke Latin and had studied the law. He knew from history that the ancient Greeks had resolved criminal cases by allowing groups of citizens to make the decisions and that similar practices had a long history among the island tribes.[6] So he proposed to settle difficult land disputes by summoning "twelve free and lawful men in the neighborhood" and asking them to determine, based on their own knowledge and judgment, who was entitled to possess the property.[7]

The idea that a group of laypeople might do better than the experts was an extraordinary one at the time, and it still is today. It required trust in people's judgment that they would find a way to sort out testimony. We don't know whether Henry realized how revolutionary this idea was. Necessity, as the mother of invention, must have played a significant role. After all, what else could Henry offer? Like some other offbeat ideas, this one actually worked. In the eyes of the people, the groups of laypeople got the job done.

The fundamental insight of Henry's solution was that of a self-organizing group. It brought together a relatively small group of people who could be expected to have different information and perspectives on the issue at hand. The authorities gave a challenge to the group. By insisting that the participants be "free and lawful," it was hoped that they were responsible people. No one was put in charge of the group. The authorities stepped back and let the jury figure out how to approach the problem and what the best answer was.

Perhaps the most startling aspect of it is that it was a radical shift in power. Henry could have followed the French practice of appointing judges who actively intervened in the proceedings, interrogating witnesses and in effect making the decisions. Such a system could have enabled him to award land to his supporters and take it away from his enemies.

By establishing jury trial, Henry was giving up the power to make the decision that he might want in any particular case. The decision might come out in favor of people who supported him or people who didn't. He gave up the power to make the decision in the specific case in return for the greater power that would be achieved by the system as a whole.

This was a transfer of real power. The decision of the jury stood, whether it pleased the king or not. The jury could see that they weren't involved in some kind of shell game in which they made a decision and then the king's men would come along and reverse it. The system worked because the jury knew that they were truly responsible for making the best decision.

By 1166, after just a few years, Henry was able to declare that the practice of assizes—self-organizing teams of diverse people thrown together and asked to solve problems for which no one knew the right answer—would become the standard way of settling difficult legal issues throughout the land.

Thus began the process of transforming English law based on evidence and inspection by self-organizing teams of laypeople. In due course, this evolved into trial by jury, a model of justice for many countries.

WHY SELF-ORGANIZING GROUPS WORK

For many centuries, self-organizing teams in the form of legal juries have been accepted around the world, largely because of the expectation that juries are less politically motivated than government-appointed judges.

But another question has always lurked in the background: What sacrifices in terms of the quality of decision making were being made by using laypeople in order to achieve impartiality? Would qualified professionals have actually made better decisions if bias had been removed?

To get the answer to this question, let's fast-forward from 1166 to 2007 and meet Scott Page, a bearded professor of complex systems at the University of Michigan. His path-breaking book, *The Difference,* puts forward an astonishing hypothesis: there may be no sacrifice. In fact, ordinary laypeople often make better decisions than experts do.[8] That's because cognitively diverse groups of ordinary people like juries in fact often do better than groups of like-minded experts.

Page came to his conclusions after playing around with mathematical models of complex organizations together with Lu Hong, an economist at Chicago's Loyola University. Together they constructed a formal model that showed mathematically why diversity can trump ability and also when it does. The model showed not merely the weak diversity thesis—that diverse groups of problem solvers outperformed groups of like-minded individuals. It showed something startling: on complex problems, groups of ordinary people who were cognitively diverse routinely outperformed groups of like-minded experts. The reason is that the diverse groups got stuck less often than the like-minded experts, who tended to think in similar ways.

Page's work also showed why cognitive diversity enables ordinary people working together to become extraordinary. When we work together with people who are not like us—people who have different interpretations, perspectives, ways of solving problems, and predictive models—we are often able to solve problems that we wouldn't be able to solve alone. This happens because when we collaborate with people who are different from us, we start to see the world through their eyes. We see a wider range of variables as relevant to the problem. We develop a fuller understanding of the causal connections between variables and a richer comprehension of the architecture of the problem. We get help in identifying our false assumptions—those many things that we firmly believe to be true but happen to be false. We start to look beyond dichotomies of either-or and see ways of connecting information in a both-and modality. We become able to synthesize apparent contradictions. A dramatic illustration of this is the success of betting markets for predicting the outcome of the U.S. presidential elections, where an amorphous population of participants has consistently done better than political experts in picking the winners.

Page's book also shows where cognitive diversity doesn't work. It doesn't work on simple problems with linear solutions, where there is a known answer. With those kinds of issues, an expert is better. And it doesn't work if people can't collaborate with each other. In addition, the more diverse they are, the more difficult the collaboration can be.

We can formulate a more complete version of the second principle of radical management in this way: "A complex problem, like discovering ways to delight clients, is best solved by a cognitively diverse group of people that is given responsibility for solving the problem, self-organizes, and works together to solve it." There's quite a lot packed into that single sentence.

First, we are dealing with a *complex problem*. It's a problem to which we don't know the solution: mysteries, not puzzles. It may be a wicked problem, where we're not sure even what the problem is. There has to be some kind of challenge that cannot be solved with an established body of expertise.

The group must be *cognitively diverse*. These are people who look at the world in different ways; they have different interpretations, perspectives, ways of solving problems, and predictive models. They may or may not be diverse in identity terms of race, gender, or religion. What matters is mind-set: cognitive diversity.

The group is then given the possibility of *self-organizing*, that is, the autonomy to decide how to organize itself and how to solve the problem. If you put someone in charge of the group or tell the group how to solve the problem, then you risk being thrown back into the world of preconceived ideas, where the solution is predetermined by the process you are using to answer it, so that better solutions are overlooked.

WHAT ARE SELF-ORGANIZING TEAMS?

Teams vary in terms of the scope of authority to do their work. At one extreme are *manager-led teams,* which have minimal authority. The leader is appointed by the organization, and the authority of the team doesn't extend beyond executing the work of the team—doing whatever is needed in terms of physical or mental effort to get the work done. An example is the typical NFL team, where the coach decides everything: the players just play.

At the other extreme are *self-governing teams,* which have maximal authority: they can set direction for the team, design the work, select the team members, and monitor and manage what has been done. Examples are a parliament, a board of directors, and a small start-up firm.

In between are *self-organizing teams.* These teams decide how the work will be organized, who will do what, and in what order; select leaders or spokespersons; and can decide who should be a member of the team. Juries are examples: they are given a clear direction but are free to organize themselves as to how they will decide the issue before them.

The group is *given responsibility:* the team has the ball. There isn't some other management person or group working at cross-purposes or second-guessing the work of the group. The team members know that they have responsibility for deciding and have accepted that responsibility.

The team is *working together*. The members of the team are looking beyond their own interest and are focused on solving the team's problem, not on pursuing their own interests. There is cross-fertilization: they are working together to solve the problem.

They are focused on *solving* the problem. This is not about making inputs into its solution. This is about taking the ball the whole length of the field. This means that the group has to have enough expertise to get the job done in its entirety. This will require in most cases a team with cross-functional expertise.

Thus, Henry FitzEmpress had stumbled on the power of cognitive diversity back in the twelfth century, even though it was only in 2007 with the publication of *The Difference* that we understood why a group of twelve "free and lawful men" with different perspectives and backgrounds with no legal training might do better in solving problems to which no one knew the right answer.[9]

THE PSYCHOLOGY OF SELF-ORGANIZING TEAMS

In management as in law, practice has been way ahead of theory. Throughout the twentieth century, organizations regularly used self-organizing teams to resolve mysteries—the wicked problems that management didn't know how to solve. For instance, task forces would often be established to resolve issues that management couldn't figure out. Once the problem was resolved, the task force was typically dissolved.

By 1986, self-organizing teams were identified as an emerging good practice to generate rapid innovation. In their famous article, "The New Product Development Game," Professors Hirotaka Takeuchi and Ikujiro Nonaka described how a range of firms had been successful in innovation.[10] Some of the examples were in Japan, like Toyota, Fuji Film, and Honda, and a couple were American firms like HP, 3M, and Xerox. They showed how these companies had set up teams that became extraordinarily innovative and productive.

Typically the companies were in crisis when they turned to this new solution. They were in tight competitive situations and needed to come up with responses to the encroachments on their market share. The successful companies had succeeded by setting up self-organizing teams. They had analyzed the competitive threat and then pulled together a team of their very best people. It was generally a cross-functional team, with people from R&D, engineering, finance, sales, marketing, and support.

They would then give the team a challenging mission. At Honda, for instance, the challenge was to design a car that would appeal to young people and yet be cheap and of high quality. Then they would step back and let the team figure how to make it happen.

At first, the people on the team would be concerned that this was a new form of layoff. After a while, they would settle down and would socialize with each other. And then they would wake up and realize that unless they got cracking, they would never finish by the deadline. So the team would suddenly grasp the urgency of the situation and start to work together.

Takeuchi and Nonaka noted that when this happened, the well-documented phenomenon of self-transcendence within the group would occur. *Self-transcendence* is a big word, but it simply means that the individuals started to feel that the goals of the team were more important than their own part in it, their own careers, their own preferred position, their prior attitudes. If they were thinking only about themselves—their own goals and their own interests—the team would get locked into suboptimal patterns of work. Takeuchi and Nonaka noted, "A project takes on a self-organizing character as it is driven to a state of 'zero information'—where prior knowledge does not apply. Ambiguity and fluctuation abound in this state. Left to stew, the process begins to create its own dynamic order."[11]

The psychology of this phenomenon was described by Mihaly Csikszentmihalyi in his classic book, *Flow*. He wrote about those times in our lives when, instead of being buffeted by anonymous forces, we "feel in control of our actions, masters of our own fate. On the rare occasions that it happens, we feel a sense of exhilaration, a deep sense of enjoyment that is long cherished and that becomes a landmark in memory for what life should be like. . . . The best moments usually occur when a person's body or mind is stretched to the limits in a voluntary effort to accomplish something difficult and worthwhile."[12]

Some of those moments have also occurred when high-performance teams emerge in a traditional workplace despite all the negative forces that tend to prevent it. Examples are included in the three boxes in this chapter that follow. In fact, as I noted in Chapter One, my research showed that most people have on occasion experienced optimal experiences in high-performance teams at work, at school, in communities, or at home.

STREAMLINING PROCEDURES AT THE WORLD BANK

Self-organizing teams in the form of task forces were widely used in the twentieth century to solve problems that management didn't know how to solve. Here is an example from my own experience.

○ ○ ○

In 1985, when I was working in the World Bank, I was asked to report to the office of the senior vice president. When I was ushered into his office, he smiled and told me that I was to lead a task force to make proposals to streamline the World Bank's procedures. The report would be due in six weeks.

My heart sank. Procedures at the World Bank had grown like kudzu; they had slowed work to a snail's pace and were stifling productivity. Over the previous fifteen years, various task forces had been appointed to clean up the procedures, and they had gotten nowhere. The time scale for solving the problem—six weeks—was ridiculously short.

I asked him cautiously what he expected the task force to accomplish. He replied that there was nothing wrong with the procedures that we had. I inquired whether there were any limits as to what we could make proposals on.

He named a certain report, which he said the board of directors needed. This report was in fact at the center of much of the current duplication of effort. It looked as if I was being set up to fail.

The task force started meeting with groups of staff to get their input. Frustration levels were high. After a few meetings, we had more than a hundred proposals for change.

The senior vice president had been adamant against any expansion of the task force's mandate. However, by my continued interactions with him, it became apparent that his opposition to expand the mandate had two sources. First, he believed that the board of directors would oppose any change beyond the boundary he had indicated; and second, he was concerned that any change might undermine his own review function. Once we had discovered that both these concerns were false, we were able to put together a proposal to solve the underlying problem and show him why a new proposal would continue to meet his own review needs and be embraced by the board of directors. He accepted the proposal and agreed to expand the team's mandate—retroactively. He became the chief advocate of the proposals, which were also wildly popular by staff throughout the organization. We had solved a problem that everyone thought insoluble.[13]

These high-performance experiences generally happened by accident, when some enterprising manager created the space for them to occur or management control was for some reason absent. The modus operandi of a high-performance team is, however, at odds with the hierarchical bureaucracy of traditional management, and so its life expectancy is typically not long.

Takeuchi and Nonaka were discussing the creation of high-performance teams not by accident but by design. For instance, the average age of Honda's team, tasked with developing a low-cost, energy-efficient, high-quality car that would appeal to young people, was only twenty-seven. At that time, Honda's top management was feeling a sense of crisis as its best-selling lines, the Civic and the Accord, were losing their appeal to young people. Takeuchi and Nonaka explained that the creation of tension, if managed properly, helped to cultivate a 'must do' attitude and a sense of cohesion among members of the crisis-solving project team.

Top management was expecting that team would produce a new version of the Civic, a long and low car. Instead, the team came up with a totally different car that was short and tall. Afterward team members said that it was incredible that they had been given this much freedom, while top management noted that they had also instilled a strong sense of responsibility in them.

In their study, Takeuchi and Nonaka found that all of the self-organizing teams set up in this way succeeded in coming up with something that had a significant impact in the marketplace. Some of them were merely adequate. Some of them were game changing. But none of them were cases where the team said they couldn't quite get it done. They all came up with something that was a significant competitive response. Takeuchi and Nonaka argued that if you set up the conditions right, self-organizing teams would normally evolve into high-performance teams.

THE BENEFITS OF TEAMS

Other reports of the gains made by self-organizing teams are similarly dramatic. In 1990, Jack Orsburn and his colleagues wrote in *Self-Directed Work Teams* that teams at Xerox became 30 percent more productive than they had been and 30 to 40 percent more productive at Procter & Gamble. Teams at Tektronix cut the product cycle from fourteen days to three days. Teams helped Federal Express cut service glitches by 13 percent. Shenandoah Life processes 50 percent more claims with 10 percent fewer people. And so on.[14]

By 1993, Jon Katzenbach and Douglas Smith in their book, *The Wisdom of Teams,* declared that teams were "the primary unit of performance for increasing numbers of organizations. . . . The performance challenges that face large companies in every industry—customer service, technological change, competitive threats and environmental constraints—demand the kind of responsiveness, speed, on-line customization, and quality that is beyond the reach of individual performance. Teams can bridge this gap."[15]

Yet despite the growing acceptance of teams, the default mental model of management has remained hierarchical bureaucracy. Teams remain an exception to bureaucracy, and when they falter, as they inevitably do in complex dynamic environments, management usually reverts back to traditional top-down control.

The interesting question is: If teams are so productive, why haven't they become the default model for organizing and managing? The idea of giving people a voice in how to do work and using teams to get things done is obviously not new. In fact, for almost a hundred years, experts have kept discovering—and rediscovering—the importance of teamwork.

In the 1920s, Mary Parker Follett was giving lectures at Harvard Business School and Oxford University on the principle of noncoercive power sharing and emphasizing "power with" rather than "power over."[16]

In the 1930s, Elton Mayo argued that attention to employees as people could relieve the monotony and boredom of their work. He claimed that the experiments at the Hawthorne Project showed that paying attention to workers and their concerns could improve performance even without doing anything about the complaints. Years later he would romanticize the Hawthorne experiments as instances where "six individuals became a team and the team gave itself wholeheartedly and spontaneously to cooperation in the experiment." As a result, "they felt themselves to be participating freely and without afterthought, and were happy in the knowledge that they were working without coercion from above or limitation from below."[17]

In 1938, Chester Barnard argued that to survive, an organization had to satisfy the motives of its members while attaining its explicit goals, and foster cooperation among its members.[18]

In 1943, Abraham Maslow put forward his theory of human motivation, with a pyramidal hierarchy of needs, both psychological and physical, and capped by the highest human need of all, which Maslow called self-actualization.[19]

By the 1950s, human resource departments were using the rhetoric of teams, team spirit, and winning as a way to creating positive attitudes toward the organizational goals.

By 1960, MIT professor Douglas McGregor questioned the assumptions of traditional hierarchy that people are lazy, which he labeled Theory X. McGregor urged managers to explore Theory Y: that people want to do a good job and wanted to have responsibility.[20]

In 1971, the report by the Department of Health, Education and Welfare, *Work in America,* commissioned by the Nixon administration, concluded that the workplace would have to change to fit the aspirations, attitudes, and values of workers. People wanted meaningful work that provides satisfaction. Job redesign and increased participation of workers were necessary for America to be competitive.[21]

In 1982, Tom Peters and Robert Waterman announced in their book, *In Search of Excellence,* that it was attention to employees, not work conditions themselves, that has a dominant effect on productivity.[22]

As recently as 2007, Gary Hamel, at the time of publication of his book, *The Future of Management,* could once again rediscover the human factor: "Probably for the first time since the industrial revolution, you can't build a company that's fit for the future unless it's fit for human beings."[23]

A HIGH-PERFORMANCE TEAM: JOHN OZIER'S TRIO OF SONGWRITERS

In May 2008, John Ozier, director of artists and repertoire at Curb Records in Nashville, talked with me about a group of country songwriters.

○ ○ ○

In the spring of 2007, songwriter Joe Leathers offered to take two colleagues to his house on Rosemary Beach in Florida. Because of that trip and the experiences that they shared, they became best friends, and they worked together in producing songs at an extraordinary success rate.

Two of them wrote a song for Garth Brooks, a big country artist. It debuted at number 1, the highest starting debut of a country single ever in country music history, and two of them were a part of that. And after that, all three of them have had songs recorded more than anyone else in town. Joe Leathers is in his early to mid-forties. He lived in Memphis, Tennessee. He is married with three kids. He worked for Bear Stearns until recently. He played college football. He's a decent guitar player rather than a great musician or a great singer. He was writing songs as a hobby.The second guy is Kyle Jacobs. He's about to turn thirty-five. He has been in Nashville for a while. He's done everything from painting houses, to waiting tables, just waiting for that big break. He's the musical genius of the group. When they got together at the start, he was engaged to be married. He told those guys about his relationship, and about two weeks after the writing retreat, he decided to call off his engagement. After that, the songs started pouring out from these three guys.

It turned out that breaking off the engagement was an important experience for the whole group. Kyle felt he couldn't love the woman in the way she needed to be loved. There were times when he regretted it.

But he felt that it was the right thing to do for her. One of the songs they wrote was, "*I Am Saving You from Me.*"

The third guy is Lee Brice. He is almost thirty. He is from South Carolina. He is the artist of the group. He is by far the best singer and the best guitar player. He has the most talent, but he needs support to keep focused.

When they're together, they all just lock in. The level of songs that they get out of each trip is so much better in terms of quality than the songs they write here in Nashville.

They complement each other. Joe provides the landscape, and Kyle provides the creative energy that Lee feeds on. It's a collective effort. Kyle and Lee write the music. Then they all collectively contribute the words, mainly from Lee's and Kyle's feelings. Joe adds color to the words.

Before the beach house, things were different. Kyle had little success. But after this writing retreat, they've all had Top Ten singles, which is extraordinary. And they just keep coming.

WHY TEAMS KEEP BEING REDISCOVERED

Why did we see this incessant "rediscovery" of the human factor and teams? How could management theorists plausibly claim the same thing over and over, shouting, "Eureka!" as though they had made an extraordinary discovery? How could managers continue to be amazed by these "discoveries"? Why did the traditional mental model of hierarchical bureaucracy remain largely unscathed?

There are a number of reasons.

Managers' Short Memories

One is the limited role occupied by history or memory in most management writing. There is a tradition of presenting everything as new. The tradition is in part driven by hype: something old is presented as something new in order to get attention and sell books or consulting services. As George Santayana noted, those who can't remember the past are condemned to repeat it.

The Confusion of Language with Reality

Another was the widespread confusion of the language with the reality. The Hawthorne experiments at the Western Electric Company from 1924 to 1932 were one culprit. Calling that cynically manipulated work group a "team that was free from coercion" did little to help the cause of real teams.

The temptation for management to use the seductive language of teams was considerable. Work could be made to sound like fun and games. The language of teams could convey the idea that the team members are all in this together, engendering excitement and catering to the human need to belong. It could conjure up dramatic feats of excellence and the desire for perfection. To have a *coach,* rather than a *boss,* carried with it the promise of helping people become better individuals rather than the soft despotism of command and control.

The words of teamwork and coaching were often used without the reality. Management called work groups "teams" yet remained in tight control of who was on the team, what work was done and how it was done, and how people would relate to each other. The use of the rhetoric of teams in this setting was hypocrisy and led to worse workplaces, not better ones.

As a result, counterfeit teams were confused with the real thing. It became another instance of Gresham's law. Just as bad money drives out the good, the prevalence of pseudo-teams made it difficult to launch real teams.[24]

In the late twentieth century, it didn't help that even when teams succeeded, firms would abscond with the winnings. Professor Paul Osterman of MIT found that five hundred companies between 1992 and 1997 that used teams did not share their gains with the teams unless they were unionized.[25]

Against this background, when managers start talking about teams, it should be no surprise that warning bells start sounding in workers' minds.

Failure to Transfer Power

Another deeper cause was the failure to discuss openly the question of power. In creating legal juries, Henry FitzEmpress had been crystal clear that the jury system involved the transfer of power for the specific issue at hand. He transferred power to decide the specific instance in order to gain greater power for the system of justice as a whole. The jury's decision stuck even if the king didn't like it.

By contrast, management was often ambivalent in setting up self-organizing teams about whether any real power was being transferred. Since the energy of a self-organizing team is sparked in part by the sense of responsibility that comes with the power to decide—a contingent transfer, to be sure, but nevertheless, a transfer of power—many of management's so-called teams weren't really teams at all. They were pseudo-teams.

Conflict with the Default Mental Model of Management

A further cause was the failure to recognize that self-organizing teams were at odds with the prevailing default model of management: hierarchical bureaucracy. As a result, when real teams emerged, particularly high-performance teams, management had a tendency to suppress them. That's because a high-performance team typically becomes more productive by breaking the rules, and a bureaucracy hates having rules broken. A group that breaks rules may be tolerated for a period, but eventually the rules take over, the group is "brought back into line," and high performance ends. The participants return to the daily grind. Enhanced productivity is not enough to save the group. In a bureaucracy, order trumps performance.

ERNST & YOUNG: CENTER FOR BUSINESS INNOVATION

In November 2008, Larry Prusak talked with me about his experience at Ernst & Young's Center for Business Innovation.

○ ○ ○

My experience of a high-performance team was in the early 1990s at the Center for Business Innovation at Ernst & Young in Boston. Tom Davenport was the first hire. I was the second. Eventually the center had around twenty-five professional people, with a mix of senior, midlevel, and junior people. They were all people who were devoted to real intellectual progress. Occasionally they would go out and assist the firm by helping the consultants make a sale. But it was mainly about ideas.

The group was in a building separate from the consultants. The nature of the physical office really mattered. It was a small building. We were always bumping into each other and overhearing conversation. It was small. And it was fun.

It was collaborative, but there was also a certain combativeness in the group. We felt that they were going to show the consultants who were very skeptical about what we were doing.

When we first presented our ideas on knowledge, for example, the consultants were dismissive. "What do you mean, knowledge? That's the same as information." We would reply, "Why do we have different words then? If it's the same thing, how come everyone doesn't know everything?"

It was very successful. Two of the big ideas in business emerged from this group—business process reengineeering and knowledge management.

Intrinsic motivation was a real force. We really loved the play of ideas. It wasn't that we weren't interested in making money or in helping Ernst & Young. We weren't wild-eyed dreamers, but nothing was going to stop us pursuing those ideas. We believed! We cared! If we had been told, "I want you to quit thinking about it," or "This isn't valuable for the firm," we would have left.

In its heyday, the center had a fair amount of autonomy to innovate. Then the firm started to put financial and political pressure on us to do things that would help to make money, and it became less productive. We weren't against making money, but that wasn't the point. That wasn't why we had joined. And so people began to lose their edge. And pretty soon the group was no longer a high-performance group.

The phenomenon of teamicide isn't unusual. Many of the high-performance teams that I came across in my research suffered that fate.

They had been killed by a traditionally minded management, either willfully to bring the team back into line with the prevailing corporate norms, or by accident, as a result of splitting the team up, without realizing that this would destroy the high level of performance that had been created.

Teams Didn't Work

Even more worrisome was that overall, taking all the studies of teams into account, teams on average didn't work. There is a sharp contrast between amazing reports from the field about the benefits of specific teams and the gloomy picture that emerges from scholarly research on the overall impact of teamwork on performance across many organizations: overall, no net improvement in performance is discernible.[26]

The claims of Orsburn and his colleagues, Smith and Katzenbach, and Takeuchi and Nonaka thus have a strong smell of survivor bias: the teams that failed are not fully represented in their writing.[27]

The gains made by successful teams are equaled by the losses encountered by unsuccessful teams. Even when managers sincerely wanted to create self-organizing teams and were ready to delegate power to the teams, they knew how to launch teams but often they didn't know how to sustain them. When teams began to go off track, management didn't react quickly enough to resolve the problem.

In a traditional management setting, poorly performing teams could continue to operate for months, years, or even decades, without anything ever being done to identify the impediments to performance, let alone remove them.

Managers Didn't Know How to Sustain High-Performing Teams

Despite the vast literature on teams, the use of client-driven iterations and radical transparency to sustain self-organizing teams and foster their evolution into high-performance teams has only recently been developed and field-tested extensively.

Of the large numbers of tools and techniques necessary to sustain effective teams and ensure that poorly performing teams are quickly identified and helped, three principles stand out as crucial:

- Do the work in client-driven iterations.
- Deliver value to clients each iteration.
- Be open about impediments.

They are not merely optional tools. They are foundational principles of radical management.

It is to these principles that we now turn.

PRACTICES FOR CREATING SELF-ORGANIZING TEAMS

To create self-governing teams that have the potential to develop into high-performance teams, managers must proceed on the basis of a realistic psychology. Those doing the work are neither inherently lazy nor inherently committed. Human beings are mixed bag, and the creation and sustenance of teams must cope with the vagaries of human nature. They must be able to handle the good, the average, and the mediocre.

In effect, a set of management practices needs to be put in place that encourages self-organizing teams to evolve into high-performance teams. When things go wrong, as they inevitably do with something as precarious as self-organizing teams, safety devices need to be in place to identify and rectify the situation quickly and decisively.

There must be a willingness to address questions of power and compensation in a franker way than has been customary in recent years.

The managers must know how to converse with people, through genuine conversations with authentic stories, open-ended questions, and deep listening, rather than simply telling people what to do or sending messages. Managers also need to recognize that creating self-organizing teams isn't easy. It isn't a quick fix and isn't something that consultants can do for them. Managers must be willing to put their own hearts as well as their minds to work.

To accomplish it, they need managerial practices that make the teams sustainable for the long haul, particularly purpose (Practice #1), passion (Practice #2), power (Practice #3), productivity (Practice #4), performance recognition (Practice #5), pay (Practice #6), and practices (Practice #7).

Practice #1: *Articulate a Compelling Purpose in Terms of Delighting Clients*

An almost universal characteristic of teams that achieve high performance is a compelling *purpose.* People will give their very best to a cause only if they believe in it and think it worthwhile. The failed teams, or pseudo-teams, as in the Hawthorne experiments, were groups of people working for bureaucratic goals—produce so many widgets. It was boring and dull.

In general, it is more difficult to articulate a compelling purpose in terms of a thing than in terms of people. Things as goals tend to be either too mundane or too grandiose.

Work becomes meaningful because there is some good in it. The most meaningful jobs are those that help other people. A generic form of a compelling purpose is to delight clients. Doing something extraordinary for others is worth fighting for, something that can get the juices flowing.

Practice #2: *Consistently Communicate a Passionate Belief in the Worth of the Purpose*

Managers need to bring their passion for delighting clients to the table. Passion is the catalyst for transformation. It's not enough to articulate the purpose of delighting clients. They must show their belief in that goal in their words and actions. They can't fake it; they have to feel it and demonstrate it daily. Their passion will be contagious. It will overcome obstacles and hesitancy in others. If they don't feel passion for delighting clients, that attitude will also be contagious.

In the world of work, the people who are the most successful are those who are doing what they love. Money isn't what drives them. What drives them are intrinsic goals, the same as those of a great musician or athlete.

In hiring, managers must find people who are going to love what they are hired to do. These are people who take pride in their work, inspire their fellow workers to greatness, and become the driving force behind the business. There is no way to find and keep such people unless the managers themselves feel the same passion.

Practice #3: *Transfer Power to the Team for Accomplishing the Team Purpose*

Managers need to give explicit attention to questions of power. Creating self-organizing teams is about management's relinquishing power on the specifics of the task in order to make systemic gains for the overall system of production.

Theorists often talk about empowerment, as though management is keeping all its prerogatives and the team is being given something additional. But let's be clear. This is about a shift in power from management to the team. Who calls what shots? Real teams are about a shift in power relations that has the potential of making the overall arrangement better for everyone—clients, workers, and the firm itself.

If managers adopt the language of teams and teamwork but don't relinquish power so that the team itself can decide what to do and how to do it, the managers will be generating pseudo-teams and all the cynicism that goes with them.

When management announces that it is about to empower a team, a certain amount of skepticism on the part of the participants is to be expected. In the room at the time are not only the manager and the workers, but also the ghosts of previous manager-worker relations, the ghosts of almost a century of pseudo-teams, the ghosts of Dilbert cartoons.

A host of questions is typically swirling in the minds of team members. Is this for real? Is the offered autonomy genuine? Or is it a management trick, where they say one thing but do another? Is it a setup as a prelude to more layoffs and downsizings? Or is it a genuine offer to do things differently?

At the same time, managers are often living with a different set of ghosts. Will the team goof off and take advantage of the autonomy to work less? One manager described the feeling to me: "It's like the nausea and vertigo I felt when I first flew an airplane at night with zero visibility."

In reality, when teams are set up correctly, visibility isn't zero. In radical management, a number of protections are in place that ensure that no large-scale disaster can happen. But at the outset, it can feel as though a horrible risk is being taken. Unless the feeling is anticipated and prepared for, it can lead to actions that undermine the shift in power.

Here we are in the heart of darkness. The essence of bureaucracy is that the manager knows best and stays in control at all times. That's the default position, and every deviation from that, in the form of teams, task forces, networks, and the rest, is perceived as a temporary aberration, with the expectation of reverting back to the manager, who remains in control at all times. In traditional management, control and predictability have priority over performance.

In radical management, the values are reversed: performance is given priority over predictability. If the client is delighted in surprising ways, so much the better. The bottom line is client delight, not a predictable outcome for the system.

This shift in power on the specifics in order to gain power for the whole is predicated on a certain amount of humility—a willingness to be vulnerable, to be wrong, to recognize that workers are sometimes more knowledgeable than managers as to what will delight clients. It also means giving up some of the psychic satisfactions of being a command-and-control manager: the thrill of exercising power and telling other people what to do, of being seen to be in charge, of living out tiny Napoleonic dreams of power, of being someone who can make an arbitrary decision just for the heck of it.

Radical managers set these petty satisfactions aside and recognize the possibility that in some respects, the workers may know best, and they cede control to these workers for a period. For some managers, this is scary stuff. It means giving up some of the ancient habits of managers since time immemorial. And it can be equally daunting for workers. It can be frightening to have responsibility and to be at risk of failure. Yet when handled right, it can be energizing for everyone: firm, client, and those doing the work.

This is not about covering up power, with the pretense that authority itself disappears in some utopian world in which work is turned into play. It means explicitly enabling the shift in power.

Practice #4: *Make the Transfer of Power Conditional on the Team's Accepting Responsibility to Deliver*

This is not an unconditional relinquishment of power. The shift is conditional on the group's actually delivering on delighting clients. It's an offer, and the team has to accept the responsibility to deliver. Then in due course it must deliver.

Chapters Seven through Nine discuss the specifics of how this condition is negotiated in a way that respects the interests of the organization and those doing the work. It involves creating a setting where a team has an appropriate role in deciding how much work can be done while maintaining appropriate quality standards and in seeing that impediments are identified and removed.

Most teams don't start with a fast, rapidly improving trajectory. They go through a process of storming and forming before they develop norms of behavior. In this initial period, management must be willing to persist and not give up at the first hiccup. They must help identify and remove impediments. In effect, management must adopt teams as the basic mental model of the way things are going to be organized.

Practice #5: *Recognize the Contributions of the People Doing the Work*

Recognizing teams that are succeeding in delighting clients is key to sustaining high performance. Recognition is not by itself sufficient, but it is necessary.

Good management requires both informal feedback and formal feedback mechanisms that systematically pay tribute to performance that contributes to the organizational goal of delighting clients.[28]

Practice #6: *Make Sure That Remuneration Is Perceived as Fair*

High-performance teams are driven principally by intrinsic rewards. People will give their best only if they feel the desire to do something because it matters, they enjoy it, it's interesting, or it's part of something important.

Extensive research shows that financial rewards—extrinsic motivation—are effective for work that has a clear goal and involves the application of straightforward principles. Financial rewards sharpen our focus on the goal but also create tunnel vision.

When the goal is clear and the work is routine, tunnel vision doesn't matter. Financial rewards will tend to generate better performance. But once the work requires the application of brain power and creativity, the tunnel vision created by financial rewards leads to poorer performance.[29]

For solving complex problems like continuous innovation and delighting clients, people need to be able to see what's on the periphery; they need to be looking around and expanding their possibilities.

Nevertheless, remuneration obviously has to be part of the picture. In one sense, the essence of work is that one gets paid for it, even if there are some jobs where people would pay to do them. In effect, the pay needs to meet a certain threshold of fairness—fairness in relation to other workers on the team, other teams, other firms, what the managers are making, and what the organization is capturing.

So pay needs to be appropriate. A set of arrangements needs to be in place where monetary rewards support self-organizing teams and do not undermine them.[30]

Practice #7: *Consistently Use Tools and Techniques That Create and Sustain Self-Organizing Teams*

Against a long management tradition of withholding power and counterfeit empowerment, it can be hard for a team to believe that it is actually being given autonomy to decide.

By its actions, management needs to signal that this is not another version of hierarchical bureaucracy. This is not top-down command and control under a new label. This includes an array of actions, including identifying team members who share a passion for the goal; getting the right mix of skills and challenge; giving employees a voice in whether they want to join the team as well as giving the members the ability to determine who else is on the team; getting a team that is the right size; getting a proper location, preferably colocation; and systematically identifying and removing impediments to getting the work done.[31]

6

PRINCIPLE #3: CLIENT-DRIVEN ITERATIONS

> That which is still small is easy to direct.
>
> **Lao Tzu**[1]

In Frank McCourt's memoir, *Angela's Ashes,* Frank's dad (a shiftless garrulous alcoholic with a soft heart) unilaterally decides that Frank is going to be an altar boy. He then proceeds to torture the little boy with a program of intense preparation. As Frank puts it: "Every evening after tea I kneel for the Latin and he won't let me move till I'm perfect."[2]

Both parents make a huge effort, and spend what little money they have, preparing young Frank for his new assignment, making sure he is prepared and looks just so. Finally the day comes where Frank's dad takes him to see the priest in charge of altar boys. Here's how Frank describes the meeting:

"Stephen Carey looks at him, then me. He says, 'We don't have room for him,' and closes the door."

Frank's quest to become an altar boy abruptly ends.

Why didn't Frank's dad save the family all of that trouble and meet with the priest before Frank was thrown headlong into a grueling preparation? Why didn't he find out whether there was any interest in having a new altar boy?

When Sam Bayer was a consultant some years ago, he used this story to spark organizations to ask themselves why they should spend a long time producing a big thing, only to find that when the thing is done, what they have produced is not what was wanted. Why not focus collective energies on finding out what people want and then figure out step by step whether what you are working on is delivering what they actually want?

Bayer had seen companies spend large amounts of resources building software. But they wouldn't know whether they would succeed or fail until they launched the software, and then their customers would tell them that their product was useless. These companies had spent time building a perfectly useless product.

In 2007, Bayer saw an opportunity to launch his own firm. He noticed that people in the business-to-business world were still placing orders with their manufacturers by phone, fax, and e-mail. This was slow and expensive, and he decided to explore whether he could help by offering a Web-based service.

His idea was to use client-driven iterations to determine whether there was a market, define the service he would provide, and then implement it. He wanted to fail as quickly as possible, recover, and keep honing in on what customers really needed. His aim was to implement this in marketing, sales, and implementation.

He got together an experienced team and, as quickly as possible, built a prototype of the software that he had in mind and the pricing model with software as a service. The team got its presentation ready and then, even before he had incorporated the company, he convened a group of potential customers to see what they thought.[3]

At the time, software as a service was an unfamiliar idea in this market. The technology was straightforward, but the pricing model was new.

He walked the people through the prototype and the pricing model and asked why it couldn't be introduced the next day. Bayer says, "We weren't asking people for ideas. We were asking people: 'Why won't this work in your organization tomorrow?' We didn't waffle around and talk about all the things it was going to do. We presented it and showed what it actually did. The comments we received went into the next iteration of the service. We were doing engineering, sales, and marketing all at once."

Bayer incorporated his company and is now the CEO of his business-to-business technology firm in Raleigh, North Carolina, called b2b2dot0 (pronounced "bee two bee two dot oh") in 2007. The business continues to grow in this same way. When Bayer launches a new feature or function, he invites customers and prospects to try it out: "You invite people to come and have a look at what you are doing. And if people show up, then for that hour and a half, you take it on the chin. The people say, 'Yeah, we like it, but it won't work because of this, or because of that.' We get thirty to forty reasons per hour as to why it won't work for them. Which I find delightful."

Bayer establishes priorities among the issues that have been raised and fixes the top ones. Then he comes back to the people and asks them, "Now why won't it work?" And they tell him why or say, "I don't see any reason why it won't, so let's go do it."

Bayer describes the work as having "a rhythm to it. There are multiple streams happening. There's an overall quarterly product rhythm. We set out a theme for each quarter. We leave a lot of room for new things to emerge during the quarter. But we have our eyes on one major release for the quarter. On the product side, on a daily basis, we are prototyping, demonstrating, because when software is a service, we can release it."

Implementation is also done in an iterative fashion. For each client, he sets up an implementation project and focuses on thirty days to get some value, then sixty days to get more value, and finally ninety days to get the full value from the project. The length of the iteration depends on the client. There might be weekly demos in some cases. And on a daily basis, they are constantly interacting with the client. In this way, the firm uses client-driven iterations on the front end, on the sales and marketing, and on product implementation. They are concurrent and intertwined.

Is it working? Bayer says, "It's a blast. It really is. It's not a bureaucracy. On a daily basis, we're seeing the impact on the business. Everyone in every role that we play, whether we are implementing product with clients or trying to drum up business, or developing partnerships, it's all direct feedback. Our work—results! Our work—results! We get it on a daily basis. We're preselected to enjoy that."

ITERATIONS AT TOYOTA

Credit for the idea of doing work in client-driven iterations is often given to Taiichi Ohno, an engineer at Toyota. Ohno himself says that some of the thinking actually came from America.

Born in Dalian, China, Ohno graduated from Nagoya Technical High School in 1932. He was an employee first of the Toyoda family's Toyoda Spinning, then moved to the motor company in 1943 and became section manager at the Honsha final assembly plant in February 1945.[4]

After the war was over, the challenge facing Toyota was how to be competitive when the U.S. auto industry was eight times more productive than Toyota. "We realized," writes Ohno, "that with our traditional methods the Japanese automotive industry would never survive. We could not even catch up unless we improved our productivity ten-fold."[5]

He wondered how Toyota could possibly improve productivity ten-fold. He heard from a colleague in the assembly section of the plant that the president of Toyota, Kiichiro Toyoda, was saying that the most efficient way to assemble cars was when each part arrived "Just in Time."[6] Up until then, the upstream manufacturing processes would deliver the parts they finished one after another. The engines would be delivered, but the cars couldn't be assembled right away because the steering wheels weren't ready. As a result, considerable time was spent waiting around for all the parts to arrive so that work could begin, followed by intense bursts of work and large amounts of overtime. Ohno saw that by organizing the flow of parts so that they arrived in a smooth sequence, or "just in time," major gains in productivity could be accomplished fairly easily.

The idea of "just in time" came from the president of Toyota, but the next step, the idea of having the client drive the iterations, came from America.

Ohno explains that in the early 1950s, one of his classmates had come back from a visit to the United States where he had taken photos. Among them were several photos of what was a new phenomenon for him. The classmate said that in the United States, "there was something called a supermarket, and there was only a young woman at the exit, and the customer pulled along something like a baby stroller, bought just what they wanted and paid at the exits. This reduced expenses quite a lot, so the customers could buy things inexpensively. If one person was enough for the store, this reduced expenses of the store."[7]

Ohno saw that the idea of having customers go to the store to buy what they wanted in the quantity they wanted, and then have the managers replenish the store with exactly the amount and the type of goods that the customers had bought, could be applied to the process of assembling cars. When parts were brought to the assembly section just because they were made, whether they were needed or not, the assembly section was forced to work in a very uneconomical way. So just like a supermarket, the manufacturing section would manufacture only the type and the quantity of parts that the assembly section actually came to pick up.

The system he developed was initially called "the supermarket system": the manufacturing section no longer delivered parts to the assembly section. Instead they waited until the assembly section came to pick up parts, and then manufactured as many parts as the assembly section had actually used. For ten parts actually used, they simply had to make ten parts by the time the assembly people came back the next time. Instead of manufacturing so as to push parts from manufacturing to assembly, manufacturing waited until there was pull from the assembly that they needed parts.

This posed a challenge for the manufacturing section to effectively produce only what the assembly section came to get. In order to do this, they had to keep lot sizes small and do changeovers from one part to another very efficiently.

In due course, the "supermarket system" came to be known as the Toyota Production System. Contrary to what common sense might indicate, once rapid changeovers were accomplished, small demand-driven iterations generally turned out to be more efficient than mass production runs.[8] Toyota's goal was "to go from . . . 'order to cash' as fast as possible at a sustainable pace—to deliver things of value to the customer . . . in shorter and shorter cycle times of all processes, while still achieving highest quality and morale levels."[9]

Initially Toyota's production system was ignored, even in Japan, because demand was strong and companies were growing quickly. Then the oil crisis of 1973 triggered an economic slowdown, and other Japanese companies saw how Toyota emerged from the slowdown stronger and more resilient. This model of manufacturing came to the United States in the 1980s.[10] In 1990, it was christened "lean manufacturing" in the book, *The Machine That Changed the World.*[11]

When lean techniques are executed well, with small batch sizes, increased flexibility, and reduced variability, cycle times can drop by factors of ten to one hundred. Inventories can be reduced by more than 90 percent, freeing enormous amounts of cash. Secondary effects include improved quality, accelerated learning, and lower production costs.[12]

Toyota uses an iterative approach not only in manufacturing but also to develop its new models. Lean analysts Mary Poppendieck and Tom Poppendieck write: "The product development process has specific synchronizing events such as vehicle sketches, clay models, design structure plans, prototype and so on. The dates for events are scheduled by the chief engineer. Every engineer and supplier knows that these dates will never—ever—be moved. They know exactly what is expected of their contribution by the date. The engineers are expected to obtain for themselves everything necessary to be ready on time. Thus information is 'pulled' by engineers as they need it instead of broadcast to long distribution lists."[13]

Fujio Cho, board chairman of Toyota says: "You realize how little you know and you face your own failures and redo it again and at the second trial you realize another mistake and so you redo it once again. . . . So by constant improvement . . . one can rise to the higher level of practice and knowledge."[14]

ITERATIONS IN BUILDING HOUSES

In the 1990s, Quadrant Homes, a subsidiary of Weyerhauser, built homes in the Seattle area in the traditional manner.[15] First, the company would buy a tract of land, assuming high demand and hoping for appreciation. Then its architects would design the home from the builder's viewpoint to incorporate the latest housing trends, meet buyer profiles, and match the competition. Next, builders would construct the home in three to four months, adding options that they thought would be appropriate. It was often only toward the end of the construction period that there would actually be a real buyer. When the buyer was in hand, Quadrant would conduct a single final walk-through aimed at fixing defects and problems to be covered under the warranty. Finally, the deal would be completed.

In a seller's market with high demand, this might have worked. But in the Seattle market where Quadrant operated in the 1990s, demand for the kind of houses Quadrant was building was mixed. Because the houses didn't sell quickly, it faced the cost of holding high levels of inventory. Buyers encountered sticker shock since the actual price of the house was often above the advertised price as a result of the high-priced options that the builder had installed. To get the home sold, price concessions had to be made, further reducing Quadrant's margins. Overall, the houses that Quadrant was building didn't respond to what home purchasers were really looking for. Customer satisfaction was low.

In 1998, Quadrant took a hard look at what it was doing and came to the realization that it couldn't grow and meet its profitability requirements with the model that it had. It saw that it wasn't in the business of building houses. Instead its goal should be "to help people realize the American dream." When it studied the market, it discovered a large unmet need among first-time home buyers who were buying existing homes that were cheaper than new homes and met their basic needs more closely. Quadrant set out to "provide more house to more homebuyers for less money than they ever thought possible."[16]

To accomplish this, Quadrant began operating in an iterative fashion, starting from what the buyer wanted. Instead of building the home and then trying to sell it, Quadrant sells the home before building it and involves the buyer iteratively in the design and building of the house. The customer can choose from multiple footprints and floor plans. Standardized customization offers the flexibility buyers want while reducing complexity for the builder.

The buyer, not the builder, chooses the options so they get exactly what they want. They can also experience what the design choices feel like in one of two showrooms and on scheduled site visits. The final walk-through inspection with a punch list of issues to be fixed has been replaced by three site walk-throughs with the buyer at key milestones, along with weekly customer calls with updates on progress.

"The word 'choice' is a big deal for us," says Quadrant vice president Ken Krivanec. "It's all iterative for the buyers. They can go from a variety of locations, to a variety of lots to choose from, to a variety of floor plans, and then on to complete customization of the house itself with up to 10,000 different permutations and combinations that they can experience in one of the showrooms."

Quadrant has also made internal efficiencies. Single long-term partners were engaged for each trade. As a result, costs have been lowered and quality raised. Quadrant is also able to compress construction time from a variable 90 to 120 days to a standardized 54 days.

Despite a difficult housing market, an iterative way of working has enabled Quadrant to continue igniting client delight.

MEANING IN WORK AND MEANING AT WORK

Toyota, Quadrant Homes, and b2b2dot0 are just a few of the countless firms that are using client-driven iterations as a means of becoming more productive. Interestingly, client-driven iterations are not just more efficient; they also can help create meaning in work.

Meaning *in* work, as Chip Conley, the CEO of Joie de Vivre Hospitality, points out in his book, *Peak,* is different from meaning *at* work: "Meaning *at* work relates to how an employee feels about the company, their work environment, and the company's mission. Meaning *in* work relates to how an employee feels about their specific job task."[17]

Some organizations are content if they have a worthwhile mission and people are paid adequately. Feeling part of an organization that is making a difference in the world can help give people a sense of being part of something more important than themselves. Having a mission that can inspire, like Apple's "Think different," Nike's "Just do it," and Joie de Vivre's "Create joy," can—to a certain extent—give people a feeling that they are working in something larger, and may even encourage them to tolerate bad working conditions.

And yet if people can't see how the specific work they are doing on a daily basis fits into this larger mission, cynicism may set in. This is the issue often faced by people working in the public sector and at nongovernmental organizations: the mission is worthwhile, but the traditional management often practiced by those organizations is dispiriting.

Radical management is about creating both meaning at work and meaning in work: that is, both a worthwhile mission for the organization as a whole and meaningful work on a day-to-day basis. The distinction is nicely depicted in Figure 6.1.

Meaning in work can be facilitated by getting work done within client-driven iterations. This is not only where the rubber hits the road but also where the people doing the work can see the impact of the rubber hitting the road.

THE USE OF ITERATIVE WORK PATTERNS

Iterative work patterns have been around for a long time. In fact, in painting, literature, music, engineering, and filmmaking, they are the

FIGURE 6.1 The Distinction Between Meaning at Work and Meaning in Work

		Meaning *IN* work: Low	Meaning *IN* work: High (Radical management)
Meaning AT work	High	The person loves the company but isn't inspired by what they do each day.	The person loves the company and loves what they do each day.
	Low	The person doesn't believe in the company and isn't inspired by what they do each day.	The person doesn't believe in the company but loves what they do each day.

Source: *Based on Conley, C.* Peak: How Great Companies Get Their Mojo from Maslow. *San Francisco: Jossey-Bass, 2007.*

norm. At Pixar, for example, the award-winning digital moviemaking firm, although each team has clear leaders, collaboration and criticism are built into the creative process. The work on each film is subjected to daily review and anyone can offer an opinion.[18] And rapid prototyping is one of the practices that underlie the success of the award-winning San Francisco design firm, IDEO.[19]

As early as the 1930s, quality management saw the introduction of iterative approaches to work when Walter Shewhart, a quality expert at Bell Labs, proposed a series of short plan-do-study-act (PDSA) cycles for quality improvement.[20] Starting in the 1940s, quality guru W. Edwards Deming began vigorously promoting PDSA, which he later described in his book, *Out of the Crisis.*[21] Quality management, however, focused for the most part on internally driven iterative work patterns. It was management that defined quality and steered the flow and direction of change. The client wasn't always the center of attention.[22] By contrast, client-driven iterations start from the client. Rather than pushing steadily improved goods and services to the client in the hope of making a sale, client-driven iterations adopt a pull approach, starting from the client.

Through client-driven iterations, firms like Toyota, Quadrant, and b2b2dot0 are able to keep inventory and work in process as small as possible and customize their product not only to meet the customer's original perceived needs but also to adjust it to meet any changes in those needs.

Conceptually, in a pure pull approach, if there is no buyer, the firm does nothing. Instead it sets about improving the firm's practices and techniques or developing new products and services. In practice, the pull approach is never purely pull. So as software developers Larman and Vodde point out, to state that pull is good and push is bad is a false dichotomy.[23] Toyota's manufacturing section has to make some product before it can be replaced by a pull from the customer. Quadrant needed to build the new home showroom and some amount of product to show to potential buyers. Sam Bayer's firm had to build a prototype before he could begin the client-driven dialogue. But the amount of time and effort spent on these push-based activities is minimized until there is a client.

Client-driven iterations have become pervasive in software development with the spread of Scrum and Agile methodologies. The traditional sequential way of managing with a sequence of specifications, planning, implementation, and delivery ran into major problems. The end result of traditional project management wasn't just that the projects didn't finish on time. Around half of all large projects simply didn't finish at all.[24]

The success of client-driven iterative methods in managing software has led to the spread of those methods to related fields. Thus, the Quality Software Engineering group at IBM is responsible for software development processes and practices across the company. As part of the effort to promulgate Scrum in developing software, an iterative process of working was adopted for doing change management.[25]

Similarly, at the Chicago software firm Total Attorneys, iterative work patterns were so successful that they spread to the staff of call centers: small cross-functional teams work in cycles of three weeks. At the Danish software firm Systematic Software, iterative methods have been spreading from software development to other parts of the firm. At the Swedish software firm Trifork, iterative methods have spread from software development to conference management. And OpenView Venture Partners, a Boston-based venture capital firm, has expanded client-driven iterations into consulting and finance.

Once a firm sees the power of client-driven iterations in one area, it becomes natural to ask: Why not do all work in this fashion?

BUSTING THE IRON TRIANGLE OF MANAGEMENT

Client-driven iterations help force progress on all three sides of the iron triangle of organization, staff, and clients. They improve productivity for the organization by focusing work on the elements that really add value and eliminating work that doesn't add value. They also eliminate unproductive planning time. It's counterintuitive but true that once an organization masters the turnaround, short production runs are usually more efficient than long ones.[26] They also reduce risk to the organization by providing management not with unreliable progress reports, but with evidence of whether actual progress is being made.

They boost job satisfaction by providing people doing the work with a direct line of sight to the clients for whom the work is being done, giving a sense of accomplishment if they succeed and a spur to try harder if they fail. And they promote client delight by giving the clients or their proxies the opportunity to guide the work to generate exactly what they want.

They do these things simultaneously, not in opposition to each other.

IMPLICATIONS FOR WORK IN GENERAL

Despite the spread of client-driven iterative methods of managing, it is fair to say that the default mental model of management in general remains the push approach of doing work in one go from start to finish in accordance with a plan.

We know that this doesn't work very well in complex dynamic environments. And we know that when the goal of work shifts from the linear task of producing goods and services to the complex challenge of delighting clients, then all work contexts become dynamic and unpredictable.

WHERE ITERATIVE APPROACHES DON'T APPLY

Doing work in iterations is not a panacea. It is less applicable in these situations:

- *Predictable environment.* Where the goal is to produce a thing and the work is stable and predictable, iterative work is effective but not necessary. Where the work is focused on a simple linear goal in a stable environment, traditional project management may work well.
- *Totally unpredictable environment.* Where the work environment is so uncertain that nothing can be planned, a flow system (in Japanese, *kanban*) may work better. The approach involves a queue, with limits as to how many things can be introduced into the queue, so as not to create a work jam.[27]
- *Client willingness.* The client is unwilling to spend the time on iterations and giving feedback ("just give me the thing on time and on schedule"). Where the contract prescribes delivery of a final product or service at a fixed time and fixed price with no possibility of discussion of what is to be delivered, there may be a tension between the language of the contract and the principles of client-driven iterations. In such cases, the organization may nevertheless do the work internally in an iterative fashion, using a proxy representative acting for the ultimate client.

So why aren't client-driven iterations already the standard pattern for doing work? One reason is historical. Organizations change slowly. The habits of managers who have worked in a sequential push fashion for decades are set and embedded in the culture of most large companies. It is common sense, obvious, and logical to do the requirements, then design, then implement. It gives the impression of an orderly, accountable, and measurable process with simple, document-driven milestones. It is a natural marriage with hierarchical bureaucracy. It ties in with thinking built on the economies of scale, mass production, and mass marketing. There is only one problem: in a complex dynamic environment and where competitive survival depends on being able to delight clients, it doesn't work.

The traditional management approach of big-chunk implementation in accordance with a plan is also based on a philosophical difference. It reflects a deterministic philosophy that imagines we can create a complete definition of what needs to be done and then realize that definition. Radical management accepts that in a dynamic, unpredictable world, it isn't possible to create a complete definition of what needs to be done. The way to cope with a rapidly changing and unpredictable environment is through short iterations that enable adjustment to change.

Big-chunk implementation is also based on an economic error. The conventional view of iterative work processes is that doing iterations and prototypes wastes resources. Why not get it right the first time and do big production runs? Why waste time on multiple cycles? Each iteration incurs a cost in cycle time and transition expenses. Extra iterations incur extra costs and extra costs are bad, so iterations should be reduced to improve efficiency. In reality, once the art of managing quick transitions between cycles is mastered, iterative work patterns are not only more flexible and deliver higher quality; when the overall costs to the organization are taken into account, they are generally cheaper.[28]

The difficulty of communications also plays a role. Iterative work patterns are hard to explain and understand. They are counterintuitive. Software developer Kent Beck writes: "I thought that for a mass-production factory to run smoothly there must be a large inventory of parts between any two steps of the process. That way, if the upstream machine stops working, the downstream machine can keep chugging away on the buffer of parts. [The Toyota Production System] turns this thinking on its head. While individual machines may work more smoothly with lots of 'work in progress' inventory, the factory looked at as a whole doesn't work as well."[29] Analogies can help communicate, as Taiichi Ohno found with the supermarket analogy and Sam Bayer has found with the story from *Angela's Ashes.*

A less obvious stumbling block is psychological. Managers are used to having comprehensive plans with Gantt charts and fixed delivery dates, often spelled out over several years. Such magisterial plans, however, can lead to magical thinking, with managers confusing plan with reality, viewing the world as an extension of their will, even losing their grasp on the real world as something independent.

Working in client-driven iterations generates self-understanding. We learn that we are not as free or as powerful as we thought. Our shared interdependence is brought into immediate and direct view. We realize that we are tied to our fellow human beings and all the frustrations and delights that this entails. These discoveries are not necessarily comfortable.

A final reason is practical. How do we slice up big, lumpy projects into iterations? We have already seen how client-driven iterations can be applied to building houses, something that doesn't at first glance look as though it can be handled in an iterative fashion. Once we understand the practices involved, virtually any work can be approached in this way.

One of the pioneers of doing work in iterations is Tom Gilb. In his book *Evolutionary Project Management,* he writes about an apparently unpromising candidate for iterative implementation: a naval radar system on a ship that wasn't due to be launched for another three years. How could it possibly be done in an iterative fashion?[30]

The project was to make a radar device that had two antennas instead of the usual one. The dual signal sources were analyzed by a computer, which presented their data. It was for monitoring the ship and air traffic surrounding the ship. It was like having two eyes.

Gilb began to solve the problem by identifying the stakeholders and the results they would be expecting. The goal was increased accuracy of perception for the Royal Navy, not the production of a black box. Gilb then asked whether the black box worked more or less in the lab. When he found out that it did, this opened the way to asking why it couldn't be tried out on one of the navy's existing ships, initially running in parallel to conventional radar. Then any problems in practice would be ironed out, and desirable new features would be added, possibly giving the test ship itself immediate increased capability. Then when the new ship was launched, the system would be far more mature and safe to use.

Iterative thinking was also used in the U.S. Navy to build submarines.[31] In October 1957, Vice Admiral Levering Smith had recently been appointed technical director of the new Polaris program, which was aimed at developing submarines that could launch missiles when submerged. The first Polaris submarine was scheduled to be operational eight years later, in 1965. That was already an ambitious target, as the Polaris program required the development of nine new technologies. In addition, Smith had a problem. The Soviet Union had just successfully launched *Sputnik I,* the first artificial satellite to orbit the world. That showed that the Soviet Union had the capability to launch long-range missiles with nuclear weapons toward the United States.

Two weeks after *Sputnik I* was launched, the deadline for completing the Polaris program was moved up from 1965 to 1959. What was already a very difficult goal had suddenly turned into mission impossible. How could such an acceleration be possible?

Smith's client was the U.S. Congress. To them, time was of the essence. Having any kind of missile-launching submarine in the water was far more important than having the perfect submarine. So Smith decided to approach the task iteratively. Instead of creating the ultimate system in nine years, he set about creating a progression of systems: A1, A2, and A3. The A1 version would contain whatever technology could be deployed in three years. The A2 version would be developed in parallel but proceed more slowly to allow it to use more desirable technologies. The A3 version would incorporate everything learned in the development of the earlier versions.

Smith succeeded. Congress gave him the money, and he delivered. What had seemed to be a mission impossible was accomplished. On June 9, 1959, the first Polaris missile was launched from a submarine. By the end of 1960, two Polaris submarines were patrolling at sea.

Unlike many other defense systems, the missile performed as promised. There was never a hint of a cost overrun.[32]

In essence, radical management and client-driven iterations imply a mental revolution, a different way of thinking about work. Once the mental revolution has occurred, the work can be divided into iterations. The key to success is delivering value to clients at the end of each iteration. It is this question to which we now turn.

PRACTICES FOR CLIENT-DRIVEN ITERATIONS

Practice #1: *Focus on Stakeholders and What Is of Value for Them*

The first step in developing client-driven iterations is to shift attention from the thing to the person and identify the primary stakeholders. Rather than focusing on what is being produced, the focus is on whom it is for.

Thus, when radical management is applied to an apparently lumpy thing like building a house, the attention shifts from the house to the person for whom the house is being built. The goal switches from building a structure to fulfilling the client's dream. The house is obviously the principal means by which clients fulfill their dream. But the house is the means, not the end. Radical management asks: Who are the people who need the house? Why do they need it? How can we delight them more or sooner? How do we turn the process of building the house into one that adds to the customer's delight? It's a change in mind-set from things to people.

Practice #2: *Identify the Principal Performance Objective for the Primary Stakeholders*

It's important not to be distracted by the apparent objective of delivering a thing. One keeps asking why, until one finds what the customer really wants. In the case of the Polaris submarine, the real objective wasn't to develop a missile-based submarine: it was the increased feeling of security generated by having a submarine—any functioning submarine, not the perfect submarine—in the water and operational.

The priority is to focus first on those elements of high value that can be delivered soonest. To the extent possible, the client should participate in setting priorities. If this isn't possible, a proxy representative does the job—someone who spends time with the client, knows the client, understands the client, and has a good sense of what would delight the client.

Radical management is thus a process of organizational learning that allows teams and organizations to discover how to delight a client at the level of the overall business, of a particular product, or an individual team.

Practice #3: *Consider How to Deliver More Value Sooner or Cheaper*

Once you have the real goal, you can ask: How can we evolve toward that goal sooner? How can we delight the client with partial steps or other means? How can we give the client a taste of what it would be like so that he or she can give us feedback? Is it meeting the client's needs? How it could be improved?

Temporary designs or prototypes can also be used. It may not matter if the design is rough and inelegant. For instance, when the San Francisco–based design firm IDEO was trying to communicate the idea of a new kind of surgical knife to a group of high-powered surgeons, the staff taped together a whiteboard marker, a black plastic film canister, and an orange clothespin-like clip. The makeshift model represented a rough physical prototype of what the surgical knife would look like. Despite its inelegance, the surgeons understood the concept and liked what they saw.[33]

Practice #4: *Decide as Late as Responsibly Possible What Work Is to Be Included in the Iteration*

By making decisions at the last responsible moment, the team has the best information to make informed decisions. It avoids wasting resources by making unnecessary inventory or early decisions that will have to be undone. This gives the greatest chance to avoid working on something that isn't needed, and to include the best possible ideas at the top of the list of priorities to be worked on.[34]

Practice #5: *Have the Client or Client Proxy Participate in Deciding Priorities for the Iteration*

Ideally no work is done until there is some indication that the customer wants something, so that the team has a clear line of sight to that customer.

When the product is intended for a mass market, it is obviously not possible to have millions of customers giving their feedback on successive iterations. Here the challenge is to have one voice that speaks for the customers, understands the customers in depth, and anticipates how the customers will react to successive iterations.

The finished product is presented to the client or customer proxy at the end of the process of iterations, and the team doing the work can see and experience the reaction.

Practice #6: *Ensure That the Team Doing the Work Knows Who Speaks for the Client*

Systematic Software, a Danish software firm, has found that a distinguishing feature of its most productive teams is the clarity of their understanding as to who speaks for the client. They know how priorities are being defined and by whom, and when and how decisions are made. In practice, this function is often being performed by many people, including the project manager, architect, team leader, and lead developers. All of these different people form part of the function that defined priorities for an iteration.

Whether it is the team itself or a separate team that decides priorities or the clients themselves, clarifying who decides on priorities is one of the first steps in setting up a project.

Practice #7: *Spell Out the Goals of Each Iteration Before the Iteration Begins*

Unless we know where we are going, it is hardly likely that we will get there. Today many knowledge workers find themselves, as did Nathalie, the software developer we met in Chapter One, in the frustrating situation of not knowing exactly what work is meant to be done. There are many possibilities, but decisions are hard to come by.

When we don't know what work is to be done, we will never know when we have finished it. Much time will be wasted in spinning wheels, going down wrong alleys, trying to guess what is needed, and then doing rework when it turns out that the team guessed wrong.

Radical management entails getting crystal clear on what work is to be attempted in each iteration and then getting out of the way to let the team get on with it.

Practice #8: *Define the Goals of Each Iteration in the Form of User Stories*

In the world of traditional management where the goal is producing goods or services, the target is relatively easy to define in terms of the abstract requirements of the final product or service. Build things. Provide services. How much? How big? How long? How wide? What color? Requirements, sometimes extending over hundreds of pages, often include low-priority things that might be needed.

When work is done in this way, clients are rarely delighted, and workers often see little meaning in their work. That's because when the requirements are spelled out in terms of abstractions, the reasons for them are typically hidden. Why this much? Why this big? Why this long? Why this wide? Our ability to understand the meaning of our work is limited and our ability to innovate eliminated.

It's hard to argue with an abstraction. The job is simply to deliver a product or service in accordance with the specifications, come what may. "Just do it" is the implication. "Don't ask questions." The possibility that there might be a better way of delighting clients is systematically removed.

Once the goal of work shifts to delighting clients, the definition of work moves from an abstraction to a client experience. The questions become: How do we get inside the mind of the clients and understand what their current experience is like? How could that experience be different as a result of what we can accomplish during the iteration? How can we understand what these clients will be experiencing that will cause delight?

Capturing the experience will normally be in the form of a story. Stories catalyze our understanding by providing direct access to other people's thoughts and feelings. They enable us to climb out of our own self-centered world and see things from their perspective. With that understanding, we can begin to imagine what kind of a product or service will be likely to delight them.

In some areas like software development, planning in the form of stories is now pervasive. It is explained in detail in Mike Cohn's book, *User Stories Explained.*[35] It is now common to hear developers talk in terms of implementing stories: "I implemented three stories in this cycle."

Software developer Mike Cohn recommends a standard form for the user story: As a <type of user>, I want <some goal> so that <some reason>.[36] (See Table 6.1.) Putting the story in the first person is important, because it draws the team into imagining the client's situation. By saying, "As a such-and-such, I want . . . ," one instantly imagines what it is like to be a such-and-such.

It's not that written requirements have to be abandoned. The goal of radical management is to find the right balance between documentation and discussion. Traditional management has focused far too much on producing abstract requirements and not enough on discussion aimed at understanding the client.

TABLE 6.1 Examples of User Stories

As a <Type of User>	I Want <Goal>	So That <Reason>
As a parent,	I want a comfortable, affordable home	so that my spouse and I can raise our family.
As the U.S. Congress, which funds the nation's defense systems,	we want a missile-launching submarine built in a timely fashion	so that we can be assured that the country is safe from nuclear attack.
As the client of a boutique hotel,	I want a comfortable room with a personal feel to it	so that I have an unexpectedly stimulating night away from home.
As the holder of a house insurance policy,	I want to know that the major risks to my family home are covered in case there is an unexpected catastrophe	so that I will not be financially destroyed by the catastrophe.
As the user of a job search Web site,	I want to be able to find and apply for jobs that might interest me	so that I can find a better position than I currently have.

Practice #9: *Treat the User Story as the Beginning, Not the End, of a Conversation*

When a user story is dropped into a traditional management setting, the likelihood is either that it will be instantly rejected (because it is a story) or that it will become an artifact, an instruction, a new abstract plan to be imposed on the team. It will be seen as a top-down, one-way communication. One part of the organization defines the requirement, and a different part implements it. Through the written document, the manager is giving an instruction, "Here's what to do," and the team is expected to do it without asking questions.

This type of boss-subordinate relationship with one-way communications is unlikely to create commitment on the part of those doing the work, particularly where the workers are at least as knowledgeable as the boss. Rather than feeling responsible for the success of the product or contributing new ways to delight the client, they will focus on what they have been told to do.[37]

Open-minded conversations have the opposite effect: the opportunity for everyone to participate elicits new insights and inspiration to contribute to the complex goal of delighting the client.

User stories are a way of shifting the focus from writing abstract requirements to discussing what might delight the client. A user story is a short, simple description of a need told from the perspective of someone who wants the product or capability. The written version of the user story is less important than the conversations surrounding the story. It enables the people doing the work to get inside the mind of clients and focus on what might delight them.

Practice #10: *Keep the User Stories Simple, and Record Them Informally*

Traditional managers visiting Toyota factories are often startled by the simple handwritten documents on which progress is recorded and lessons are learned and shared on single sheets of paper.[38]

Similarly, in the high-tech environment of software development, visitors are often surprised to find that instead of planning being done with sophisticated computer programs, user stories are typically displayed on handwritten cards or sticky notes and prominently displayed in the workplace itself.

Why this preference for handwritten paper notes ahead of computers? Computers are wonderful things, but when information is stored on a computer, it is available only when it is actually accessed and then usually only one person at a time. Moreover, once the information is in the computer, it tends to become a formal, fixed artifact, with all the risk of generating magical thinking that the plan is reality. Having handwritten notes, cards, and charts that are visible to all in the workplace and adjusted as necessary can be a constant reminder of the fluid nature of reality.

Using a lightweight, temporary form of recording like cards or sticky notes also serves as a constant reminder that the written version of the story is a starting point for a conversation, not the final word.

Practice #11: *Display the User Stories in the Workplace*

A board on which the stories are posted should be visible to anyone in the work space to show what is being worked on, what has been completed, and what remains to be done in the iteration. People can see at a glance where a project stands. The board on which stories are recorded becomes an information radiator.

Practice #12: *Be Ready to Discuss the User Stories with the Client or Client Proxy*

The story card serves as a catalyst for a two-way conversation between the development team and the client or client proxy. The team promises to talk to the client proxy before beginning work on the story; the client or client proxy has to be available when the team is ready to talk.

The user story is thus useful not as a thing in itself but as a catalyst for conversation. Those doing the work can get inside the mind of the client and figure out what might delight him or her.

The availability of the client or client proxy for conversation is important because it allows the team to accept work in an iteration without having resolved every issue. Similarly, the team's availability to talk to the client or client proxy helps remove concerns by the manager that every last detail must be written down.[39]

Practice #13: *Find Out More About the Client's World*

Crafting user stories requires knowledge of the context of the client. Becoming de facto ethnographers who visit and live with clients is part of the process of understanding their situation.

Usability expert Jeff Patton talked to me about his experience designing software that would be used by people receiving groceries at the loading dock of a grocery store:

> I was building software that would be used in the backs of grocery stores—people who received items on the docks of grocery stores, using handheld devices. I didn't want to try to build the product without an understanding of that world. So I called the grocery stores and arranged to visit, and see what goes on at the backs of grocery stores. Because it wouldn't do any good if I understood and the team didn't, I grabbed members of the team and we went to a grocery store. We spent the day finding out what it was like receiving vegetables at the back of grocery stores. At the end of the day, we were better equipped to design software for people who received groceries at the back of grocery stores because we had lived that experience.

Similarly, when Toyota was designing the Lexus, it sent teams of its designers to California, to live in a beachfront house at Laguna Beach and breathe the world of country clubs, fancy restaurants, and golf courses so that they would understand what is important in that world.[40]

The recent emergence of narrative medicine, in which doctors are trained to listen to and understand the patient's story, is another illustration of the growing recognition of the importance of understanding client's story.[41]

Practice #14: *In the User Story, Include a Test to Determine When the Story Has Been Fully Executed*

So that you know when you are done, you specify in advance the test of what is meant by "done." The user story includes a test to determine when the story has been executed. In software development, an emphasis on testing is critical to delivering value to clients. The interaction of multiple computer programs is such that automated testing is typically built into the work cycle.

In less structured forms of work, being clear about the definition of completion is also important. Every user story should result in customers or clients who feel as if they have accomplished something.

Practice #15: *Provide Coaching to Encourage Good Team Practices*

Just as customers don't know what they want until they see it, teams don't know good work or team practices until they have experienced them. They may eventually discover them for themselves. However, the process of learning can be expedited if the team has access to good practices from within the team itself or from coaches outside the team.

A study at Yahoo! showed that the provision of external coaches had a high payoff in terms of team productivity.[42] Traditional management tends to ignore such studies, because the mental model is that the managers are responsible for productivity. The perspective of radical management is that the productivity of the team represents the very future of the organization. Skimping on coaching can be a highly counterproductive form of economizing.

7

PRINCIPLE #4: DELIVERING VALUE TO CLIENTS IN EACH ITERATION

> As a strategic weapon, time is the equivalent of money, productivity, quality, even innovation.
>
> **George Stalk Jr.**[1]

Picture this. You're driving along the freeway in Los Angeles, making steady progress, when suddenly you come to a halt at the tail end of a lengthy queue of traffic. You inch forward for what seems like hours. When you eventually get moving again, you look for the cause of the jam, but you can't find it. No police. No accident. No crushed cars. No breakdown. No dead animal. No debris strewn on the road.

So you wonder: "Why did everyone stop? How odd!"

You imagine that it will never happen again. But it does. Again and again.

Eventually you realize that you have encountered the curious phenomenon of the phantom traffic jam. Whole sections of engineering theory are devoted to phantom traffic jams. The mathematics of such jams, which the researchers call *jamitons*, are strikingly similar to the equations that describe detonation waves produced by explosions. Once a jam starts to form, it happens very quickly, and once it's formed, it's almost impossible to break up. Drivers just have to wait it out.

Phantom traffic jams are puzzling because our intuitive thinking about systems is not very reliable.

We imagine that traffic delays start only when utilization of the roads approaches 100 percent.

We expect that delays will be linear: a little bit of a traffic jam will cause a little bit of a delay. It will take a lot of traffic to cause a big delay.

We expect that once the cause of the jam disappears, the flow will resume more or less straight away.

We anticipate that the variability of inputs, like the arrival of slow-moving big trucks or a cluster of cars all arriving into the system at the same time, won't have much impact on the flow of traffic.

Yet all of these commonsense propositions are false.

It's not the case that everything flows smoothly until utilization reaches 99 percent. In fact, traffic flows start slowing once utilization reaches 50 percent and significantly after 80 percent utilization. And the delays that occur are not proportional. They grow exponentially. Clearing the queue takes much longer than creating it. Forty-five minutes of blockage in Los Angeles takes a lot longer than forty-five minutes to clear. And the variability of inputs isn't neutral. It can have a massive impact on the flow of the system. When slow-moving trucks arrive or clumps of cars arrive simultaneously, the system once more tends to jam.

Here is the solution to solving the problem of traffic jams that inexplicably and suddenly erupt: in order to get people where they want to go faster, we have to slow the flow of vehicles into the system to a level that it can comfortably handle. In other words, in order to go faster, we have to go slower. We know this. Mathematics describes it, and experiments confirm it. But we still have a hard time believing that it's true.[2] And it is even harder to believe with similar phenomena in the workplace.

UNDERSTANDING PHANTOM WORK JAMS

In the workplace, the idea that we might have to go slower in order to go faster is counterintuitive. Let's look at a couple of simple examples.

A House Renovation

Björn Granvik lives in Malmo, a small town at the southern tip of Sweden. At work, he is the chief technology officer of the software firm Jayway. In the evenings and weekends, he works on renovating the house that he occupies with his wife and three children. The house used to be a school, and so it is rather large, but it doesn't have many rooms. Transforming it into a livable house has required a massive effort.

When he started the renovations, his wife would stand in the corner in one of the rooms and say, "Björn, here's something over here that doesn't work." And Granvik would run over and start trying to fix it.

But then he would hear her from somewhere else in the house, calling, "Here's something even worse." And he would leave whatever he was doing and go over to try to fix that. So he kept running among projects in the house. There was so much to do that he was constantly jumping from one project to the other, hardly ever finishing anything. So one day he said to his wife, "This doesn't work. We can't go on like this."

Granvik had encountered a phantom work jam! Too many inputs had jammed the system. Given his experience with the practices of radical management and the simplicity of the situation, the solution was fairly obvious. "I know that there are a bunch of things to do," he told his wife. "But we need to do them in some kind of order."

So he cleared a space on the door of the refrigerator and said that they would have two lists, each with three available slots. One list would be for all the big things that needed to be done—things that take a lot of time, like fixing the leak in the roof. The other list would be for small items: something that would take less than an hour to do, for which he could squeeze in an hour here or there—for example, "Hang ten photographs on the wall."[3]

"Anything we put in these slots," he said, "we can talk about. And we can get them going. I will concentrate on these three things. If something else comes up, we can put it on the side of the refrigerator, but I will not look at it. There's no point in talking to me about this, because although I will listen, I won't do anything about it. I will only work on the top-priority items in the three slots."

So he and his wife began working this way, and it went really well. He was happy because his wife stopped bugging him about things that weren't on the priority list. And she was happy because things that she really wanted done were actually accomplished.

The interesting thing was that it turned out that Granvik's client—his wife—was equally happy if he hung ten photos or fixed the leak in the roof. Fixing the leak in the roof is a big, expensive project that takes considerable time and effort. But the amount of joy that comes from it was no bigger than a tiny task like hanging the ten photos.

By focusing on what his client really wanted at that particular moment, he found that increasing client delight didn't necessarily cost more. A small thing delivered sooner could delight more than a big thing delivered later.

In order to become more productive and generate more delight for his wife, Granvik had to restrict the flow of work. To go faster, he had to go slower.

Like traffic systems, workplaces encounter problems when they take on more work than they can comfortably handle. This was Granvik's initial situation. He was being asked to take on more work. He accepted the request and ended up taking on more than he could handle. So he suffered a phantom work jam: he slowed down.

And it wasn't just that there was too much to do. When a lot of things are in process, work becomes less productive. It takes longer to finish something when it is done in pieces. All the tools are not at hand. The worker's mind isn't necessarily focused on what has been done already and what needs to be done next. Time is lost catching up on what was done before. Work done in fits and starts is unproductive. To maximize the value to clients, work has to be done from start to finish in one go.[4]

Paradoxically, an apparently good thing—listening to clients—can thus become a problem. Initially, because Granvik listened to his wife and responded to what she wanted, he was hardly able to finish anything. If he had continued in this mode, he might even have entered a client-driven death spiral.

In Granvik's case, it was his wife who was piling on the work. As long as Granvik was face-to-face with her and they had a friendly, nonhierarchical relationship and he understood the issue, it was simple to fix. But when it's a manager who is piling on the work and no one is paying attention to how it is affecting the speed of delivery of value to the client, solving the problem can be more complicated.

The Health Sector

Let's look at two examples in the health sector drawn from Mark Graban's book, *Lean Hospitals*: a center that provides outpatient chemotherapy treatment to patients with cancer and a laboratory that provides test results to doctors.[5]

At the outpatient center, patients have appointments in the morning to have their blood tests, see their oncologist, and make sure that they are ready to receive a fresh chemotherapy treatment. If everything is okay, they go to another part of the building where the chemotherapy treatment is given intravenously to them while they sit in lounge chairs. It's not a pleasant experience, so patients like to come in the morning and get it over with as soon as possible.

In principle, patients would have the blood tests, see the doctor, receive their chemotherapy treatment (which often lasts for several hours), and then go home. In practice, by the middle of the day, all of the lounge chairs for patients were full and the nurses so busy rushing about, monitoring the intravenous flows and changing the drugs for each patient, that a number of patients would end up having to sit around waiting their turn. Why, they would ask, did they have to sit around for so long in addition to several hours of chemotherapy treatment? The complaints grew so loud from both patients and staff that management was considering expanding the facility and hiring more staff.

What has happened here? The chemotherapy center encountered a phantom work jam! Analysis showed that too much work was coming into the system, causing it to freeze. It also showed that although the center was overloaded in the middle of the day, it was underused later in the afternoon.

Why was that? The oncologists worked in another part of the building separate from the chemotherapy treatment center and didn't see patients waiting for too long. It turned out that they prepared their schedules on the assumption that most patients would want to start their chemotherapy treatment in the morning and get it over with. This would have made sense if the center was dealing with only a few patients. But when all the oncologists were proceeding on this basis, they unwittingly created a phantom work jam.

Once the problem was understood, the oncologists were able to space their appointments more evenly throughout the day, and all the patients could be treated immediately and finish their treatment without any extra waiting. The nursing staff found the even workload easier to handle. There was no need to expand the facility or hire extra staff. In order to give a higher value experience to patients, they simply had to slow the intake.

In another example from the health sector, a regional laboratory at Kaiser Permanente would receive a giant cooler of specimens from twenty-nine medical centers at 3:00 P.M. They would receive a second one at 7:30 P.M. and a third one at 10:30 P.M. The lab facilities and staff were overworked from late afternoon to early morning. In some cases, doctors would be waiting for the results to decide what treatment step to follow, but they wouldn't receive news of abnormal results until three or four o'clock in the morning.

Everyone was frustrated. The workers in the lab were stressed by the sudden huge influxes of work. The doctors were frustrated because they couldn't get their results in a timely fashion and so critical decisions were being delayed. And the patients were left worrying.

They were experiencing phantom work jams! Analysis of the situation showed that both the staff and the lab were underused in the late morning and early afternoon. After that, too much work was coming into the system and causing it to freeze. The underlying problem lay in sending a few large containers of specimens to the lab. This made sense to those responsible for deliveries because it saved on the cost of shipping. But that decision to optimize the cost of shipping caused suboptimal performance for the system as a whole.

For the system as a whole to perform faster, the intake into the lab had to slow down. The courier service was asked to deliver smaller and more frequent batches of specimens starting in the morning. When they did that, the cost of delivery increased, but the lab was able to complete most of its work in the afternoon shift, thus reducing overtime. The lab was also able to call doctors about most of the abnormal results by 5:00 P.M. or 6:00 P.M. the same day, thus enabling the doctors to decide on the next steps in treatment sooner, and patients found out sooner what was needed.

Those who had originally organized the shipments of samples were looking at work from the perspective of a thing: how to perform the shipment more efficiently. They weren't asking themselves: "Who are the people we are doing this for, and how can we get more value for them sooner?" If they had asked those questions and considered the needs of the doctors and patients, they would have seen that bulking up deliveries was causing a phantom work jam. They were making the work of the lab staff and the doctors more difficult, causing frustration and delaying critical decisions for the ultimate client: patients.[6] By not having a clear line of sight to the people for whom they were doing the work or focusing on getting more value to them sooner, they ended up causing suboptimal performance.

IDENTIFYING AND REMOVING PHANTOM WORK JAMS

Granvik's renovations, the chemotherapy treatment center, and the regional laboratory are examples of phantom work jams where people initially didn't recognize what was happening.

In large hierarchies with multiple vertical layers of authority and many different departments and divisions, phantom work jams are occurring all over the organization on a daily basis, and typically no one recognizes them or does anything about them. Work sits waiting in queues. Approvals are holding things up. Customers are trying to get answers and waiting for responses. Well-intended cost savings or big production runs implemented in one part of the organization are slowing things down in another part of the organization, retarding the overall delivery of value to clients.

Big production runs are a particular problem. They maximize work in process and inventory: both are because of the direct costs of working capital and warehousing. There are many indirect costs and noxious secondary effects.[7]

In traditional management, typically nothing is done about delays and phantom work jams until they become so extraordinary that people complain or customers defect. Eventually something may be done, but it may take months, or years, or even decades. Even then, the action taken often fails to solve the problem. The most frequent remedy, a reorganization, may take place with the goal of speeding things up. The reorganization draws the vertical or horizontal boundaries of the hierarchy in different places in the work flow. The result may be removal of the old sources of delay but often the creation of new sources of delay arising from the new boundaries. Traditional managers fail to see that the source of the problem lies in the boundaries themselves. Phantom work jams are inherent in the boundaries of hierarchical bureaucracies.

What can be done? In the world of lean techniques, teams are trained to pinpoint delays and eliminate waste.[8] Value stream mapping is used to help identify and eliminate delays in getting value to clients. It analyzes the flow of materials and information currently required to bring a product or service to a customer. In effect, the workplace is viewed from the ultimate customers' point of view, with the object of accelerating or eliminating any step or activity that does not add value to them.[9]

Lean techniques represent an obvious improvement over traditional management, although they tend to leave the source of the problem untouched: hierarchical bureaucracy. Radical management goes a step further. It incorporates expediting value to clients into the structure of the work itself. Radical management organizes work not in hierarchical divisions and departments, but rather by having projects done by cross-functional teams working in client-driven iterations and examining each iteration in terms of its contribution to delivering value to a client. It gives a clear line of sight to everyone in the organization for each iteration as to whether and to what extent the ultimate client is being delighted. Radical management thus makes the elimination of delays in getting value to clients an integral part of everyone's job.

The questions that radical managers ask themselves are not merely about whether the goods or services have been delivered, but whether the client is being steadily more delighted:

- If asked at the end of each treatment, would the patients using our chemotherapy center recommend us to others?
- As we build our houses, does each step in the process contribute to the happiness of the family who is going to live in it?
- As we construct our submarine, is each interaction with the legislature contributing to reassurance about security?
- As we go about issuing insurance policies, is each step in the process giving a sense of security to the families we're insuring?

- As we run our boutique hotel chain, does each stay generate a feeling of being at home away from home?
- As we develop software, do users see each new feature as useful?
- Overall, as we run our business, how likely is it that the people who work in our organization will recommend it to their friends and colleagues?

In dealing with the responses to these questions, radical management gives priority to time ahead of cost. That's because being more responsive in terms of time also tends to lower costs. In lean manufacturing, it was found that by relentlessly improving the capacity of the overall system to deliver value to customers sooner, overall costs tend to come down of their own accord.[10]

THE MANAGEMENT MIND-SET PROBLEM

Why doesn't traditional management focus on getting value to clients sooner? In part, it's a problem of management mind-set. Traditional management instinctively focuses on deliveries of things, such as chemotherapy treatments or specimen analyses in individual divisions and departments. Because the client is not kept in mind as the principal goal, traditional management instinctively thinks in terms of reducing costs of things in the system rather than looking at the people for whom the work is being done and getting more value to them sooner.

A look at standard management texts is revealing. They contain everything you need to know about traditional management with sophisticated analyses on how to optimize bureaucracy: game theory, decision trees, what-if analyses, marketing and advertising expenditures, make-or-buy options, downsizing, outsourcing, mergers and acquisitions, risk, technology and alliances, inward versus outward orientations, and so on.

References to the time taken to get value to a client appear, if at all, at the back of the book, and then only as a low-level operational issue. In traditional management, time is not considered a strategic issue. The idea of competing on the basis of time is so unfamiliar that it is hardly treated at all.[11]

As a result, traditional management typically doesn't explicitly monitor the time it takes to deliver value to customers, and rarely does so as carefully or intensively as the more easily measurable financial measures of cost and profit. Yet time turns out to be a more important factor in organizational performance than traditional financial measurements. That's because when you put a primary focus on cost, you end up having to make trade-offs between cost and responsiveness. When you focus on time, you tend to get both greater responsiveness and lower cost.[12]

The False Trade-Off Between Time and Quality

Another constraint to taking time seriously is the false trade-off between time and quality. Going fast is associated with cutting corners and lowering quality. Therefore, the traditional manager feels justified in aiming for quality ahead of speed.

The message of this book is different. It is saying that in radical management, the trade-off is often false: you may not need to choose between speed and quality; you may be able to have both. By focusing tightly on what people really want and getting that to them sooner, you get speed and quality at lower cost—a triple win.

At the same time, it is important to keep in mind that speed itself is not the goal. The ultimate goal is delighting clients more and sooner. Focusing on speed per se may generate quality problems and so frustrate clients. Greater speed that results in quality problems may result in a negative quality spiral.

By contrast, when quality is maintained and clients are delighted sooner, costs decrease because there is less work in process. Moreover, the firm earns money sooner and so needs less cash. The primary focus is on performing at a level of quality that delights clients and then provides that sooner.

The Psychological Constraint

There is also a psychological constraint. Even when we discover something that is counterintuitive and know that it is true, we may still have difficulty in believing it.

Intellectually we may know that it's not the speed of any specific component that matters, but the speed of the entire system. We may hear that the speed of the entire system is often inversely correlated with the speed of individual components. We may deduce that going slower in some components enables the system as a whole to produce faster.

For most of us, this is hugely counterintuitive. Until we see it with our own eyes, we find it hard to believe. That's why for people to accept it emotionally, they have to see it demonstrated. Simple games sometimes help. (See the "Learning to Understand Systems" box.) These games show the importance of looking at the system as a whole and focusing on the overall speed of getting value to clients. They demonstrate the importance of focusing on getting more value to clients sooner—that is, the time spent from order to delivery, rather than the speed of individual components of the system. It means looking at work from the ultimate client's point of view and optimizing that experience.

LEARNING TO UNDERSTAND SYSTEMS

The penny game involves four people turning twenty pennies from one side to the other. Each person must turn each penny over once. The game starts with batches of twenty, then batches of ten, then batches of five, and finally batches of one. With the help of five stopwatches, the times taken by each individual and by the group as a whole are recorded. Participants are usually startled to find that as the batch sizes get smaller, the pace of work of the individuals slows, but the overall completion of work becomes faster.

Similarly the envelope game consists of having people fold and insert paper in an envelope, seal twenty envelopes, and affix stamps. Participants are usually startled to find that doing the envelopes completely one by one generally gets the job done faster than folding all the paper, then closing all envelopes, and finally affixing the stamps.

Cultural Barriers in High-End Professional Work

Cultural barriers to delivering more value to clients sooner also play a role. The barriers vary from sector to sector. In software development, the biggest hurdles are usually having management establishing clear priorities for the work of a team before the beginning of a work period and then allowing the team to work without interruption on those priorities for the course of an iteration.

In high-end knowledge firms, an even bigger constraint tends to be getting the degree of collaboration that high performance in cross-functional teams requires. In such settings, cross-functional teams may exist, but they are often teams only in name. The reality is that teams become a means to divide and conquer: each expert participates in the team as the owner of a piece of intellectual turf. There may be collaboration at the border, but within each area of expertise, the expert is the czar. The idea that other members of the team might contribute to another expert's area of expertise, make suggestions, or even suggest improvements as to how the work should be done is a strange, almost unthinkable thought.

The expert owns the territory precisely because of expertise. The idea that experts might have something to learn from others less expert than themselves would put in question the experts' self-image. The thought that a junior member of the team might make a suggestion to improve the work of the senior member is as unthinkable as the thought that a nurse might tell a surgeon how to improve the conduct of an operation. This is silliness, of course, but it is the silliness of highly intelligent and articulate people.

We know from Scott Page in Chapter Five that ordinary people who are cognitively diverse tend to outperform groups of like-minded experts. We know that teams of experts who are operating in intellectual silos are not performing as well as they might if there was collaboration across areas of expertise. And we know that teams performing work in intellectual silos are maximizing the amount of work in process at any one time. Large amounts of work in process retard getting value to clients. We also know that if all members of the team are working on "their own thing," the work of the team proceeds at the pace of the slowest team member. The possibility of getting more value to the client sooner ceases to be feasible.

In short, these teams are operating in a suboptimal fashion. This is one of the reasons that people working in such firms are on the job for long hours under considerable personal stress.

In such settings, the possibility of changing the work culture can seem unthinkable. Within the firm, this way of working is simply the way the work has always been done. It is the unquestionable reality of what it means to work in the firm.

From there it is a short step to conclude that this is the way that it will always be. The thought that large numbers of clever and talented people working very hard for very long hours are actually working in an unproductive fashion is culturally unacceptable, however intellectually robust that thought may be.

Are such firms a lost cause for radical management? Are they doomed to remain in this suboptimal way of working until newer, upstart, more productive firms emerge, are recognized as better, and take the place of their more prestigious predecessors?

TACTICS FOR INTRODUCING RADICAL MANAGEMENT

Several tactics for introducing radical management into even the most intractable high-end knowledge culture are available.

Tactic #1: The Future Is Already Here

Given the global scale of radical management practices in software development, software teams within most big organizations are already implementing the principles of radical management. Teams that are experiencing success in implementing radical management may constitute Trojan horses for introducing the approach more broadly within their firm. It's an argument by analogy: if it worked in software development, why not more broadly in the organization?

Tactic #2: Interacting with Other Organizations

Considerable evidence shows that radical management can lead to major gains in productivity. At a minimum, it's one of the strategic options to consider, because the potential productivity gains are game changing in nature. In any service business, an organization has to be ready to deal with firms that have adopted better management practices. Thus, it will need to familiarize itself with what is involved in radical management. In the process of acquiring that expertise, managers might decide that the firm should consider the implications for its own work.

Tactic #3: Getting a Better Work-Life Balance

Another angle of attack is through work-life balance issues. Many, if not most, staff in high-end knowledge firms are working long hours and under considerable stress. The usual proposals put forward to deal with this dispiriting but well-compensated existence is for people to carve out more time for their private life. This usually doesn't work well because the pressures from work remain inexorable. At best, staff end up working at home. The paradox is that although these talented and intelligent people are working very hard, they are not working productively.

A similarly dispiriting scene existed in software development for many years until the way of managing the work was changed. When more productive practices were introduced, overtime vanished, and late nights at the office became the exception, not the rule.

Convincing people that working very hard for long hours is not productive can be difficult. Having done it for so long, they see it as simply the way things are. However, as the new generation of people joining the workforce are increasingly looking to the quality of working life as a key factor in deciding which firms to work for, hiring the best people will be a force for change.

Tactic #4: Smaller Tasks

One of the constraints in getting people working together collaboratively is having large tasks where the possibilities of collaboration are hidden. But if the task is broken down into its component parts, it will become apparent that although some parts of it require unique expertise, other parts are less specialized, and the resources of the team can be brought to bear on those parts and get them done expeditiously.

○ ○ ○

These tactics, however, deal with symptoms. They don't get at the real source of the problem, which is the apparent impossibility of discussing productivity issues in such organizations. These firms are characterized by a lack of openness about the impediments to getting things done better. It is to this issue that we now turn.

PRACTICES FOR DELIVERING VALUE TO CLIENTS

Practice #1: *Focus on Finishing the Most Important Work First*

In manufacturing, lean manufacturing focuses on eliminating wasted time (any time spent in a queue). In knowledge work and innovation, the equivalent focus is on the things that are most likely to delight clients soonest and getting those items finished as soon as possible.[13]

Typically if you ask a group of people to allocate work among themselves, each person will take the task that he or she likes doing best. This maximizes the amount of work in process and thus delays overall completion of the work.

In radical management, the focus is on deploying optimal resources to finish the most important task first. Only once those resources are deployed should attention shift to the next most important task.

Practice #2: *Ensure That User Stories Are Ready to Be Worked On; Prepare Work Before Beginning to Work On It*

A big influx of inputs into any system will cause it to jam. Just as loading a road system to capacity will cause a phantom traffic jam, so will loading a work unit to capacity. It will cause delays, management and worker frustration, and ultimate client dissatisfaction. To avoid phantom work jams, care must be taken to carefully control the work coming into the unit and avoid loading the work unit even close to full capacity. For instance, Systematic Software noticed in 2008 that several of its software teams were much more productive than the others. One of the successful practices they used was making sure that work was ready to be worked on before an iteration of work began.[14]

Practice #3: *Have the Team Itself Estimate How Much Time the Work Will Take*

In traditional management, managers decide how much work will be done. In radical management, the self-organizing team is given responsibility for estimating how much time any individual piece of work or story will take.

The object is to bring everyone's judgment to bear on the issue. Radical management uses tools to incorporate everyone's voice into the discussion. In complex knowledge work like software development, which is inherently dynamic and unpredictable, methods have been developed known as story points and planning poker.

In software development, the nature of the work is usually described in user stories and the quantity of work measured in story points, as described in Mike Cohn's book, *Agile Estimating and Planning.*[15] To calculate the total story points of a set of tasks defined in terms of user stories, you find the user story involving the least amount of work in the group of tasks and assign it a value of 1 story point. You then use planning poker to compare the amount of work in this user story with the amount of work in each of the other user stories to be worked on and assign story point values to each of those. The sum of the story point values of all the user stories is an estimate of how much work is involved in finishing all the tasks.

The estimated velocity of a team is the sum of the story point estimates of the work that the team estimates can be completed in the cycle. The actual velocity of the team is the sum of the story point estimates of work actually completed in the cycle.

Most software development teams use a rule of giving credit only for fully completed items. When tasks are only partially completed, the work counts as zero, which maintains the discipline of delivering value to clients in each cycle. Working in this way, the team can see how much value can be delivered within a cycle and begin to make more reliable estimates of outputs.

Planning poker is a technique for rapidly estimating, prioritizing, or evaluating a set of items by a group of people. It is simple, quick, and fun.[16] It draws on the talents of the entire group of people present, not just those who speak loudest or most often. It engages people actively in the discussion, flushing out different opinions and clarifying the reasons behind the differences. It slices through hierarchical differences among a group as well and gives everyone an equal voice. It encourages expertise-based results rather than status-based outcomes. It is widely used to estimate effort or relative size of tasks in software development. It can be used to establish priorities or preferences among competing items for a wide variety of tasks.

PLANNING POKER AND THIS BOOK

Planning poker was used as part of the process to decide on the title for this book. In August 2009, about twenty-five titles were being considered. Finally, a meeting of around twelve people was held at the publisher's office to make a decision. There were differing views about which title would be best, and each participant seemed to have different favorites. But in less than an hour, planning poker had narrowed the list of titles to a mere handful. A short discussion, largely drawing on the conversation that had already taken place, was followed by a new round of planning poker, and the winning title quickly emerged.

Thus, people with sharply differing opinions made a complex decision relatively quickly. All participants could see why their favorites had not been selected. Everyone had contributed to the decision and knew that they were heard. A consensus was reached easily and collaboratively, with the entire expertise of the group brought to bear on the issue at hand.

The idea behind planning poker is simple. Each item is briefly presented to the group. Participants ask questions if they don't understand the item being presented, but there is no discussion of how the issue is to be decided.

When everyone is clear on the issue and what the item is, all participants simultaneously signify their opinions on an agreed scale with an agreed methodology. The simplest methodology is for people to use fingers to vote on a scale of one to five or one to ten.

If the estimates of all the participants are the same or very close, the group can reach a decision and move on. If there is significant divergence among the ratings, the group needs to hear from the outliers as to why they held different views (Figure 7.1). When the discussion has fully explored the differences, the group then votes again to see whether there is now a consensus or whether there are still unresolved issues.

A more elaborate version of the approach uses numbered cards with a modified Fibonacci series: 0, 1/2, 1, 2, 3, 6, 8, 14, 20, and 40, so that the discussion focuses on broad orders of magnitude.[17]

A common problem in organizations is a confusion of estimates and commitments. For instance, I might estimate that I can complete a task by June, but I commit to delivering it by August in case something unexpected comes up.

Often what happens in traditional management is that my "estimate" that I can finish in June is passed on to a higher-level manager, who may then pass it on to a client. My estimate has now become a de facto commitment because the client is expecting the output by June and will be upset if it isn't ready then. Or worse, the higher-level manager makes an arbitrary

FIGURE 7.1 Voting in Planning Poker

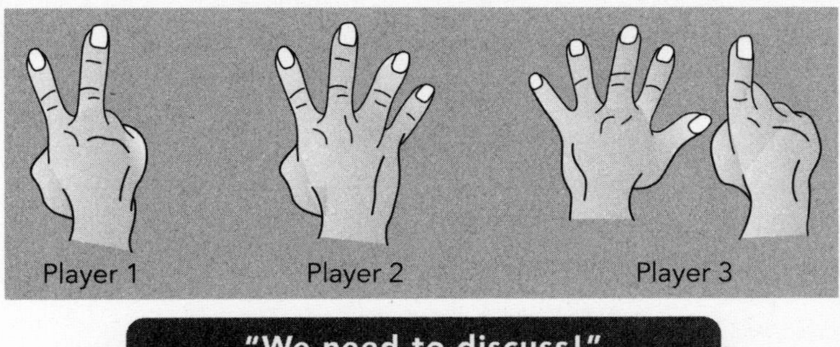

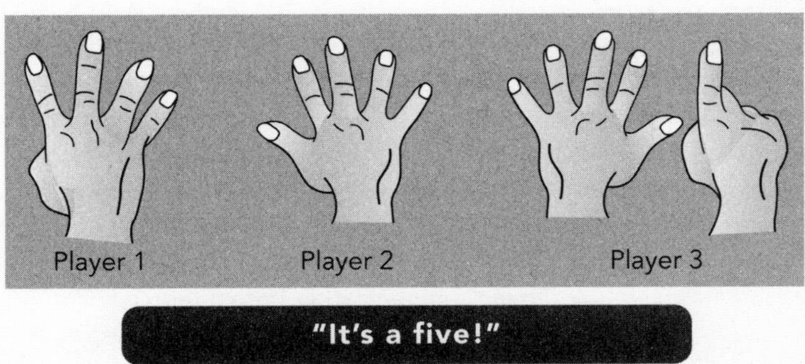

decision that the task should finish by April and informs me afterward without asking my advice. Now we are in the traditional squeeze play of traditional management.

Being careful to distinguish between estimates and commitments and to avoid second-guessing those doing work as to how much time work will take are keys to a quality workplace.

Practice #4: *Give the Team the Responsibility for Deciding How Much Work It Can Do in an Iteration*

In order for work to get done efficiently, people must have the time to do the work that they have committed to complete. In effect, in order to avoid phantom work jams, new work arriving must be limited to match capacity. In a repetitive situation, a company may have a good sense of how much effort will be required in any development cycle and can stagger cycles so that the demands on each function are more or less leveled.[18]

In knowledge work, where it is much more difficult to determine how much effort will be involved in accomplishing anything, experience suggests that the team itself be given responsibility for determining how much work can be accomplished in an iteration. The knowledge workers are best placed to know what the work entails and what is involved in delivering value to clients at the end of the iteration.

Practice #5: *Let the Team Decide How to Do the Work in the Iteration*

In traditional management, managers decide how the work is to be done. This is the essence of Taylorism: experts find the "one best way" to do the work and managers then instruct the workers how to do it.

In radical management, management steps aside and draws on the talents, ingenuity, and insights of the cross-functional team to find the best way to attack the task. Traditional management is typically concerned about the risk of delegating such a decision to a team. But the risk isn't significant when the work is being done in iterations.

Practice #6: *Encourage Open Communication Within the Team*

"Death by meeting" is a common joke in offices. Meetings are derided and parodied. Some books even recommend scrapping meetings altogether.[19] However, open communication among team members is the source of high performance, so that different cognitive perspectives and experience can be brought to bear on the problems collectively facing the team.

Daily stand-up meetings, planning at the start of iterations, and retrospective meetings at the end of each iteration are essential elements for systematically ensuring this degree of open communication.

Practice #7: *Systematically Identify and Remove Impediments to Getting the Work Done*

In the daily stand-up meetings of a self-organizing team, each member systematically answers three questions: What did I do yesterday? What am I going to do today? What impediments are getting in the way of what we need to accomplish? Often the impediments facing any team will exist not only in the team itself, but also in the context surrounding the team, particularly management actions or the organization's policies and practices.

The willingness of management to encourage the identification of such impediments and take action to remove them is one of the make-or-break aspects of radical management.

Practice #8: *Don't Interrupt the Team in the Course of an Iteration*

Self-organizing teams are exactly that. Management needs to step out of the way and let the team get on with the work for the duration of the iteration.

When traditional managers begin to implement radical management, this is typically one of the points of difficulty. Traditional managers find it hard to resist the temptation to interrupt the team during an iteration rather than wait to the end of the iteration and have their requests integrated and prioritized with all the other things that need to be done. When they interrupt the team in this fashion, they show that the team is not truly empowered to do the job that was agreed on. The air goes out of the balloon, and any chance of high performance is undermined.[20]

Just as a judge doesn't interrupt a jury while it is deliberating, so radical management requires that the team be allowed to work uninterrupted for the course of the work iteration. If new issues that need attention keep cropping up in the course of an iteration, then the iterations need to be shorter, or resources should be allocated for unanticipated emergencies, or the team needs to switch to a flow approach.[21]

Practice #9: *Have the Team Work Sustainable Hours*

The extraordinarily long working hours that are common in high-end law firms, consultancies, and investment banks are incompatible with high levels of performance of knowledge work.

What tends to happen in work settings with such long working hours is that time is spent on activities that do not add value to any client. Instead, energy is often spent on networking, socializing, attending dreary information sessions, and tending to one's career.

Surveys indicate that the percentage of time actually spent on work that adds real value to clients—the focus factor—is low. One survey of managers from many organizations showed most estimates of the focus factor to be between 15 and 35 percent, while those higher in the hierarchy were in some cases less than 5 percent.[22]

In radical management, the focus is on maximizing work that adds value to clients and reducing or eliminating activity that does not. The net result of this effort is that work, even in high-end consulting firms, can come down to forty hours or less—and accomplish more.[23]

Practice #10: *Fix Problems as Soon as They Are Identified*

Toyota discovered that the cost of not fixing problems immediately is enormous, and so a tremendous emphasis is placed on detecting mistakes early and fixing them immediately—even stopping the whole production line to achieve this.[24] Failure to follow its own principles is behind some of Toyota's current troubles (see Chapter Nine).

Practice #11: *Measure Progress in Terms of Value Delivered to Clients*

Traditional management relies on progress reports. Radical management counts only finished work—work that actually delivers value to clients at the end of an iteration.[25]

Practice #12: *At the End of the Iteration, Get Feedback from the Client or the Client Proxy*

Feedback may occur in several different ways. When the iteration is delivered to the customer, the customer deploys it for use and provides user feedback. In other cases, the result of the iteration is delivered to the customer, who evaluates it and provides feedback. Or the customer is given access or a formal demonstration. The iterations may also be done internally. The team gets feedback from a client proxy, that is, someone who knows and understands the client.

Practice #13: *Calculate the Velocity of the Team*

Getting work done in iterations enables the velocity of the team to be calculated.

Iterations help establish the cadence of work. Every week, or fortnight, or month, something gets done. After a time, people begin to count on it. They can make plans based on a track record of delivery. The amount of work that can be accomplished in an iteration becomes apparent. The team can calculate its velocity and so understand whether it is improving. (See Practice #3.)

From an organizational point of view, the more important measure than team velocity is cycle time. In development, how long does it take to go from concept to client delight? Or in production, how long does it take to go from order to client delight? Nevertheless, the team velocity is an important component of overall cycle time.

Practice #14: *Conduct a Retrospective Review of What Has Been Learned in the Iteration and How the Next Iteration Can Be Improved*

Radical management is predicated on continuous learning. At the end of each iteration, the team reviews what has been learned, including impediments that have been identified in the course of the iteration, and decides what improvements are to be explored in the coming iteration.

8

PRINCIPLE #5: RADICAL TRANSPARENCY

> The truth will set you free. But first, it will piss you off.
>
> **Gloria Steinem[1]**

In the pantheon of the twentieth-century managers, Robert McNamara stands out: dashing, analytical, and quick. President John Kennedy called him the smartest man he'd ever met. After a brilliant career at the Ford Motor Company, of which he became head in 1960, McNamara was the U.S. secretary of defense from 1961 to 1968 and president of the World Bank from 1968 to 1981.

McNamara transformed the World Bank from a small, sleepy, financial boutique into a large, bustling, modern corporation, expanding lending more than tenfold in the course of his thirteen-year tenure. He dramatically increased the World Bank's role in agriculture and education and opened up new lines of business in health, population, nutrition, and urban development. He articulated a new role for the World Bank in alleviating global poverty, passionately calling attention to the plight of the poorest 40 percent of the world's population who had been essentially untouched by development lending.[2]

On his arrival at the World Bank in May 1968, McNamara quickly took charge. John Blaxall, a young economist at the time, recalls being summoned to McNamara's office shortly after his arrival, being handed a stack of annual reports, and asked to assemble multiyear financial statements—something that hadn't been done before. McNamara penciled in his left-handed scrawl on a white-lined pad the headings that he wanted. The columns across the top were the past five fiscal years, and the rows were the standard balance sheet and income statement items. How soon could he have it ready? Blaxall gave him a date and observed with concern that McNamara carefully wrote it down.[3]

Within six weeks, McNamara had a set of tables covering all major aspects of the Bank Group's activities, with totals for each five-year period and detail for the past five years. Blaxall recalls McNamara poring over the sheets full of numbers, exclaiming with some animation: "This is really exciting, John!"

McNamara then asked the senior managers in the President's Council of the bank to fill in the numbers for the next five years for the activities under his responsibility. The immediate reaction was that it couldn't be done, to which McNamara replied that they should do it anyway—and have it ready within a month.

It is not surprising that the five-year lending plans submitted by the geographical units had little correspondence to the five-year plans prepared by the technical units. And the financial projections put forward by the disbursement department were unrelated to either.

It was at this point, in early summer 1968, that McNamara announced to the senior managers that in the future, the World Bank would have only one sheet of music from which everyone would play. Ensuring the necessary consistency would be a key role of the programming and budgeting department. The game plan was not a narrative but rather a set of standard tables—a bunch of numbers—through which McNamara managed the organization for the next thirteen years.

Some elements of the World Bank's activities, however, weren't captured by McNamara's standard tables. One occasion in particular brought this home to me.[4] This was in the late 1970s when McNamara had agreed to come to one of the staff meetings of the Western Africa region, where I was working. He offered to answer any question.

Any question?

Being an incautious kind of person, I spoke first and asked him the question that was on everyone's lips at the time: Was there any tension between his policy of pushing out an ever-increasing volume of development loans and improving the development impact of the projects that were being financed by the loans? In effect, was there a tension between quantity and quality?

His reply was chilling. He said that people who asked that kind of question didn't understand our obligation to do both: we had to lend more money and we had to have high quality. There was no conflict. People who couldn't see that didn't belong in the World Bank.

Next question!

And so the meeting moved on to other topics.

Years later, project audits would confirm the very tension that people were concerned about in the late 1970s. The audits documented that McNamara's push to rapidly expand lending was accompanied by a declining quality of projects.[5] What's worse, economic studies also revealed that the push for more lending contributed to a ballooning debt problem in the developing countries, a debt crisis that was a precursor of the 2008 global financial meltdown.

But more fundamentally, what that incident in the late 1970s brought home to me was that this style of management, dazzling as it was, prevented discussion of real issues in the workplace.[6] It was striking to see how McNamara's internally contradictory statements were made to stick by the sheer force of his presentation. He staked out positions on both sides of the issue. Yes, he stood for quantity, and yes, he also stood for quality, and if there was a quality problem, no, it wasn't his responsibility. Someone else must be responsible.

Next question!

When a CEO is talking like that, and very forcefully, it is no longer possible to discuss openly the issue of whether the organization is pushing too much lending out the door.

THE STRUGGLE BETWEEN TRUTH AND POWER

The struggle between truth and power is ancient. As long ago as the ancient Greeks, the sophists held that playing games with language, presenting falsehood in the guise of truth, was a key to power and winning.

In 1837, Hans Christian Andersen advanced our understanding of the phenomenon with his tale, "The Emperor's New Clothes." The tale has a familiar part and an unfamiliar part.

The familiar part is that the emperor of a prosperous city is swindled into buying an imaginary suit of clothes. The cloth, he is told by a pair of scoundrels, is invisible to anyone who was either stupid or unfit for his position. The emperor cannot see the nonexistent cloth, but he says that he can for fear of appearing stupid; his ministers do the same. When the scoundrels report that the suit is finished, they pretend to dress the emperor in a suit of clothes. The emperor then goes on a procession through the capital showing off his new "clothes." During the course of the procession, a small child cries out, "But he has nothing on!" The crowd realizes the child is telling the truth. That is the familiar part of the story.

The unfamiliar part of the tale is that the truth that the child has inadvertently blurted out makes no difference. Neither the emperor nor the attendant nobles pay any attention to it. The emperor holds his head high and continues the procession, as do the other courtiers. The charade continues.

In this tale, Andersen put his finger on a key feature of all hierarchies: the mere exposure of falsehood doesn't put an end to it or change behavior. False statements that support the power structure of a hierarchy have precedence over true statements that put the power structure in question. Everybody in the power structure tends to go on acting as though right is wrong and black is white because their own role in the structure depends on defending it.

Some writers have noted that this style of communication was the norm in the heyday of the Soviet Union. It resulted in concealing issues for long periods rather than solving them. Eventually the issue would become too big to conceal, and it would suddenly explode into the open. In those settings, language was being used not to clarify reality but to obscure it.[7]

Nontransparency isn't limited to the former Soviet Union. It is characteristic of communications in any hierarchy—the more despotic, the less transparent.

Other writers have described this phenomenon with a more expressive term than *nontransparency.* In 2005, Princeton University Press published a book by Harry Frankfurt, an Ivy League philosophy professor. In this book, entitled *On Bullshit,* Frankfurt pointed out philosophically that bullshitting is different from lying.[8] Lying is saying what you know is wrong. Bullshitting is saying things where you don't really care whether they are true.

If we accept Frankfurt's thesis, we can exonerate McNamara of lying when he said that there was no conflict between pushing out more and more lending and maintaining the quality of loans. In his heart of hearts, I'm sure he believed it deeply. He just wasn't interested in finding out whether it was true. It was a statement of will rather than a statement of fact. He was exhibiting a lack of attentiveness to the truth. He was bullshitting. He was doing it very eloquently and forcefully, but it was bullshit.

The point here is not to pick on McNamara as an individual. The issue isn't the individual bullshitter. If you had asked any of the other legendary managers like Jack Welch or Harold Geneen a similar question, you would have gotten a similar answer. These managers stayed above the fray by denying that there was an issue, or if there was one, it wasn't their responsibility.[9]

The issue is institutionalized bullshit. Institutionalized bullshit systematically drives out truth, and truth is what is needed for consistently achieving the complex goal of delighting clients.

When you have a CEO denying that there is any tension between pushing out lending and the quality of the loans, and impugning the integrity of anyone who raises that question, it's difficult for any team to discuss issues openly. If they do, it is *their* integrity that will be put in question. They will be seen as rocking the boat and not being team players. As a result, most teams go with the flow and lose any possibility of achieving high performance. A few courageous teams may speak out about the issue and point to the truth. But those teams are rare, and their life expectancy is typically not long.

THE BLUE PILL VERSUS THE RED PILL

Jeff Sutherland, whom we met in Chapter Three, clarifies what's at stake by reference to the science-fiction movie *The Matrix.* In one scene, a character called Neo is offered a choice of taking a red pill or a blue pill. If he takes the blue pill, he will wake up and everything will look the same—the same sugar-coated semblance of reality that he's been living with for so long. If he takes the red pill, he will be able to see things as they really are.

In the movie, Neo takes the red pill. When he wakes up, he finds himself naked in a liquid-filled pod, with his body connected by wires to a vast mechanical tower covered with identical pods.

Similarly, in the world of work, people have the option of taking the blue pill or the red pill.

Taking the Blue Pill

In traditional management, managers take the blue pill. When they wake up, everything looks the same. They see no issue in expanding quantity with fewer resources.

Workers are issuing progress reports to managers saying that everything is okay and that their work is proceeding according to plan with only minor issues.

People are telling customers, "Your call is important to us," when they both know it isn't so, and that is seen as normal.

The amount of time spent actually doing useful work is quite small. Most of the workday is spent talking about work or doing rework of something someone didn't like or tending one's career. That is normal.

Phantom work jams are occurring all over the organization on a daily basis. No one notices them or does anything about them.

If anyone brings up a real problem without a solution, they are silenced for not being a team player.

Accountability is one-sided. Managers are searching for workers who have made mistakes so that they can be punished, and the workers are doing their best to make sure the search is unsuccessful.

Management is frustrated, and customers are upset. That is also normal.

There is talk of improvement of morale. Karaoke competitions are held. Retreats are staged. Managers come and go. It makes no difference. Nothing changes. It's simply the way things are. This is normal in the world of traditional management.

This is what happens when you take the blue pill.

Taking the Red Pill

For those who take the red pill, waking up is a shock. Now we see that everything is broken!

We suddenly realize that the managers are not leveling with themselves and the workers. There is a tension between quantity and quality that is not being addressed.

It dawns on us that the subordinates are not leveling with the bosses: the progress reports are not revealing what is really going on or the real problems being encountered. No one wants to hear about those problems.

Now we see that people are saying things they don't believe just to get through the meeting.

We see that the work is agonizingly slow. Phantom work jams are everywhere, and something urgently needs to be done to fix them.

We suddenly realize that accountability is two-sided: if the workers have failed, the managers have also failed.

Now many of the bureaucratic practices of the organization appear comical or pointless.

Now we see the karaoke competitions, the employee-of-the-month competitions, and the lunches with the CEO for what they really are: distractions from the real problems in the way the work is organized.

Now we can see that people are living only a fraction of their true potential. Never experiencing the exhilaration of what it means to be fully functional now appears tragic.

We feel an irresistible urge to do something about it.

That's what happens when we take the red pill: we experience an urge to establish radical transparency.

THE PARALLEL TO SCIENCE

A similar awakening occurred in science in the seventeenth century. People like Francis Bacon took the red pill and started saying that we have to stop taking on faith what Aristotle said and find out what actually happens. We have to pay more attention to truth than to authority.

Initially there was resistance in the universities.[10] It took decades before rigorous observation was embodied consistently in scientific practice. But eventually it happened. In science, truth generally triumphs over power.

Scientists didn't necessarily become paragons of honesty in all their dealings with other human beings, as Francis Bacon's conviction for corruption in 1621 demonstrated. Scientists merely adopted certain practices to encourage openness in regard to scientific experiments and principles.

In management, we are now on the brink of an equivalent revolution. Until recently, most organizations have been taking the blue pill and opting for the status quo: living with the system of traditional management that dominated the workplace of the twentieth century.

As in any other hierarchy, an elaborate set of falsifications and mystifications is deployed to maintain the power structure. As long as the goal of management is the simple linear one of producing goods and services, those falsifications and mystifications are tolerated. That degree of nontransparency is good enough to get by. But once the organization takes on the more strenuous and complex challenge of delighting clients, nontransparency isn't good enough. The reason is that in the organization that aspires to delight its clients, managers and workers must become more open with each other about the impediments that prevent high performance.

They cannot consistently delight clients if discussing impediments is a matter of tactical calculation, or if people are telling each other what they want to hear or only so much as they need to know. Achieving the complex goal of client delight requires total openness about any impediments to the work: everyone levels with everyone else. There is total openness within the team, of the team in relation to management, and of management in relation to the team.

This is not about returning to some golden age when people were honest and everyone spoke the truth. Historically there was no golden age: we have been living with nontransparency for millennia. Nontransparency has always been the norm for communications in hierarchical bureaucracies. That's because a hierarchical bureaucracy is a hermetically sealed container, whose continued existence depends on the participants' speaking consistently with the underlying assumptions of the power structure, even when they are at variance with external reality. By contrast, radical management is an open system that depends on the ascertainment of truth—what will delight clients—in order to achieve its goals.

Several centuries ago, science managed to pull itself out of the hole of myth and legend dominated by authority, although there are exceptions even today. Nevertheless, by and large, science has implemented principles and practices that enabled progress toward intellectual integrity.[11]

Now management must do the same. Radical management means seeing the workplace as it is, rather than as we would like it to be, and being willing to do something about it. In this way, it can kindle the spirit of innovation and ignite client delight.

Radical transparency cannot be accomplished by exhortations. It is established and maintained by systematic management practices. Some of the principles and practices that facilitate radical transparency have already been touched on, particularly client-driven iterations focused on delivering value in each iteration. As a result, a team's progress, or lack thereof, is visible early and often.

Additional steps are needed to establish radical transparency within the team, the team in relation to management, and the management in relation to the team. Several practices are particularly noteworthy:

- *The daily stand-up meeting.* Teams typically hold a daily meeting where people stand in order to keep it brief. Team members share with each other the answer to questions: What did you do yesterday? What are you going to do today? What impediments are you facing?
- *Identification and removal of impediments.* A make-or-break aspect of radical management is managers' encouragement of staff to identify impediments and their prompt action to resolve them.
- *Simple visual displays that everyone can see.* It is striking to visit the workplaces of computer experts and find the walls covered with handwritten sticky notes, cards, and charts. The displays serve as ever-present information radiators. Anyone can walk by and see what has been completed, what is being worked on, and what is coming next. There is no need for progress reports. The reality is always visible.

These three practices don't guarantee transparency, but they do make transparency easier and covering up more difficult. Transparency is essential to radical management. If people don't level with each other, radical management turns into a fantasy. The fog of bureaucracy will descend, and the workplace will lapse back into the command-and-control world of traditional management.

THE SCOPE OF RADICAL TRANSPARENCY

I am not proposing that everyone be totally honest about everything. That would be unrealistic. Normal politeness and business sense require occasional dissimulation of the truth. As Jeremy Campbell argues forcefully in *The Liar's Tale*, harmless lies are part of the inevitable social routine of any society: they make the world run more smoothly and avoid needless embarrassment.[12] Nor is this about a free-for-all airing of problems, grievances, and complaints. The focus is on total openness about the work—specifically, the identification and removal of impediments to getting the work done.

Just as scientists didn't necessarily become paragons of honesty in their personal dealings with other human beings, managers will not miraculously become totally honest human beings. Rather, this is about managers' adopting certain practices that reinforce openness about impediments affecting the accomplishment of the work.

Genuine Responsibility and Accountability

Why didn't greater openness emerge in traditional management? One reason is that it wasn't necessary. The traditional management that we inherited from Major George Whistler from that train wreck back in 1841 has a number of assumptions: failure is assumed to be rare; the goal of producing goods and services is a straightforward linear task that is in principle achievable 100 percent of the time; roles are defined; duties are specified; deadlines are set; if failure has occurred, it involves personal dereliction of duty; and those responsible for the failure should be punished.

Another reason is that the managerial attitude toward failure creates a self-fulfilling prophecy. By punishing failure, failure becomes ever harder to find. As the story of Nathalie, the software developer in Chapter One, illustrated, the language of traditional management is often deliberately couched so as to facilitate deniability and prevent the discovery of failure. Traditional management has routines to cover one's own backside, up and down the line.

In a world where no one ever clearly succeeds or fails, merit is wholly subjective, responsibility dissolves, and accountability goes out the window. Performance is at best variable. In big bureaucracies, failures can go on for months, years, even decades, without being rectified. Over time, problems build up behind the scenes and then suddenly they explode into the open.

In some organizations, radical management is unthinkable precisely because it would expose the personality conflicts that now lie hidden, particularly in top management teams. Although conflicts are hindering performance, the concern is that if the conflicts were exposed, the goals, methods, and membership of the team would have to be reconsidered, and fundamental issues of governance would have to be addressed. This would be painful and disruptive, and thus unthinkable.

Radical management means not only thinking about such possibilities but also doing something about them. It starts from different assumptions about failure and how to respond to it.

With the shift in the goal from the simple linear task of producing goods and services to the complex task of delighting clients, failure can no longer be assumed to be rare. The bar has been raised. Failure will be more frequent. Indeed, in a dynamic, unpredictable world with a complex goal of delighting clients, some failure is a certainty. Radical management accepts the inevitability of failure and puts arrangements in place to learn rapidly from failure and so progress toward success.

Its approach is to fail fast and fix it quickly. With short work cycles and practices that encourage openness, failure stares everyone in the face almost as soon as it happens. The team knows and management knows, so there is nowhere to hide. The principles and practices of radical management make crystal clear, iteration by iteration, whether management is spelling out what needs to be done and whether the team is delivering that.

Making failure so visible can make individuals and organizations uncomfortable, particularly those that have been living with nonaccountability for a long time, perhaps decades. If at the end of the iteration, the team doesn't deliver on its goal, then it is a failure of both the team and management. A retrospective is held to figure out what went wrong. Maybe the goal was too ambitious; perhaps it was impossible. Maybe the project wasn't ready to be worked on. Maybe the team didn't identify the impediments. Maybe the impediments didn't get removed. Maybe the team had the wrong membership or the wrong skills. Maybe management interrupted the team. Whatever the cause, the diagnosis will determine the next step. Failure is faced up to so that issues can be fixed and high performance can emerge.

The Courage to Be

I can't say that I feel proud for having allowed myself in that World Bank meeting in the 1970s to be browbeaten by Robert McNamara into silence. I didn't feel good about the obvious conflict between quantity and quality. Living in a fog of institutionalized bullshit isn't healthy for the human spirit. It creates distrust of oneself, disconnection with others, and the betrayal of stakeholders. It leads to a divided life.

Radical management is about opening up the windows, letting in bright sunlight and fresh air, and discovering what's going on instead of covering it up. It means aiming high and failing often, but taking responsibility for failure and addressing it. It's about living a life where actions have consequences. It's exciting, frightening, challenging, and thrilling. It's about truly living.

PRACTICES FOR ESTABLISHING RADICAL TRANSPARENCY

Radical Transparency Within the Team

Radical transparency within the team enables the self-organizing team to improve. A team that doesn't know how it is doing or what its members are doing usually lacks the clarity and traction to improve. Radical transparency provides that clarity and traction.

Practice #1: *Have the Team Estimate How Much Time Work Will Take*

In traditional management, managers typically decide how much work will be done and how long it should take. In radical management, the team is given this responsibility. The belief is that the people who know most about how long things will take are the people actually doing the work. When members of the team themselves make the estimate, they take responsibility for it and learn from the experience.

Practice #2: *Let the Team Decide How Much Work to Undertake*

From the prioritized list of tasks provided by the client or client proxy, the team decides how much work it can accomplish within the work cycle. The team commits to deliver work that is of value to a client or stakeholder within that cycle and lives with the consequences of its decision.

Practice #3: *Calculate the Team's Velocity After Each Iteration*

The team establishes its velocity for each work cycle: how much work that adds value to clients can it accomplish during a given time period? This enables the team to understand its own trajectory and whether it is improving. (See Practice #3 in Chapter Seven on team velocity.)

Practice #4: *Have the Team Members Stay in Contact with Each Other on a Daily Basis*

Teams typically hold a daily stand-up meeting in which team members share with each other the answers to questions: What did you do yesterday? What are you going to do today? What impediments are you facing?

Initially it can be uncomfortable having to justify oneself to others. But over time the members of the team connect with each other. It's no longer just one person's problem if something is not going as well as hoped for. Now it's the team's problem, and everybody can work together to solve it.

Practice #5: *Conduct Retrospective Reviews at the End of Each Iteration*

At the end of each work cycle, the team conducts a review of what it has accomplished, as well as what could have gone better, and it then plans the next iteration of work. The team systematically inspects and adapts how it is doing the work.

Practice #6: *Use Informal Visual Displays of Progress*

Radical management aims to maximize transparency by having simple visual displays available at all times in the work space. The displays serve as information radiators.[13]

When information is available to a select few, only those few can take responsibility. When information is stored in computers, it is available only when people go and look for it; it isn't constantly visible.

"Visual controls," writes David Mann, "might seem like an embarrassing return to the information Stone Age." However, accuracy, proximity, and flexibility are great advantages: "Hand-created data, especially when you know whose hands created it, including the real possibility that the hand was or could have been yours, have a much lower intimidation value than the crisp, precise-looking management document someone has posted on your team's information board."[14]

Transparency of the Team in Relation to Management

Radical transparency of the team in relation to management provides management with timely and reliable information about how the team is doing, as well as information about impediments. In this way, the risk that the team will go off on a tangent is reduced.

Practice #7: *Deliver Value to Clients at the End of Each Iteration*

At the end of each iteration of work, the team produces not progress reports but items of finished work—something that is of value to the client or stakeholder. The focus is on completing work at the earliest opportunity, because finished work is more transparent than reports about work.

In the traditional organization, having more work in process is seen as progress. In radical management, as in lean manufacturing, work in process is viewed as a problem because it entails hidden costs that will have to be spent in order to complete the task. The more time it takes to do that, the more costly and problematic work in process becomes.

In each iteration of work, management can see what the team promises and what it delivers. By doing work in short iterations, the team cannot go too far wrong without that fact becoming visible to everyone. By focusing the team on delivering something of value at the end of each iteration, management and stakeholders can see what is happening. As a result, management can adjust in time if the team is going off track and can also shift priorities in an orderly fashion as new issues emerge without disrupting the work of the team.

Because the people doing the work are getting continuous feedback as to what is—or is not—delighting the client, they can align their activities with the true goal of work: continuously delighting clients.

Practice #8: *Systematically Identify Impediments in the Daily Stand-Up Meetings*

Impediments to improved effectiveness are also systematically exposed by the team to the management. In traditional organizations, people who bring bad news to the attention of the management tend to be punished unless they also bring solutions. In learning organizations, people are rewarded for bringing forward solutions. By contrast, in radical management, people who bring bad news to the management's attention are celebrated, even if they have no immediate and obvious solutions for the problem.

A well-known example is the way that workers on Toyota's production line are congratulated if they spot a quality problem on the line: the line stops until the problem is understood and fixed—something that is almost inconceivable in traditional organizations.

The shift in language from "What are the problems?" to "What are impediments?" is significant. "Problems" may arise from unhappiness for any number of reasons. "Impediments" relate to goals. "What is preventing us from delighting clients?" An airing of impediments focuses the discussion on what is getting in the way of reaching the common goal.

Transparency of Management in Relation to the Team

Management is also transparent in regard to the team by providing a unified and fully reconciled list of requirements at the start of every work iteration. It then refrains from making any changes in priorities until the next iteration. This makes it totally transparent to the team what is expected of it, while leaving the team free to decide how much of this work can be accomplished and how it should be accomplished.

As a result, work is focused on items of highest priority, and no time is wasted on items of low priority that happen to have been included in the original specifications.

Practice #9: *Set Priorities for Work at the Beginning of Each Iteration*

Management has to allow the team to self-organize and draw on its talents, energies, and insights. It thus creates a workplace in which a team takes responsibility for accomplishing something tied to objective standards.

The difference between responsibility that is assigned and responsibility that is personally accepted is significant. It is even more so when allocated responsibility does not respect the intrinsic requirements of excellence that the work itself requires.

In the world of traditional management, if people are asked to do twelve units of work when they know they can perform only eight units of high-quality work in the time allotted, their options are unsatisfactory. They can tell the boss that it isn't possible and risk being labeled as troublemakers. Or they can try to work evenings and weekends and so produce the twelve units of work, in the process interfering with their private life. Or they can cut corners by doing the best they can and hope that their boss doesn't notice that the quality has declined.

In such a world, there is social pressure to conceal problems. Managers may be honest individuals, but here there is social pressure to be less than fully frank. Since everyone is expected to do the same, a facade of not leveling becomes the cultural norm. In this way, good people slide into not being fully open, not calling a piece of shoddy work just that, not pointing out that the company is making money with bad profits, and so on.

In this world, the manager inhabits a moral maze where those higher in the hierarchy are inclined to absent themselves from the details of the production process, calling for results with an apparent indifference as to how they are achieved, and not inquiring into what kinds of compromises might have been made in the process. These are the practices that lead to the buildup of bad profits in the background, with brand liabilities that eventually have to be repaid.

To avoid having these issues arise, management sets the direction and the priorities for work, but it is the team itself that decides how much work can be done in an iteration and how to go about that work.

Practice #10: *Go and See What Is Happening in the Workplace and in the Marketplace*

Taiichi Ohno begins his book *Workplace Management* by noting that while a fool is wrong 70 percent of the time and a normal person 50 percent of the time, even a wise man is wrong 30 percent of the time.[15] Knowing this, even a wise man has to have humility: he may be wrong even in matters in which he is certain he is right. A willingness to check things out—the true scientific spirit—and accept the possibility of being wrong then becomes a key attitude in radical management.

Practice #11: *Establish a Clear Line of Sight from the Team to the Client*

The team is able to see whether and to what extent the client is delighted by its work. Among the actions that management takes are ensuring that the client or the client proxy is available to discuss the user stories as needed and giving feedback on whatever is delivered at the end of each iteration.

Practice #12: *Systematically Help Remove Impediments*

Management supports the daily stand-up meetings that systematically identify impediments. It informs itself of these impediments and takes steps to remove them.

In some cases, impediments concern actions by management or organizational policies or procedures. There may be good reasons for these actions, policies, or procedures. Management works with the team to find solutions to the perceived issues.

Practice #13: *Accept Two-Sided Accountability*

If subordinates have failed, managers should accept that they have also failed. As management theorist Samuel Culbert says, "The consequence of a failed performance should be personal development, new perspective, improved judgment, skill enhancement, and general all-around learning. If the cohort is one's boss, so much the better. In a straight-talk relationship, both have the opportunity to learn. Subordinates learn what they need to do differently to achieve desired results, and bosses learn what type of support and guidance the subordinate needed but did not receive."[16]

9

PRINCIPLE #6: CONTINUOUS SELF-IMPROVEMENT

> "Whether top management, middle management, or the workers who actually do the work, we are all human so we're like walking misconceptions believing that the way we do things now is the best way."
>
> **Taiichi Ohno[1]**

"Can anything stop Toyota?" In 2003, that was the title of a *BusinessWeek* article about how Toyota, through its inexorable commitment to continuous improvement, was set to dominate the global auto industry in a way that no other company ever had.[2]

Today the question has a different meaning and refers to runaway cars. In early 2010, Toyota found itself the subject of state and federal investigations, congressional hearings, news media inquiries, and a rash of lawsuits for failing to deal with a safety issue. How had such a renowned company managed to become the butt of late-night comedy—a one-word joke conveying corporate incompetence or worse?

I'll get to all that soon enough, as well as what it shows about radical management. But first, let's find out what Toyota taught other companies about improving quality.

THE EXPERIENCE OF CONTINUOUS SELF-IMPROVEMENT

Some years ago, shortly after being appointed as a group leader in Toyota's factory in Georgetown, Kentucky, Mike Hoseus was sent to the Camry plant in Toyota City, Japan, to spend a month seeing what it was like to work on the production of a Toyota auto factory.

"I was installing liners underneath the wheel," Hoseus writes,

> when my air gun slipped, and the driver bit scratched the paint on the inner lip of the wheel wall. I gasped and looked around—no one saw me do it—but they had told me to pull the andon cord if I made or caught any defect. It was my moment of truth. My first reaction was to let it go. No one would probably see the scratch anyway, and no one would know that I made it. But my conscience got the better of me and I wanted to see whether they really meant what they said about admitting mistakes. So I pulled the andon and the team leader came to fix the problem and showed me how to hold the bit with a free finger in order to stabilize it better. But he did not seem angry at me for making the scratch.

Later at the break, Hoseus was wondering what the team would say. Would he be criticized or looked down on for having made a mistake? To his surprise, they applauded him for having admitted making a mistake. Hoseus says: "I felt like a million bucks and guess what I did the next time I made a mistake?"[3]

The concept of rewarding workers for pointing out problems as soon as they are discovered is so at odds with traditional management that outsiders often have difficulty believing that it actually happens.

In traditional management, an employee who points out a problem without having a solution at hand is typically punished as a whistle-blower—someone who is rocking the boat. Some inroads on this attitude were made in the learning organization, popularized by Peter Senge, where anyone who points out a problem is rewarded, provided that he or she also has a solution to the problem.[4] Radical management goes further: employees are rewarded for identifying problems even if no solution is in sight.

THE CONCEPT OF CONTINUOUS IMPROVEMENT

Taiichi Ohno, whom we met in Chapter Six, pioneered this radical notion at Toyota in 1955. He had discovered that the cost of not fixing problems immediately after they were discovered was huge. So he developed the idea of giving the responsibility to workers to stop production at the first sight of a problem and get to the root of it so that it never occurred again. He installed andon cords so that those doing the work could pull the cord and halt production if they noticed defects or other problems.

Ohno's achievement wasn't simply installing the cords. That was the easy part. The difficult part was to create the attitudes throughout the workforce so that workers pull the cord when they see a problem and managers reward them for doing so. It's difficult because the implicit respect for workers is the direct opposite of traditional management in which the system is seen as more important than people and quality is the responsibility of overseers.

The attitude of continuous self-improvement has two components, and both are radically different from traditional management. One component concerns the goal: relentless improvement. Traditional management sets a limited goal of "good enough" quality, which translates into an acceptable number of defects and an acceptable range of standardized products that, it is hoped, meet customer requirements. Continuous improvement means having the entire workforce find ever better ways to give more value to clients—higher-quality and safer products, continuously declining costs, and endless product variety.

The other component concerns the means of achieving the goal: the workers themselves. By making workers (the people who are there on the line who see things as they happen) responsible for identifying and getting to the root causes of problems, the firm improves faster than in traditional management, where the responsibility for quality rests solely with managers, who are remote from the action.

For over fifty years, Toyota combined these two components and inculcated the attitudes necessary to make them work. It developed a corporate culture that was based on them, and the results were extraordinary. Its cars were top-rated around the world: reasonably priced, problem free, and long lasting. From tiny beginnings, Toyota grew rapidly and became the world's largest car manufacturer, as well as an innovator in environment-friendly technologies. Its approach worked just as well in the United States as it did in Japan.

THE TOYOTA APPROACH AT FREMONT

Fremont, the fourth largest city in the San Francisco Bay Area, is ethnically and culturally diverse. According to the city's publicity, residents are attracted to it for its high-ranking public schools, its numerous well-kept parks, and a variety of recreational amenities, including beautiful Lake Elizabeth, Central Park, and Mission San José.

In 1963, General Motors was attracted to Fremont by the high transportation cost of shipping cars to California. To GM, it made sense to locate a plant in this large and growing market. And so it built a car manufacturing plant that at its peak employed seventy-two hundred workers.

The factory fared badly. The United Autoworkers (UAW) union filed thousands of grievances each year. Absenteeism, slowdowns, drug abuse, alcoholism, wildcat strikes, and even sabotage were widespread. There was a climate of fear and mistrust between management and the union. First-line managers were frightened of the workers and carried weapons for their personal protection. George Nano, union representative at the plant described labor relations succinctly: "It was war."[5]

By 1982, GM was the least productive of the Big Three U.S. auto manufacturers, and its Fremont plant was the least productive plant in the entire GM system. GM's managers studied the numbers and took the logical, rational, difficult, hard-nosed management decision: they closed the plant.

Enter Toyota from stage right, riding a white horse.

At the time, Toyota was looking for an opportunity to establish itself as a Japanese firm that was friendly to the United States. It was facing growing hostility to its steadily expanding market share at the expense of the Big Three automakers in Detroit. What better way to do this than by performing mission impossible: reopening the failed Fremont plant in partnership with the American icon, GM, and turning it into a success?

So in 1983, Toyota offered to reopen and operate the Fremont plant. GM accepted the offer because it needed a facility to produce its new small car, the Nova, and it hoped to learn about Toyota's production system.

Toyota and GM signed a joint agreement. They each invested about $100 million in the venture, which was named the New United Motor Manufacturing (NUMMI). Under the joint venture, NUMMI would produce cars for Toyota—the Corolla and later the Tacoma pickup—and GM—the Chevy Nova and later the Prizm. Toyota was responsible for running the plant, including product design and engineering. Toyota and GM each assumed responsibility for marketing, sales, and service for their own branded vehicles. GM would assign managers and coordinators to NUMMI on a rotating basis to learn the Toyota production system.

In managing the plant, Toyota agreed to take on the very problems that had caused GM to close the plant. First, it offered to take back the workers who had been so unproductive under GM's management. The demographic composition of the resulting workforce thus closely resembled that of the original GM plant, suggesting that almost all of the old employees who wanted to work at NUMMI were in fact rehired. Then Toyota accepted the same union that had stymied GM, UAW, and agreed to pay union-scale wages. It even accepted the very union leaders who were behind the slowdowns and the wildcat strikes of the previous two decades.

So Toyota faced all the principal difficulties that had caused GM to fail at Fremont, except for one: GM's traditional management practices. The result? The Corollas, Novas, and pickups produced there soon had the highest internal GM quality audits. NUMMI produced the same number of automobiles as the old GM Fremont plant but with much higher quality and just over half the workforce.

THE IMPACT OF THE TOYOTA APPROACH

In the late 1980s, a comprehensive study documented the gains that had been made by firms using the approach that Toyota had deployed at NUMMI. It was a collaborative study that looked at a large number of auto plants in Japan, the United States, and Europe. The results of the study were reported in 1990 in a landmark book, *The Machine That Changed The World,* by James Womack, Daniel Jones, and Daniel Roos.[6] The book recorded extraordinary differences in outcomes between factories using Toyota's approach (which the book called "lean") and those run on traditional lines (which it called "mass manufacturing").

On the design side, the lean approach was more productive on every measurable aspect. Average engineering hours per new car was 1.7 million compared to 3.1 million. Average development time was 46.2 months compared to 60.4 months. The average number of employees involved was 485 compared to 903. In manufacturing, the differences were equally striking: the lean approach produced a higher-quality product, produced at dramatically lower cost, with quicker turnaround times, and fewer defects, that met customers' needs more closely.

It wasn't a difference between Japanese factories and U.S. factories. In fact, some of the best factories were in the United States, and some of the worst were in Japan. What made the difference was how the factory was run. Nor was it a question of who was running the plant. In the study, the top-rated plant in terms of quality and productivity wasn't a Japanese plant at all. It was a Ford plant in Hermosillo, Mexico.

Given the extraordinary differences in outcome, one might have expected rapid adoption of the results by all the companies. But that's not what happened. Despite NUMMI, GM continued for the most part to operate in a traditional manner, progressively losing market share until it went bankrupt in 2009 and was rescued by the U.S. government. Ford also largely ignored what it had learned at Hermosillo and continued in the path of traditional management, until in 2006 it appointed a CEO, Alan Mulally, who believed in the Toyota approach. Only then did continuous self-improvement take off at Ford as a whole.[7]

Ford and GM were not alone in having difficulty learning from Toyota. In 2003, the foremost foreign expert on Toyota, Jeff Liker, wrote in his book, *The Toyota Way*, "What percent of companies outside of Toyota and their close knit group of suppliers get an A or even a B+ on lean [manufacturing]? I cannot say precisely but it is far less than 1 percent."[8]

"Far less than 1 percent" is a low number. And it's not that Toyota has been secretive. On the contrary, it has been a model of openness, inviting visits from its competitors, publishing extensively about what it does and how it does it, and doing joint ventures with its competitors.

Why is it so difficult to emulate what Toyota does? Before you can emulate what Toyota does, you have to understand what it is doing. When you are looking at the world through the spectacles of traditional management, this turns out to be difficult.

UNDERSTANDING WHAT TOYOTA DOES

Jeff Sutherland, whom we met in earlier chapters, believes that in order to understand how to manage in the twenty-first century, you have to be able to understand what Toyota does and how it does it.[9] So he got a group of senior executives to read *The Toyota Way*. They responded that they couldn't understand *The Toyota Way*. (These executives had been to Harvard Business School, or its equivalent, and they couldn't understand *The Toyota Way*!) So then he asked, "Well, what do they understand?" The reply he got was that they understood Taiichi Ohno's book, *The Toyota Production System*.[10] Ohno's book, short and clear, is packed with insights about what Toyota does and how it does it.

Ohno's book is enlightening in many ways. Who better to learn from than the inventor of the Toyota Production System? The absolute elimination of waste, the pull approach to production, the leveling of flows, just-in-time systems, automatic detection of abnormal conditions: all of these production innovations Ohno lovingly describes in his book.

Ohno's book is a hymn of praise to the management of things. He mentions people and teams in passing, but the main focus of the book is on engineering practices. Nowhere in the book is there a discussion of the radical shift in attitude involved in requiring those doing the work to identify problems as soon as they are discovered.[11] The book is all about production processes and the elimination of waste from those processes. If Ohno's book is the only one people read about Toyota, they could easily conclude that the Toyota way is essentially a set of low-level engineering practices about eliminating waste.

As it happens, Toyota spent the 1990s working on its own formulation of the Toyota Way so that it could effectively transplant its culture to factories and salesrooms in other countries. The result was an internal document entitled "The Toyota Way 2001."[12] The conclusions are represented in Figure 9.1.

The Toyota Way 2001 has two main pillars: "continuous improvement" and "respect for people." Each pillar rests on foundation stones. "Continuous improvement" rests on "challenge," "relentless search for improvement" (*kaisan*), and "go and see for yourself on the shopfloor" (*genchi genbutsu*). "Respect for people" rests on "respect" and "teamwork."

The picture is interesting as much as for what is not there as for what is there. There is no sign, for instance, of the elimination of inventory, the pull system of production, just-in-time systems, the leveling of production flows, or automatic detection of abnormal conditions—the key elements of Ohno's *The Toyota Production System*. This doesn't mean that those elements have been rejected. Rather, the implication is that those elements are lower-level details—mere consequences that flow from the more important high-level principles of the Toyota Way.

FIGURE 9.1 The Toyota Way, 2001, as Conceived by Toyota

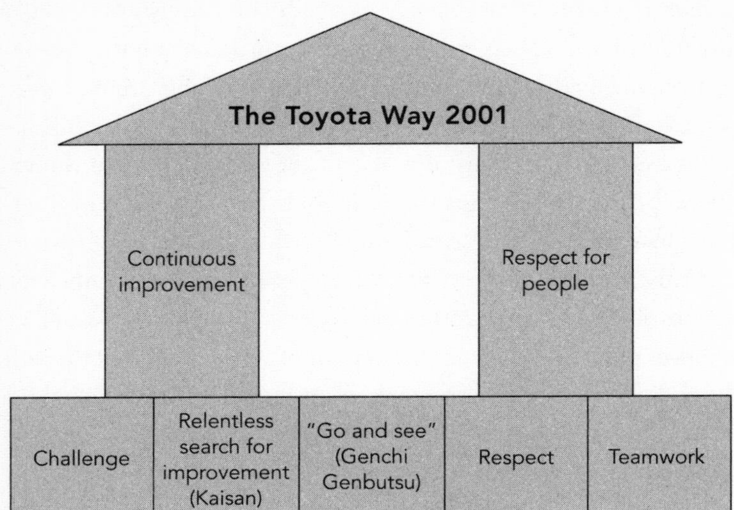

From this perspective, we can begin to grasp why Sutherland's executives were able to understand *The Toyota Production System* but not *The Toyota Way*. The former book is perfectly compatible with the assumptions of traditional management: the elimination of waste from production processes. It can be implemented by traditional managers without any change in basic assumptions.

However, implementing what Toyota actually does requires a fundamental shift in mind-set from the assumptions of traditional management. Instead of the system being more important than people, respect for people becomes the engine of continuous improvement at Toyota.

Looking at the world through the lens of traditional management, where people are regarded as fungible components of processes, Sutherland's executives had trouble understanding a company where respect for people and teamwork are fundamental assumptions of the company. What would it be like to run a company like this? It was at odds with everything they had learned in business school and management textbooks.

Not surprisingly, when the Toyota approach is understood simply as the elimination of waste in production processes and is implemented within the framework of traditional management, without appropriate respect of people, the result is very different from what actually happens in Toyota (Figure 9.2).

When the focus of management is eliminating waste in production processes without respect for workers, all of the effort for improvement falls on the managers. They are the last to find out about a problem. By the time they hear about it, the errors are expensive to fix, and there are fewer eyes and minds available to find solutions.

In the Toyota approach, respect for people provides the engine for continuous improvement. It results in a fundamental difference in attitude of those doing the work, as shown in these quotations:

> "It's the way they treat people. You've got a say now in how your job is done. It makes a person feel important."

> "I look forward to coming to work here. There's more responsibility and challenge but with no one pressuring me. People get along well. People listen if you have ideas."[13]

FIGURE 9.2 The Toyota Way 2001, as Implemented by Traditional Management

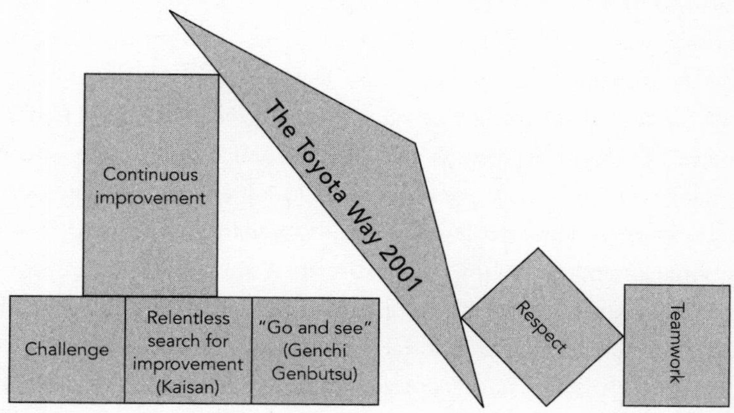

The responsibility for quality, according to O'Reilly and Pfeffer, "is pushed down to the worker. . . . Problems are resolved at the lowest level possible. . . . Responsibility lies with the individual to call attention to a problem whenever a defect is observed. . . . This is almost the opposite of the old GM assembly line, where few people beyond the superintendent had authority to stop the production line."[14]

Toyota's success rested on "the values of trust, respect and continuous improvement that characterize relations within the plant, and the consistency with which these are applied in *all* the operating systems and management practices. The consistency in alignment is manifest in how people are selected, trained, rewarded and supervised."[15]

THE MEANING OF LEAN

The Machine That Changed the World is in many ways a wonderful book, but it has also contributed to the confusion as to what Toyota does to achieve the results that it has accomplished. Womack, Jones, and Roos contrasted what it called "lean manufacturing techniques" with "mass manufacturing." It called what Toyota was doing "lean production" "because it uses less of everything compared to mass production—half the human effort in the factory, half the manufacturing space, half the investment in tools, half the engineering hours to develop a new product in half the time. Also it requires keeping far less than half the needed inventory on site, results in many fewer defects, and produces a greater and every growing variety of products."[16]

As a result of *The Machine That Changed the Word,* lean manufacturing has come to be seen as a set of production techniques aimed at eliminating waste.[17] It is presented as a low-level engineering issue—something to be deployed in factories—rather than a strategic issue for top management as to how the entire firm should be organized and run. When lean manufacturing techniques aimed at eliminating waste are shoehorned into a traditional management environment, without respect for people, the results are very different. The engine for continuous self-improvement is missing.

Even when an oasis of excellence is established within an organization being run on traditional management lines, as at Ford's Hermosillo plant, the experience doesn't take root and replicate throughout the organization because the setting isn't congenial. The fundamental assumptions of the Toyota approach are at odds with those of traditional management.

Implementing continuous self-improvement requires a fundamentally different kind of mind-set from traditional management. It involves creating an environment in which the organization draws on the full talents and capacities of the people who work there. It means generating a context in which workers want to improve and are given the means to do so, so that they do evolve into a high-performance mode. It's about powering up the internal energy of teams so that they transcend their limitations and create products or services that generate client delight. When a firm like Toyota makes this its foundation and embeds it in the corporate culture, it operates at higher levels of productivity, wins market share from competitors, and delights its customers.

Toyota spent decades nurturing the culture to reinforce these attitudes. With its organizational foundation and a highly skilled workforce committed to a career at Toyota, what could go wrong?

As it turns out, plenty.

In the early years of this century, Toyota was over-committed to growth and was poorly placed when the U.S. car market collapsed in 2008. It began to suffer its first losses, and was forced to postpone the opening of new plants. After GM pulled out of the NUMMI partnership, it ended its involvement there.

Even worse was to come. But before I get to that, some background on the history of unintended acceleration in automobiles will help clarify the context in which Toyota's troubles emerged.

UNINTENDED ACCELERATION

On Sunday evening, November 23, 1986, millions of Americans saw a frightening segment on *60 Minutes* that reenacted their worst nightmare about driving: unintended acceleration. The program showed an Audi

5000, a German luxury car, moving along normally and then suddenly accelerating on its own when the brake pedal was pushed. The segment included interviews with six people who had sued Audi after reporting unintended acceleration, including one woman whose six-year-old son had died in the accident. It later transpired that the frightening video sequence of the car accelerating on its own was the result of the car's having been modified by the television producers with a concealed device that caused the car to accelerate.

The lawsuits of the six people who sued Audi were unsuccessful. Independent investigators concluded that the problem was most likely due to driver error, since even with the throttle wide open, the car would simply stall if the brakes were being used. But the damage to the brand was done. The incident devastated Audi sales in the United States, falling from seventy-four thousand in 1985 to twelve thousand in 1991, and resale values fell dramatically as well. It took some fifteen years for Audi sales to recover in the United States.

In 1989, the National Highway Traffic Safety Administration (NHTSA) released a study concluding that the unintended acceleration cases, including all the ones that prompted the *60 Minutes* report, were caused by driver error, such as a confusion of pedals. Nevertheless, such "driver error" in the case of Audi resulted in over seven hundred accidents, hundreds of injuries, and six deaths—an incident rate that was several dozen times higher than in other cars of that era.

Although Audi escaped any legal responsibility for these accidents, critics argue that the higher incidence of driver error in its vehicles was not unrelated to the design of the car. In the Audi 5000, the brake and gas pedal were unusually close to each other, and the brake pedal was very narrow. When Audi made changes to the design, the number of incidents of unintended acceleration dramatically dropped.

Whatever the cause, one lesson from the Audi experience is that a single highly publicized incident of unintended acceleration can be devastating to a brand.

So in the 1990s, when the possibility emerged of introducing a brake override system that guaranteed that the brake would always overrule the accelerator, and so prevent the possibility of unintended acceleration, Audi and many other car manufacturers, including GM, Ford, Chrysler, and BMW, opted to install it. By contrast, a number of Japanese companies, including Toyota, Honda, Mitsubishi, and Mazda, had confidence in their engineering to automatically detect abnormal conditions and decided that a brake override device wasn't necessary.[18]

THE SAYLOR CASE

In the years following the Audi experience, incidents of unintended acceleration continued to be reported to the NHTSA from all makes of vehicles. NHTSA called the frequency of such incidents "unremarkable," given the millions of cars involved.[19] They were viewed through the lens of the 1989 NHTSA study, which had concluded that incidents of unintended acceleration were the result of driver error.

Unintended acceleration thus attracted little attention until August 28, 2009. On that day, Mark Saylor, an off-duty California Highway Patrol officer, dropped his Lexus off for work at the dealer in San Diego. The dealer gave him a 2009 Lexus ES350 as a loaner. Shortly afterward, Saylor was driving the Lexus along the highway with his family when it accelerated of its own accord to 120 miles an hour.

In a 911 emergency call made from the car as it sped along the highway, Saylor's brother-in-law, Chris Lastrella, was heard saying: "We're in a Lexus . . . and we're going north on 125 and our accelerator is stuck . . . we're in trouble . . . there's no brakes . . . we're approaching the intersection . . . hold on . . . hold on and pray . . . pray." The Lexus slammed into a Ford Explorer, plowed over a curb, and crashed through a fence before it flipped and burst into flames, killing Saylor along with his wife, Cleofe; their thirteen-year-old daughter, Mahala; and Lastrella.

The incident received wide publicity. The combination of the dramatic 911 call, the horrifying accident that ensued, and the implausibility of "driver error" by a highway patrol officer created a national furor.

A CRISIS OR AN OPPORTUNITY?

When an organization encounters an incident that receives alarmingly negative publicity, two very different outcomes are possible. It can result in disastrous brand damage for the organization, which had happened to Audi two decades previously. Moreover, with the advent of twenty-four-hour cable television news and the Internet, what used to happen in days or weeks can spiral out of control within minutes. The other outcome is that the incident can constitute an opportunity for the organization to show what the company really stands for and so strengthen the brand. Thus, Johnson & Johnson showed in its handling of the poisoning of Tylenol capsules in 1982 that decisive action aimed at protecting the public, combined with prompt, clear, accurate, and authoritative communication, can end up strengthening a brand.

As it turned out, Toyota's actions and communications with the public over the six months after the Saylor accident were at best clumsy. As a result, the incident grew into a major crisis for the company.

First, the company was slow to get to the root cause of the problem. On October 30, 2009, Toyota began sending letters to some 4 million owners notifying them of an unspecified upcoming recall to fix the unintended acceleration issue due to wandering floor mats that had a tendency to jam the accelerator pedal. It wasn't until almost five months later, in January 2010, that Toyota announced that it would be recalling a further 2 million cars for sticky accelerator pedals.

Second, in the months following the Saylor accident, as people were waiting for news of solutions to the apparent problem, further bad news started trickling out about the origins of the problem. It brought to light a history of events that tended to put in question everything that Toyota had come to stand for. Thus, it emerged that Toyota had been alerted by NHTSA in 2004 that its vehicles had a slightly higher-than-average occurrence of unintended acceleration. Given its fifty-year record of continuous improvement, the expectation would be that Toyota would immediately deploy its best engineers to get to the bottom of the issue and not rest until they had done so. Instead, Toyota dismissed the incidents as driver error and negotiated with NHTSA a narrow recall of floor mats on a limited number of cars. In 2009, in a briefing to the new head of Toyota in America, the negotiations with NHTSA and the limitation of recalls to fifty-five thousand floor mats were even celebrated as a "$100 million win," as though to imply that Toyota cared more about profits than about safety.

Third, throughout much of the six-month period following the Saylor accident, Toyota's top management was invisible. On October 2, 2009, the newly appointed CEO of Toyota, Akio Toyoda, publicly apologized to the Saylor family relatives and to every customer affected by the recall. But then he largely vanished from view until late January 2010. Eventually he reemerged to give testimony at congressional hearings in Washington, D.C., in February 2010. But his absence from the media in the prior months had left a void in which speculation and innuendo spread about what Toyota was up to.

Fourth, during this period, Toyota spokesmen issued inconsistent statements about what might happen or what could be done. They thus created confusion as to whether Toyota knew what it was doing and whether it was deliberately stonewalling or obfuscating the issues.

Fifth, Toyota did little to counter the news of further reported incidents of unintended acceleration. Moreover, the alarming elements of the earlier history kept emerging as a result of the media discoveries rather than being voluntarily disclosed by Toyota. The constant flow of bad news helped keep the story alive and strengthened the impression that the company was hiding something. It also left people wondering what other bad news had yet to come.

Sixth, Toyota appeared to be working at cross-purposes with the NHTSA. In the letters sent to car owners on September 29, 2009, Toyota said "no defect exists." On November 2, 2009, NHTSA took the highly unusual step of publicly rebuking Toyota, calling a company press release reiterating the statements made in the thirty October letters to owners "inaccurate" and "misleading." Toyota publicly apologized.

NHTSA was frustrated by Toyota's slow response to the problem of sticky accelerator pedals. Its acting administrator even went to Japan to try to get the attention of management and was brushed aside. The U.S. secretary of transportation had to personally call CEO Akio Toyoda to stress the seriousness of the problem. After two months of silence, Toyota finally announced at the end of January 2010 that it had developed a solution.

But the damage was done. As a result, *Toyota* had become a one-word metaphor for anything that wouldn't stop.

Congressional hearings were held. At the hearings, senior Toyota managers disagreed as to whether the problem was solved. Toyota's CEO apologized yet again and announced that Toyota would be installing a brake override in its vehicles in the future.

But it was too little, too late. What had begun as a significant but manageable problem had turned into a full-scale corporate crisis.

THREE FACTS

Amid the swirling media controversy as to what the problem is and whether it has been solved, three facts are solid.

Toyota (Still) Makes High-Quality Cars

For decades, Toyota set the gold standard in making cars. Over fifty years, its cars were reasonably priced and consistently at or near the top of quality ratings. This continues to be the case. This assessment is not changed by what has emerged in the unintended acceleration. Overall its record on safety and quality is still much better than that of most other companies.[20]

Toyota Failed to Fix a Significant Problem for at Least Five Years

Toyota learned in 2004 that its vehicles had an above-average level of incidents of unintended acceleration. Toyota then took five years before it issued recalls for two root causes—first wandering floor mats that jammed the accelerator (announced in September 2009) and then accelerator pedals that stuck (announced in January 2010). The NHTSA has associated over fifty deaths with incidents of unintended acceleration.

We can only speculate on why Toyota didn't get to the root causes of the problem sooner. Everything in its history indicates that it would be the last company in the world to sweep a problem under the rug.

What caused Toyota's failure to get to grips with this issue? Was it, as Akio Toyoda suggested, that managers had become "confused" about its traditional priorities of safety first, then quality, and, only then, volume? Was it that Toyota had begun to espouse the traditional management goals of growth at any cost, and drastic cost reductions even at the expense of quality? Was it that Toyota had adopted the explicit goal of reducing recalls? Was it false reliance on automatic detection of abnormal conditions? Had Toyota grown too fast to train staff? Was it the hubris of the engineers who had enjoyed so much success with the Lexus and the Prius that they saw no need for a brake override device?

We may never really know precisely what combination of factors caused the problem. But we do know that there was a failure to fix a problem for a number of years—something that is out of keeping with Toyota's long history of fixing problems as soon as they are found.

Toyota's Communications Were Clumsy

For the six months following the Saylor incident, Toyota's communications with the public gave an appearance of obfuscation, stonewalling, and even deliberate hiding of the truth. Misstatements and inconsistencies compounded the problem. No one appeared to be in charge. The firm appeared to be dragging its feet. It often responded with "no comment."

When incidents occurred, Toyota spokespersons said that "no decision had been made whether to investigate." Whatever the substantive merits of the case, Toyota's actions comprise a classic study in how not to communicate when a crisis emerges.

By mid-March 2010, Toyota was finally beginning to get a grip on communications. It was aggressively and publicly investigating each reported incident. It was able to establish at least a suspicion about the genuineness of some of the highly publicized incidents. It began using social media to elicit conversations as to what it should do next.

Yet the key to truly great communications is total transparency. In mid-March 2010, Toyota's CEO was still blaming the problem of unintended acceleration on its growth, which was so rapid that it had led to a failure to train new staff adequately. The implication is that the issue arose because of engineering lapses at the periphery of the company's activities.[21] In reality, the decisions on design and recalls were, and still are, tightly held at Toyota's headquarters in Japan; that is, the decisions are being made by Toyota's best and most experienced specialists. So it remains an open issue as to whether Toyota has fully come to terms with the root cause of the problem.

FOUR LESSONS FOR CONTINUOUS SELF-IMPROVEMENT

Toyota's experience with unintended acceleration offers some lessons about continuous self-improvement.

Continuous Self-Improvement Requires a Particular Mind-Set

Continuous self-improvement is not a bunch of low-level production techniques to eliminate waste at the factory level. It's a deeply rooted set of values and attitudes focused on fixing problems as soon as they occur. This mind-set rests on the realization that not fixing problems as soon as they are discovered is much more costly in the long run. It can flourish only if the entire organization looks at the world in this way.

We learn about the character of an organization not from the fact that it encounters adversity but how it deals with it. Opting to fix a problem at once, even when it is inconvenient or costly or inconsistent with an organization's production goals, tests the mettle of individuals and the organization. Continuous self-improvement is not a technique that one learns in a book. It's about having the courage to act, even in the face of adversity.

Continuous Self-Improvement Is Fragile

What is shocking about Toyota's response to the reports of unintended acceleration is that the engineers seemingly forgot their fifty-year history and responded like traditional managers. Instead of pulling the andon cord at the first sign of a possible problem, finding the root cause, and fixing it, they spent five years sweeping the problem under the mat. Clearly the mind-set on which continuous self-improvement rests is fragile. If it can evaporate at Toyota, it can evaporate anywhere else.

Communications Are Crucial

It's not enough to be continuously improving. The organization's customers need to know about it. All large organizations inevitably encounter accidents and emergencies from time to time. These incidents can be an opportunity for the organization to be proactive, and improve and strengthen its brand. Or the organization may be perceived as stonewalling and lose both credibility and brand value. Being ready to respond to a crisis through prompt, decisive, and authoritative communications is crucial.

In the early stages of Toyota's crisis, on October 4, 2009, a Toyota spokesperson said that it was "conceivable" that Toyota would introduce a brake override device in its car—something that many other car firms had already introduced.[22] It was only four months later, in February 2010, that Toyota announced that it would do this in 2011.

If the CEO of Toyota had followed Johnson & Johnson's example, he would have announced early in the crisis that whatever the cause of the problem, Toyota was taking responsibility for what had happened.

Moreover, he would have announced the decision to introduce a brake override device on all affected cars as soon as possible. If he had done these things, it is likely that Toyota would have been given credit for taking responsible action and enhanced its brand, rather than having its reputation tarnished by months of speculation and innuendos of stonewalling and avoiding its responsibilities.

Continuous Self-Improvement Is a Top Management Responsibility

Productivity gains of continuous self-improvement occur at low levels of the organization where the work is getting done. But the basis for continuous self-improvement is laid at the top.

Continuous self-improvement is a matter of high-level strategy, not a low-level operational issue, that is, a way of running factories. It begins with top management focusing the whole organization on the goal of delighting clients and providing a clear line of sight so that everyone in the organization can see to what extent he or she is contributing to the goal. It continues with structuring the work around self-organizing teams and supporting those teams with whatever they need to achieve the goal.

Responsibility for making this happen sits at the top of the organization. If top management has focused the firm on efficiently producing a certain quantity of goods and services, with top-down communications telling people what to do, then hierarchical bureaucracy will infect everything that happens in the organization.

At Ford, brilliant implementation of continuous improvement at Hermosillo in the early 1980s went nowhere until 2006, when its new CEO, Alan Mulally, imbued with the Toyota philosophy, arrived and focused the whole organization on continuous self-improvement.[23]

Toyota's CEO also seems to have got the message. When Akio Toyoda returned to Japan on February 28, 2010, after his grilling by the U.S. Congress, he held a rally for Toyota employees. He wore a gray workman's jacket, and in a voice wracked with emotion, he told two thousand assembled workers and a far greater audience that was gathered in front of live television monitors around the world, "Let's go with high spirits, have fun, and be confident while staying humble. We are making a new start today."[24]

High spirits, fun, confidence, humility. Time will tell, but this is beginning to sound like the communication of a radical manager. And it is to the issue of communications that we now turn.

PRACTICES FOR CONTINUOUS SELF-IMPROVEMENT

Practice #1: *Give the Team a Clear Line of Sight to the Client*

At the end of each iteration, the team presents what it has done to the client or client proxy and gets to hear what the response to their work is. This is direct contact with the world, which kicks back if it is unhappy and sings with delight when it is unexpectedly surprised by value it hadn't anticipated.

Practice #2: *Give the Team the Opportunity to Excel*

The team is given a challenging mandate and responsibility for coping with it and then allowed the space to make its contribution. It may fail to do so, but not through lack of opportunity.

The team gives its best and learns from its mistakes, and the next time it gets a little closer to the ideal.

The only failure is not to experiment and find out.[25]

Practice #3: *Align the Team's Interests with Those of the Organization*

If a team is concerned that any savings it generates will result in staff layoffs, then clearly it will make slow progress in identifying improvements. The experience in lean manufacturing is that a policy in which savings are deployed for better products, better service, and better price rather than layoffs is central. Otherwise teams will not identify inefficiencies, eliminate tasks, or streamline unnecessary processes.[26]

Practice #4: *Calculate the Team's Velocity*

Rather than the carrots and sticks of traditional management, radical management uses transparency to inspire the self-organizing team to progress toward high performance. The team knows its own velocity, can see how well it is doing, can identify impediments, and can aspire to do better.

Practice #5: *Get to the Root Causes of Problems*

The daily stand-up session, the retrospective review, and the planning session for the next iteration of work are opportunities to get to the root causes of problems. In all three gatherings, impediments are systematically identified.

Asking "why" five times and doing experiments to determine whether there is a better way can help to get to the underyling problem.[27]

Practice #6: *Systematically Remove Impediments from the Team's Work*

The practices of traditional management—interrupting teams, telling people what to do, nontransparency—are systematically dispiriting. By contrast, radical management systematically addresses the identification and removal of impediments.

Practice #7: *Share Rather Than Enforce Improved Practices*

Knowledge is spread laterally as an opportunity to improve, not as a top-down instruction to implement. Knowledge about practices is shared as an invitation to explore their applicability and adapt ideas to the team's own context.[28]

Practice #8: *Foster the Formation of Horizontal Communities of Practice*

Management facilitates horizontal communications by fostering opportunities for people facing similar challenges to meet, in person or electronically, and share relevant experiences and learning.

Practice #9: *Remain Systematically Open to Outside Ideas*

The best teams systematically expose themselves to outside ideas.[29] Being willing to listen and consider the possibility that one's strongest beliefs are wrong requires an open state of mind, intellectual curiosity, and a kind of serious playfulness.

Practice #10: *Embrace the Need for Continuous Improvement*

Radical management starts from the assumption that every process can be improved. An assumption that there are no limits to improvement is the spur to continuing improvement. There is thus no such thing as "best practice."[30]

10

PRINCIPLE #7: INTERACTIVE COMMUNICATION

> The modern organization cannot be an organization of "boss" and "subordinate": it must be organized as a team of "associates."
>
> **Peter Drucker**[1]

Imagine a warm summer's evening. A young man has invited a young woman on a first date. They have been to dinner at a wonderful restaurant. They have enjoyed each other's company. They have laughed at the same jokes. They have enjoyed the same food. As they learned about each other, they experienced the wonder of being on a mutually exhilarating journey. Now the evening is about to end with a lingering kiss.

Then suddenly the young man pulls out his wallet and says, "I've had a wonderful evening. How much do I owe you? Will a hundred bucks cover it?" She slaps his face, and the relationship is over.

Suppose, alternatively, that instead of offering the young woman a hundred dollars, the young man had said, "I'm the boss now. Here's what you have to do over the coming weeks; otherwise I'll be terminating this relationship." To which, the young woman replies: "Save your breath, buster! We're terminating it right now!"

In either case, the young man has made a social category mistake. The social category of dating exists in what is sometimes called the gift economy of social norms. There's give and take, but actions are not seen as having a market price or determined by one person being the boss of the other.

Suggesting that the young woman's actions have a dollar value instantly moves the relationship out of dating and into the world of market pricing. Or if the young man asserts that he is the young woman's boss, he will have inexplicably turned the date into an unpleasant boss-subordinate relationship. Either way, the damage is done. She is not the kind of woman who sells her company for money or takes orders from her boyfriend. The social relationship is over.

THREE DIFFERENT WORLDS

Behavioral economist Dan Ariely points out in his book *Predictably Irrational* that we live simultaneously in different worlds: one where social norms prevail, another where market pricing determines the rules, and still another where authority ranking prevails.

The social norms of the gift economy are wrapped up in our social nature and our need for community. They are usually warm and convivial. The world of market pricing is very different. There's nothing warm and convivial about it. As Ariely points out, "The exchanges are sharp-edged: wages, prices, rents, interest, costs and benefits.... When you are in the domain of market norms, you get what you pay for—that's just the way it is."[2]

In relationships based on authority ranking, superiors are accepted as having the right to direct and control the activity of subordinates. The relationship may be anywhere on the spectrum from warm and convivial to harsh and sharp-edged. Pulling rank and asserting pure authority can quickly turn a convivial hierarchical relationship into one that is harsh and sharp-edged.[3]

TABLE 10.1 Types of Social Relationships

	Social Norms	Authority Ranking	Market Pricing
Work	Everyone pitches in and does what he or she can, without keeping track of inputs. Tasks are the collective responsibility of the group.	Superiors direct and control the work of subordinates and control the product of subordinates' labor.	Work for a wage calculated as a rate per unit of time or output.
How decisions are made	Group seeks consensus, unity, the sense of the group.	Superiors make decisions by authoritative fiat or decrees.	The market decides, governed by supply and demand.
Strengths	Energy, enthusiasm	Decisiveness	Objectivity
Weaknesses	Difficulty reaching closure	Inflexibility, lack of responsiveness	Lack of collaboration
Examples	Families, communities, sports teams, high-performance teams	Military, hierarchical bureaucracy	Labor unions, stock markets, commodity trading

When social norms, market norms, and authority ranking operate in separate domains, life ticks along in a predictable fashion. But things get tricky when these three interact.

In 1992, anthropologist Alan Fiske suggested that social norms (which he called communal sharing), authority ranking, and market pricing are three of the elementary social relationships that dominate human relationships in all cultures (Table 10.1).[4]

Dealing Simultaneously with Three Different Worlds

In dealing with their employees, managers are today necessarily operating simultaneously in all three worlds: market pricing, authority ranking, and social norms. They can't avoid being in the world of market pricing because work necessarily involves remuneration. They can't avoid being in the world of authority ranking, because someone has to take legal decisions on behalf of the organization. And they can't avoid being in the gift economy of social norms, because they need the workers to offer the gift of their energy, ingenuity, and spirit to accomplish the task of continuous innovation.

The gift can't be commanded because that leads to grudging implementation. Nor can it be bought. If the organization tries to buy it, the organization risks getting the equivalent of the slap on the face that the young man received from the young woman when he offered her money in return for the evening.

The challenge for managers is that in trying to elicit the energies, imagination, and creativity of their workers, they need to be predominantly in the world of social norms, against a history of relationships dominated by market pricing and hierarchical ranking.

The tensions among these three worlds are significant. The hard, sharp edges of money-based discussions or the sneer of cold command can slice through the warm, convivial world of social norms like a knife and kill it on the spot. How can managers overcome the baggage of market pricing and authority ranking and communicate in the world of social norms?

Managers can't treat workers like friends and family one moment and then in an impersonal, authoritarian way or a bargaining mode the next when this becomes more convenient or profitable. This is not how the world of social norms works.

The world of social norms is fragile. To be operative, the norms have to be front and center at all times in the relationship. That's because the social norms of the gift economy are allergic to communications that smell of market pricing or hierarchical ranking. Studies show that the mere mention of money or pulling rank is enough to kill the warmth and conviviality of a social relationship. Even thinking about money is enough to make people less willing to help others.[5]

Communications Within Marriages

Coping simultaneously with the conflicting norms of these three different worlds isn't easy, but the issue isn't unique to the workplace. For instance, if the young man we imagined at the start of the chapter had not mentioned the hundred dollars and his relationship with the young woman had blossomed into love and marriage, then money issues would inevitably have entered into the picture. How much money does each person bring to the marriage? Do they pool their money or keep separate accounts? Who earns money? Who pays for what? If it's a warm, mutually sharing marriage, these issues will tend to be resolved in a friendly, respectful fashion, subordinated to the overriding convivial relationship of social norms.

But if money questions dominate the marriage, so that arguments about money and who owes whom for what become predominant, with constant haggling over prices and exchanges, then all sharing and giving will go out the window. It will become a tense, market-priced business arrangement, in which divorce may be the eventual outcome.

If the young man had not pulled rank on the young woman and the relationship had continued into love and marriage, questions of authority would also have emerged. Within the marriage, who has the power to decide what? Are decisions taken jointly, or is one person in charge? Is this true for all subjects, or do they have different authority in different areas? If the relationship is warm and mutually sharing, then these issues will be resolved in a friendly, respectful fashion, subordinated to the overriding social norms.

THE COMMUNICATION CHALLENGE FOR MANAGERS

The communication challenge for managers is thus not unique, but it is significant. Clearly managers will not succeed in eliciting their employees' talents by pulling rank through top-down communications, sending messages, or merely telling people what to do. Nor will they succeed by offering to buy people's enthusiasm and spirit. These are gifts that can't be bought.

Communication in radical management entails a shift from the model of, "I've got something to tell you and I'm hoping you're going to see it the way I see it, and if you do that, I'll pay you for it," into, "I've got a spark. Let's build a fire together." In effect, radical management uses an interactive mode of communication that breeds on the connections among people.

Interactive communication is the usual mode of communication in the world of social norms. It is characterized by authentic narratives, open-ended questions, and conversations. Just as in a flourishing marriage, questions of money and power may be present. But if the communication is interactive and genuinely respectful, the social norms of a healthy reciprocal relationship will predominate.

Authenticity is central to radical management. At its simplest level, it means that words, beliefs, and actions are consistent.[6] Spelled out more fully, it means that because radical managers know who they are and what they stand for, others come to know them and respect them for that. Because they are attentive to the world as it is, their ideas are sound. Because they level with people they are speaking to, they are believed. Because their actions are consistent with those values, their values become contagious, and others are keen to share them. Because they listen to the world, the world listens to them. Because they are open to innovation, happy accidents happen. Because they bring meaning into the world of work, they are able to get superior results.

This is the ideal of authenticity. This is what a good manager looks like, feels like, speaks like, and acts like. In this way, we can recognize genuine authenticity when we see it and not be confused into thinking that an all-knowing fast-talking tough guy, like Robert McNamara, is a good manager.

As to why the people heading organizations today don't always correspond to this ideal, there are various reasons. At the outset, the people who aspire to become heads of organizations require a certain amount of boldness and ambition. Moreover, the selection process tends to favor those who put on a good front. The events that happen to people as they try to attain their goal and get ahead of their competitors for power can also reinforce the dark side of their characters. Once they attain their goal, the seduction of power itself has the potential to corrupt. Yet behind all these practical reasons lies a certain conception of what it is to be a good manager. Business schools and textbooks tend to reinforce the traditional notion of someone who knows how to play hardball and takes no prisoners.[7]

Radical management requires managers at all levels who know how to connect with and understand others and who are willing to face up to and take responsibility for the consequences of their actions. The concept of authenticity needs to find its way into business schools, textbooks, and selection processes. Attention needs to be paid to obvious gaps between what organizations say they are doing and what they are actually doing. (See Chapter Four.)

THE POWER OF NARRATIVE

A key ingredient of authentic communication is narrative. It's no accident that those who have been successful in propagating the practices of radical management in software development, like Jeff Sutherland, Ken Schwaber, and Mary Poppendieck, are excellent storytellers.[8] In many ways, they exemplify the interactive and seriously playful mode of communication that is crucial in generating and sustaining the high-performance teams of radical management.

Leadership storytelling can be learned. It is not about acquiring something totally new, but rather applying something we already know how to do for constructive purposes in an organizational setting.

As I explained in my books, *The Leader's Guide to Storytelling* and *The Secret Language of Leadership,* we all start spontaneously telling stories at the age of two and go on throughout our lives communicating through stories.[9] In organizations, we have gotten in the bad habit of communicating through abstractions, leaving people bored or confused. Storytelling is our natural language. People naturally think in stories, dream in stories, plan in stories, and make decisions in stories. Communicating in story is easier for both speaker and for the listener.

To illustrate what I mean by an interactive mode of communication, let's examine what happens in one of the most frequent and mundane of management interactions: a talk to a group of people. Let's compare the communications of a traditional manager with that of a radical manager.

Communicating as a Traditional Manager

The traditional manager comes to the meeting with a message to impart. The presentation is typically an abstract talk that proceeds independently of the listener. Without noticing whether anyone is really paying attention, the manager announces his or her idea—perhaps yet another reorganization—the premises of which are entirely management's. Decisions have already been taken. The manager assumes that the audience will accept what he or she is about to say because of his or her hierarchical position.

The audience's spontaneous reactions—smiles, frowns, applause, or disapproval—are essentially irrelevant distractions to what the manager is saying. The audience never enters the picture as an active participant. Even when they are allowed to ask questions or make comments, it is expected that the comments and questions will be safely contained within the confines of the manager's agenda. The success of the communication is seen as depending on whether the manager has been able to transmit the message.[10]

Traditional managers speak to employees as employees, and power is the currency of the communication. These managers present themselves as the superior of the subordinates, although out of feigned politeness, traditional management refrains from calling subordinates "inferiors."

In reality, the subordinates may be superior to their "superior" in many respects: knowledge, skills, courage, integrity, or something else. As a result, traditional managers are continuously involved in exaggerations and mystifications to preserve a facade of superiority. It is in this facade that traditional managers place their hopes of getting things done. Yet in the world of knowledge work, it is perceived for what it is—a facade. As a result, if traditional managers mention or allude to social norms in such a setting, they sound fake because the relationship is hierarchical.

Communicating as a Radical Manager

For radical managers, the situation is different. These managers don't come to the meeting empty-handed. They come with ideas—perhaps to introduce the principles of radical management, but also to interact with the audience, learn from their viewpoints, and discover new truths. The interaction is a conversation, not a telling.

Even before the presentation has begun, radical managers demonstrate openness. They might welcome the audience individually or physically acknowledge their presence. They do this because it's difficult to be unresponsive to someone who is actively signaling responsiveness and reciprocity.

A radical manager, on beginning to talk, recognizes that the audience is not necessarily paying attention, and so takes active steps to get attention. As discussed in *The Secret Language of Leadership,* the talk begins with things that are already of interest and relevance to the audience, before moving on to the idea to be discussed.[11]

Once the audience is paying attention, the radical manager shifts, as discussed in *The Leader's Guide to Storytelling,* to springboard stories of successful implementation of the idea under discussion. The stories—simple, true, positive, and perhaps a little unexpected but still plausible—enliven the audience's interest and are easy to understand.[12]

The reactions of the audience to these stories are central. They represent essential markers as to whether and how the narratives are resonating and as to how the manager should proceed from that point.

The radical manager adjusts what is said in light of the audience's reactions, and the audience sees that. This prompts new reactions from them, which leads to new adjustments by the manager. The manager is aware of the audience just as the audience is aware of the manager.

The radical manager uses narratives to elicit responsiveness. The responsiveness of the audience is contagious. Each listener is aware of the reactions of other listeners to the manager, so if other listeners are laughing, there is a tendency for every listener to laugh.

When the radical manager invites reactions from the audience, the responsiveness of the presentation to the listeners will have created a mood of possibility. It becomes plausible for the audience to offer their own stories, which may have different underlying assumptions from those of the manager. The discussion can broaden into areas that might otherwise be impossible to broach. As a result, what begins as a simple talk by the manager to the subordinates can suddenly become an opportunity for new ideas—new truths that fuse the inputs of multiple participants.

The talk I have just described would be only one part of a manager's busy day, which may have scores of such interactions. By being open and interactive with all the people who fill the day's calendar, the radical manager is not only communicating ideas but also opening up new horizons and possibilities and encouraging collaboration.

The stories that the radical manager has elicited in the minds of the listeners are in some ways more important than the manager's own stories. These stories are now owned by the listeners. They represent the embryonic plans of action that the audience will take. If the stories are positive and energizing, the implementation will be positive and energetic too.

The radical manager communicates as one human being to another. Hierarchy is present but in the background. Appeals to the audience to contribute with spirit and enthusiasm sound authentic and appealing. The relationship is interactive as is natural and normal in the world of social norms.

By contrast, the traditional command-and-control manager spends a day full of encounters that end in adversarial, tension-filled, power-driven outcomes, with few new opportunities emerging. On the surface, it is a day of apparent order and focus, with the traditional controlling manager "winning" most of the encounters as a result of hierarchical power. But the audience's apparent submissiveness is deceptive. In fact, the listeners' minds are filled with stories that are negative and cynical. Implementation will be difficult because the listeners will withhold the gift of enthusiastic support for change and refrain from fully engaging in the workplace.[13]

THE CONCEPT OF CONVERSATION

A key ingredient in the communications of radical management is the concept of conversation—a dialogue between fellow human beings. The relationship between the speaker and the listener is symmetrical and reciprocal. Communications proceed on the assumption that the listener could take the next turn in the discussion.

In organizations, the differences in hierarchical status between the speaker and the audience may be vast. The speaker may be a boss talking to subordinates or a subordinate talking to a higher-level boss or bosses. In radical management, the speaker ignores these differences in status and talks to listeners as one person to another. In this way, the radical manager slices through the barriers that separate individuals.

By contrast, the command-and-control manager speaks in abstractions and exploits differences in status and adversarial relationships. Thus, when the manager asserts, "We must do X," the listeners' options are to accept or reject the proposition. If they accept it, they are submitting to authority. If they reject it or argue about it, they are rebelling against authority. Either way, they are in a hierarchical, adversarial relationship. The risk of the organization's losing the precious gift of employees' energy and enthusiasm is significant.

When a radical manager converses in narratives, there is no issue of submission or rebellion. The listeners don't need to accept or reject the narrative because the radical manager and the audience live the story together. It is a mutually shared experience, something in which the audience has actively participated. The normal response is neither acceptance nor rejection but rather to tell another story. It might be a story in the same vein, or it might be prefaced by, "I have a different take on that!" followed by a story that reflects another point of view. Either way, one story leads to another. It's not a normal response to say, "That story is right" or "That story is wrong." A story is neither right nor wrong. It simply is. In this way, storytelling is naturally collaborative.

PUTTING THE BOUNDARIES IN THE RIGHT PLACE

Over a quarter of a century ago, management theorist Charles Handy noted the tendency in organizations toward bigness and consistency. According to Handy, "Size . . . brings formality, impersonality, and rules and procedures in its train. There is no way out of it. When someone cannot rule by glance of eye and word-of-mouth because there are just too many people, he has to lean on formal systems of hierarchy, information, and control."[14]

And yet there is a way out. The key is figuring out where to put the boundaries and controls. Radical management doesn't abandon boundaries or controls. In some areas, it is more open and creative, and in others, it is even more rigid and structured than traditional management. Thus, it insists on the goal of delighting clients, on self-organizing teams, on setting priorities before work, on iterative patterns of work, on the team's taking responsibility for what is to be done, on delivering value at the end of each iteration, and on accountability for the outcome. But it insists on these elements in order to create an open space where self-organizing teams can flourish. It uses structures and boundaries to prevent bureaucracy from infecting the work itself.

The living part of the organization thus coexists with the structures because they enable creativity. We see examples of this phenomenon everywhere. In nature, we see the fantastic diversity generated by a few basic structural elements: no more than a hundred varieties of atoms and a couple of primary colors lead to a universe of infinite beauty and diversity. In the twelve notes of the musical scale and the twenty-six letters of our alphabet, we see how these rigid structures have enabled the creativity of music and literature. Without structure, there is nothing for creativity to build on. Radical management thrives on structure that enables, rather than restrains, creativity.

Narrative modes of communication are extraordinarily relevant in dealing with the challenge of being rigid in some areas and open and creative in others. Suddenly the tasks of getting people to understand

and implement complex new ideas, working together and sharing knowledge to generate enthusiasm and flair become feasible.

In *The Leader's Guide to Storytelling* and *The Secret Language of Leadership,* I have explained in detail how to use the power of storytelling to handle the various challenges that leaders face, including sparking change, communicating who you are, enhancing the brand, getting people working together, transmitting knowledge and values, and leading people into the future.

The radical manager uses those practices to ignite support for the other six principles of radical management, particularly:

- Using leadership storytelling to inspire support for the goal of delighting clients
- Using conversations to create and sustain self-organizing teams
- Communicating the goals and progress of work done in client-driven iterations through user stories
- Modeling truthful communications that support and reinforce radical transparency
- Coaching teams to get on a trajectory of continuous improvement so that they become more productive than the norm and find work deeply satisfying

PRACTICES FOR INTERACTIVE COMMUNICATION

Practice #1: *Use Authentic Storytelling to Inspire a Passion for Delighting Clients*

For most organizations, radical management entails a hefty change agenda—often a fundamental shift in culture. As I explained in *The Leader's Guide to Storytelling,* this won't happen without compelling leadership storytelling—springboard stories about how other organizations have done it and stories about how it is already happening within the organization. These stories can inspire other managers and staff to try it out.

Practice #2: *Focus the Goals of the Team on User Stories*

Radical management involves a shift from seeing teams and organizations as entities that produce things (goods and services) to that of groups of people who delight clients sooner, more often, and more profoundly. This can happen only if the team knows the client's story and hence knows what might delight the client (see Practice #8 in Chapter Six).

Practice #3: *Deploy User Stories as Catalysts for Conversation*

As discussed in Practices #8 to #12 in Chapter Six, stories aren't artifacts or instructions or commands. They are opportunities to conduct a conversation between the client or client proxy and the people doing the work. The object of the conversation is to deepen understanding as to what might delight the client.

Practice #4: *Use Stories to Focus Teams on Achieving High Performance*

Why do some self-organizing teams evolve into high-performance teams, while others flounder for months or even years? Getting the context right is a big part of it. But even when the context is right, it still may not happen. Sometimes it's a matter of having the right mix of skills. But sometimes it's also the team's internal dynamics.

Much hogwash has been spoken and written about "motivating" individuals and teams through the use of incentives and disincentives. The reality is that carrots and sticks don't motivate knowledge workers.[15] Instead, skilled leaders find what drives people into action and discover ways to connect that to the goals of the team. The idea is to identify what puts people in motion and then get them more of that.

Ultimately the evolution of self-organizing teams into high-performance teams depends on team members' mutual respect and trust. When people have this kind of respect, they feel they have the support of others in the group. They view the group's resources, knowledge, perspectives, and identities to some extent as their own. They feel as though they have new capabilities and begin to include others in their concepts of themselves. They feel a sense of exhilaration as they learn new things from and about their partners. In a sense, their sense of self expands. They become larger persons.

Aristotle wrote about this phenomenon in terms of the concept of *philia.* This is usually translated as friendship, but it is more than mere liking or friendship. It connotes the passion associated with love, but without the sexual connotation. High-performance teams routinely talk about their relationships as a form of love.[16]

It is also admiration, but it's not a mutual admiration society: these relationships have a constructive frankness because the participants care enough to say the things that mere acquaintances wouldn't. The team members discover what is wonderful in the other person, but the quality is not preexisting: it is mutually created. In effect, it is a deep appreciation for the character of the other person.

In order for the team members to reach this level of respect, they have to know each other more deeply than the superficial relations of the hierarchical bureaucracy where one leaves one's personal identity at the workplace entrance. They need to know the stories of the people they are working with.

Practice #5: *Use Stories to Help Team Members Understand Who They Are*

One reason that the team members may not know whether they can trust or respect the other members is that the other team members themselves don't have a clear image of who they are, and so are unable to project a personality that is fit to be trusted. In such situations, as I explained in *The Leader's Guide to Storytelling,* teaching the team members to learn how to craft and perform the story of who they are can enable them to come to terms with what sort of person they are and communicate that to the other members of the team.

Practice #6: *Use Stories to Inspire Group* Philia

The classic way in which groups have been inspired to work together is a narrative pattern that is as old as the ancient Greek historian Thucydides and as modern as the political campaign of Barack Obama (Figure 10.1).[17] Having the group craft and perform this combination of stories communicates to both themselves and others what they have in common and why they might evolve into a high-performance group.

The first story, the story of "who I or we have been," establishes an emotional connection between the speaker and the audience. The second story, of "who we are," reminds the group of the common elements that already bind them together. The third story, of "who we are going to be," generates a new story in the minds of the listeners about how they are going to act together in future.

It is the alignment and narrative coherence of the three stories that makes communication compelling. The present emerges inevitably from the past, and the future flows seamlessly from the present.

Practice #7: *Stimulate the Muscle Memory of High-Performance Teams*

The underlying idea of radical management—energetically collaborating with others to do the very best you collectively can—is strange but also familiar. Almost all of us have had the experience of being in a group that is highly productive and vibrantly alive at one time or another. This isn't the invention of a management consultant. It's something we already know. The experience has probably existed since time immemorial, when our hunter-gatherer forebears were living in caves and fighting off wolves.

If we take the time, we can refresh that memory and recreate it. That earlier experience was a premonition of the future. If we can recall that earlier experience, it can be an easy mental leap to a realization of how easy and fruitful it can be to recreate it today.

FIGURE 10.1 The Group Story Sequence

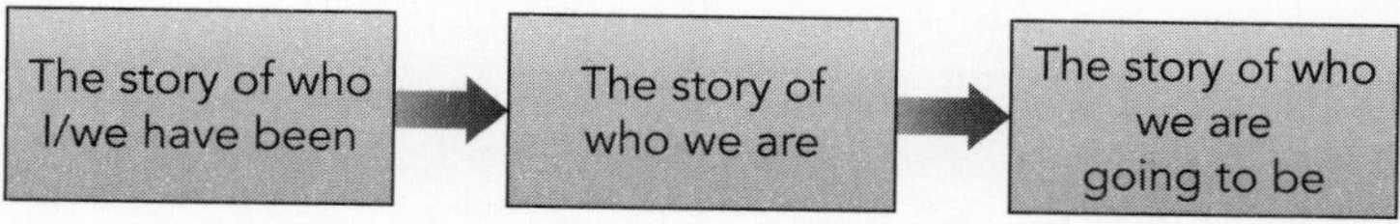

One way of drawing on that memory is to have the team members tell each other stories of their own experiences of high-performance groups that they have experienced in the past. This may enable the group members to start to see each other as people who have had such experiences. In doing so, they are seeing the other members of the team when they have been at their best. The process can give rise to the implicit question: If we have all been in high-performance teams in the past, why can't we get into this mode now?

Practice #8: *Tell Springboard Stories of Other High-Performance Teams*

To encourage memories of high-performance teams, a leader might tell stories about successful high-performance teams in other similar organizations, with the objective of stimulating the narrative imaginations of the team members with the thought, *If people like that, who are very similar to us, could do it, why not us now?*

Practice #9: *Practice Deep Listening to Each Other's Story*

Deep listening of the stories of the other members of the team can help people become more familiar with those they are working with. Managers can help create safe spaces where such deep listening can take place.

On the surface, these may seem like exercises. But when they work well, the participants lower their social guard. They make themselves vulnerable and learn about each other's hopes and fears. They discover what's wonderful in each other. They are suddenly looking at themselves through the admiring eyes of others, and vice versa. They can see themselves as more noble, generous, and open and begin to act with them in these ways. They become "new people."

Winning the mutual respect that generates high performance is not risk free. Those who recognize that radical management is something worth fighting for, taking risks for, will also see that not risking anything is an even greater risk.

Practice #10: *Give Recognition for Identifying Impediments*

Radical management is about systematically identifying and eliminating impediments to improved performance. Team members are not just encouraged to suggest improvements; they are required to identify impediments even when no solution is in sight.

Part 2

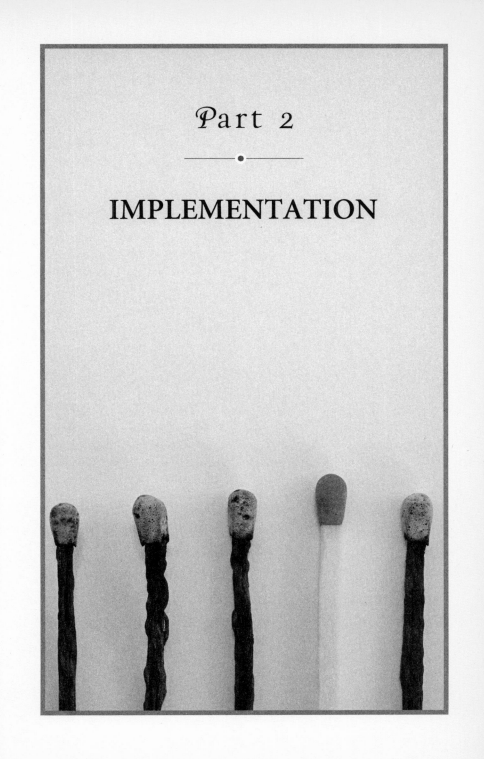

IMPLEMENTATION

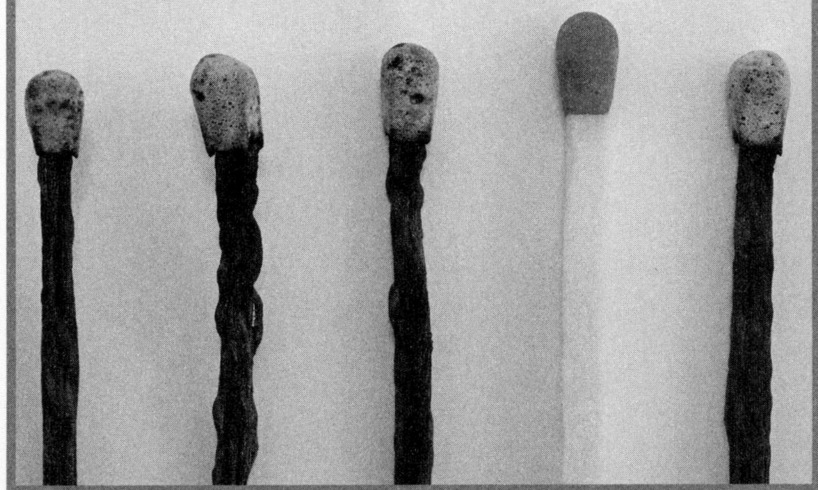

11

A RIVER OF CASCADING CONVERSATIONS

> The more we learn to use this method, the more we find that what it does is not so much to teach us processes we did not know before, but rather opens up a process in us, which was part of us already.
>
> **Christopher Alexander[1]**

A century hence, when historians come to write the history of the current age (assuming our species survives so long), they will, I believe, be puzzled as to why so many people managed—and so many more people allowed themselves to be managed—in ways that were known to be unproductive, crimped the spirits of those doing the work, and frustrated those for whom the work was being done. Why, they will wonder, did this continue for so long on such a wide scale?

One school of historians may focus on the pervasive feeling of complacency. Another may marvel at the superficiality of popular proposals to deal with it by contriving "a sense of urgency."[2] Still others may dwell on the sense of resignation felt by most of those involved—the feeling that no matter what is done, it won't make any difference. After all, how could traditional managers avoid turning radical management into a mirror image of the very practices they were supposedly trying to change? How could they walk on a bridge before they had even begun to build it?[3]

Thought therefore must be given, before heading pell-mell into the implementation of radical management, not only to the principles of radical management, but also to the principles of radical change management. If you have mastered the arguments of this book so far, you will have already guessed that radical change management is not an eight-step top-down hierarchical rollout of a program, embodying a preconceived idea, articulated in some back room by outsiders, and then imposed with one-way communications that tell people what to do.[4]

You will know that kind of thinking and acting is precisely what has brought us to the current impasse. You will expect it to be a process that gives due respect to the interests not only of the organization but also of those doing the work and of those for whom the work is done. You will intuit that communications will be interactive and respectful of the individuals involved while giving due attention to productivity and innovation.

And you will be certain of one thing: that radical change management will not be a simple recipe that you can wrap up and take back to your organization to apply without modification tomorrow morning, with any expectation of success. You know that you will have to create a story of your own—one that fits your own context—its possibilities and its constraints. You also know that you will have to adapt the story on the fly as conditions shift.

Even so, the evolving story that you must create may benefit from learning about other experiences of organizational change that have occurred principally by communicating interactively rather than relying on authority or money. Knowing how others have coped with analogous challenges and avoided common pitfalls may help make your own story more robust.

I begin with my own experience.

MY INITIATION INTO RADICAL CHANGE MANAGEMENT

Over a decade ago, I found myself in a large traditionally managed organization with an idea and not much else.[5] The idea was to inspire a major change in the organization. I had no budget, no support from any senior manager in the organization, and no organizational mandate to introduce or even to explore the idea. All I had was a passionate belief in the idea and its value, a certain amount of determination to make it happen, and some understanding of how the organization functioned.

Four years later, that idea—an airy nothing—had become a central strategic thrust of the organization and had spawned over a hundred communities to champion it. Thousands of people were deeply involved not only inside but also outside the organization, pushing the idea forward on multiple fronts in a giant social network. The organization was benchmarked as a world leader in the field.

This hadn't happened through a traditional change management approach, with the top management imposing the change. Any such approach would have been resisted fiercely. Instead it happened rapidly and enthusiastically because it grew organically, one conversation at a time, until many people became promoters of the change. It was like a bacterial life-form, unexpectedly swelling here and recoiling there in response to social, technical, economic, and cultural events.

From the outset, it was all about learning. "My" idea wasn't something that I had invented. I had heard what some other organizations had done and the benefits that they had been able to generate. I found out all I could about their experiences. I visited them and saw what they were doing and the obstacles they were encountering. I examined the parallels to our own situation. I sensed that in some respects, what they were doing could help us a lot, but in other respects, the idea would have to be adapted.[6]

After fine-tuning the idea, I began having conversations with colleagues and asking them why the idea wouldn't work for us. Initially, to my surprise, they couldn't understand what I was talking about. It was only after many failed attempts at explaining the idea that I stumbled on the power of storytelling as a tool for leadership communication. I discovered stories that could powerfully and succinctly communicate a complex idea and inspire people to see its potential value. In the course of those conversations, I could see that once people understood the idea, they were excited by it and began adapting it to their own settings. Their enthusiasm in turn energized me to press ahead and do whatever was necessary to make it happen.

I talked to people in corridors and cafeterias—wherever I could find listeners. By the time I got to present my idea to the senior managers of the organization several months later, I was able to do so in a way that had many of them imagining a new and more exciting future.

Although it wasn't necessary at the start, eventually getting the blessing of the very top of the organization was essential. As with any other idea involving substantial change, some of the senior managers were alarmed by the potential for disruption to the status quo and did their best to slow down or prevent its implementation. Support from the top was needed to neutralize the worst of this high-level sabotage.

Even when I had a mandate to begin exploration of the idea, I had little budget and no power to tell anyone to do anything. In fact, that didn't matter much because budgets and power don't usually generate genuine enthusiasm for change.

The momentum that had already been generated by innumerable conversations meant that there was no need to create a sense of urgency by contriving a phony crisis. The challenge was not one of jump-starting people with a lot of dead batteries. It was more like figuring out what to do with a stampede that was already under way. The main challenge was one of channeling forward movement in a common direction, heading off diversions and helping stragglers catch up. In the process, I cobbled together resources and people into coalitions that made the change happen.

To help manage, I pulled together a diverse group of enthusiasts who believed in the cause and self-organized themselves into doing whatever it took. The members of the group got to know each other. We regularly had lunch in a tapas bar across the street from where we worked. As we shared dishes at the round table where we always sat, we also shared intelligence on new possibilities that were emerging, as well as on what bad things had just happened. We brainstormed how to turn setbacks into opportunities.

As we began to appreciate what each other could contribute, we began to admire what was open and generous in each other. In response, we all started acting with each other more openly and generously. Ordinary people began accomplishing extraordinary things.

We had many disagreements and even fights, but there was enough trust and respect that the disagreements strengthened the group instead of splintering it. There was a lot of kidding around. The discussion was playful and creative, and it enabled the tension from the disagreements to be released.

We invited others to join the movement and become friends of the idea. In fact, as Seth Kahan explains in his book, *Getting Change Right,* we spent a good deal of time figuring out how to tell as many people as we could and as fast as possible.[7] The dialogue flowed like a river and penetrated parts of the organization our team had not formally reached.

In implementation, the idea continued to evolve. We discovered that information technology was less effective than we had expected, and so we deemphasized that. Communities of practice turned out to be much more important than we had expected, so they became central.

We convened those who understood and supported what we were up to—our evangelists. We met with directors and project managers who had the most to gain from the idea. We brought in key players who were at least initially opposed, because their participation could make or break some of our efforts.

We invited anyone who was interested to be part of our work. We created working groups and met with clients. We visited other firms that were pursuing similar strategies and invited them to visit us and critique what we were doing. We met with outsiders and business thought leaders.

We lived in a river of conversations. The interactions spread and permeated the tiniest crevices of the organization. Everywhere we went, we sought to get people thinking about what the idea might mean to them and their work, how they could become involved, and the benefits it could bring to the people they were working with. The stories that we were telling them were less important than the stories they were creating for themselves.

The pace of the change was unnerving. The movement traveled so fast and far that it often outreached where our little team was able to go.

Having practically no budget turned out to be almost a blessing in disguise. Money creates distractions that tend to take people's eyes off the activities that add value to clients—talking with people and discovering together what's possible.

In due course, we needed resources, but they emerged as we needed them. When we needed people, they were given to us on loan. When we needed to put on a big event, we made it enticing enough that people paid to be a part of it. In this way, the resources came as value was generated.

Having discovered the power of leadership storytelling, we communicated principally through stories, particularly a kind of story that sparked action—a kind of story that I have called *springboard stories*—stories that spring an audience to a new level of understanding.

Stories were effective at all levels of the organization—whether it was the CEO and the board of directors or people working on the front lines of the workplace or people outside the organization. Springboard stories communicated the spirit of our idea and generated new stories in the minds of the listeners, which drove them into action and sparked more stories, which they told to others.

The idea that we had was not a precooked message that was rolled out or imposed. Instead, it was a cascade of conversations that spread an emerging, evolving idea through a dialogue that aroused passion and created its own social network.

We energized the most influential players. We saw that people were at the heart of the change and took the time to engage others. We went after them and gave them exciting ways to be part of the action.

We took steps to understand the territory of change, figuring out the culture and how to go forward. We listened to others in order to create a map of the opportunities and obstacles.

We formed groups of people who shared our passion for the idea and put this passion into practice. These groups advanced our cause, creating systemic demand for change rather than having to push people into doing things.

We set out to create dramatic surges in progress. Special face-to-face events accelerated our program. We created gatherings that brought players together in high-value experiences designed to move things forward in leaps and bounds.

We approached problems with a SWAT team mentality. As with any other major change, obstacles and hurdles were everywhere. We expected trouble, and we got it. But we did not see difficulty as a hindrance to our success. Rather it made many valuable contributions to our overall achievement. By learning about problems early, we were able to find ways to fix them quickly.

When other members of our group and I left the organization, the idea didn't die because it wasn't dependent on us. People went on implementing it, not because they had been told to but because they believed in it.

What did implementation feel like? I wouldn't describe the period as contented, blissful, or consistently pleasurable, even though there were moments when each one of those feelings was present.[8] It would be more accurate to say that the experience overall was exciting, exhilarating, hair-raising, rewarding, challenging, and meaningful.

In effect, radical change management involves taking responsibility for what needs to happen. It means standing up for what we believe in, sometimes in the face of opposition from those in power and confronting significant risks. It entails stretching, growing, and living up to more of our potential. It means discovering the courage to be.

SOME PRACTICES OF RADICAL CHANGE MANAGEMENT

That was my first encounter with implementing change without large authority or budget resources. The idea in question was knowledge management, not radical management. As it happens, the organization was the World Bank, but it could have been any other large organization. The experience embodies the characteristics of radical change management. Your story will be different in its particulars from that experience, but the fundamental characteristics of the change process are likely to be similar.

First, *the impetus will begin with a single individual.* That individual may be anywhere in the organization. It may be the CEO. In a large organization, it is more likely to be someone in middle management.[9] It may even be someone at the working level. Change will begin when that person takes responsibility for the future and decides, "This needs to happen, and I am going to help make it happen."

Second, *the change will happen organically.* One person starts talking to and inspiring other people, who in turn have the courage, determination, and communication skills to inspire fresh groups of people to imagine and implement a different future. In turn, they become champions and inspire others.

Third, *a small high-performance team will be needed to inspire and guide implementation.* Dutiful or representative performance won't get the job done. This will be a group that is creative and energized, trusts one another, and is willing to do whatever it takes.

Fourth, *the change will happen quickly or not all.* Once organizational change takes off, it will happen rapidly. The process is viral in nature. The idea is either growing, spreading, and propagating itself, or dying and deenergizing people and spawning new constraints. There isn't much in between. A top-down process that is grinding it out, step by step, unit by unit, is usually generating massive quantities of antibodies that will lead to mediocre implementation or even total failure.

Fifth, *the change idea itself will steadily evolve.* This is not a matter of crafting a vision and then rolling it out across the organization. This is about continuously adapting the idea to the evolving circumstances of the organization. As the organization and everyone in it adapt the story of change to their own context, each individual comes to own it.

Sixth, *the change process will run on human passion*—a firm belief in the clarity and worth of the idea and the courage to stand up and fight for it. No template or detailed rollout plan can inspire the energy, passion, and excitement that are needed to make deep change happen. Most of the paraphernalia of the top-down change programs will in fact be counterproductive to authentic implementation and will generate deep-seated opposition to the change.

Seventh, *it will be focused, disciplined passion.* This is not an approach where anything goes. There will be a tight focus on the goal and continuing alertness to head off the diffusion of energy into related or alternative goals. Progress will be assessed and adjustments made based on what has been learned. There will be systematic feedback on what value is being added. There will be freedom to create, but within clearly delineated, adjustable limits.

Eighth, *outside help will be used but not depended on.* Because there is nothing new under the sun, the experience of others should be drawn on. It is foolish to go it alone. Intellectual energy is generated by cognitive diversity and interactions with people with different backgrounds and ways of looking at the world. At the same time, it is equally dangerous to follow external advice slavishly and let others dictate the change. The external advice will be received, evaluated, and adapted to local needs. In the process of adaptation, the idea will become owned. Things are not done simply because outsiders say so; they will be done because they make sense for this context.

Ninth, *the top of the organization must support it and be supported.* Although implementation of radical management cannot be accomplished by top-down directives or rollout programs, the support of the very top of the organization is key to creating the umbrella for change, for setting direction and heading off the inevitable threats to the idea. Yet the top alone cannot make it happen. In a large organization, the top will need many others to communicate the idea throughout the organization in an authentic way.

Finally, *the idea will be more important than any individual.* Top-down change programs typically die when the manager leaves. The replacement manager is a new broom who sweeps clean what has gone before. By contrast, when a change has taken root in an organic fashion, the idea continues to live because it is owned by a wide array of people.

Keeping those ten characteristics in mind may help you figure out what radical change management will look like in your context (but see the box for possible difficulties with implementation). Let's look at how they have played out elsewhere in implementing radical management.

WHERE IMPLEMENTATION WILL BE PROBLEMATIC

- *The team has latent personality conflicts.* The transparency of radical management will quickly bring latent problems to the surface. Teams that have been limping along in a mediocre fashion and nursing unresolved personality conflicts will find the hidden tensions suddenly exposed. If the conflicts are severe, the team will either disintegrate (so that a new team can form) or return to traditional modes of working at low levels of productivity.
- *Management is not on board.* Radical management is a fundamental transformation in the way work is managed. It will relentlessly expose impediments to improving productivity. If management is not ready to tackle that challenge, greater transparency may generate so much divisiveness that the work is brought to a halt. Similarly, if the firm has opted to preserve its corporate culture rather than improve productivity, radical management will not prosper. For example, in an elite consulting

firm, it can be unthinkable that high-level experts in one field would allow others to collaborate on their field of expertise. The notorious unwillingness of some surgeons to collaborate is another familiar example, as I show in my book, *The Leader's Guide to Storytelling.*

- *The firm has standardized on low-cost mediocrity.* Airlines and fast food chains have largely gone this route. With some exceptions, their work is standardized and workers are tightly programmed, and the product is low cost with predictably low quality. The experience is deadening for the workers, who have no voice in how to do the work and are unable to make improvements in the way the work is done. Such firms may prosper until competitors appear that are able to figure out a way to introduce low-cost methods of high-performance teams, just as cafés offering cheap, bad coffee have been largely eliminated by firms like Starbucks.
- *The client doesn't want it.* In some cases, the client is locked into a traditional way of doing business and wants the delivery of a defined product or service. It doesn't want to have any interaction aimed at improving the product or service or finding cheaper ways to get more value from the interaction. In these situations, an organization may still apply a partial form of radical management internally, even without the client's participation.

The Journey of Total Attorneys

At Total Attorneys, a Chicago-based organization of 160 people that provides office services to small legal firms, it was the CEO who launched the process. Ed Scanlan was asking himself why the firm was able to get more done in forty-five days with three guys than he had just accomplished in six months with several departments. So he began looking into different ways of working. An iterative approach resonated with him because it was similar to what he had been doing when his firm started.

He started talking with some of the people about radically shaking things up. At this point, the firm had a design department, a development department, a quality assurance department, and a project management department. What would happen is that a designer would design a screen. That would get lobbed over to the developers, and they would execute it. They would then send it back to design because something didn't work. Then design would send it back to development. There would be a week's lag between each step.

Scanlan began talking with his staff about getting into cross-functional teams. He didn't want to issue a diktat. He preferred to let things evolve more organically. At that point, the departments were just starting to break out into small cross-functional teams.

They did this for about three months, without any formal framework, to see how effective it was. Scanlan saw that employees were finding a greater sense of ownership in the work because they weren't punting something to another department. They were instead turning to the designer next to them on their team and asking that person to make the quick change and then turn that around and start coding.

Yet Scanlan felt the teams were throwing terms around loosely and lacked a common vocabulary for this new way of working. He wanted to take it to the next level. So he discussed bringing in a trainer to help develop a formal framework. Some people had done it before and were really excited about the prospect. Others were hesitant. Scanlan had to do some stumping around the office to get everyone into it. In due course, the leadership and a majority of the teams agreed that it would be worthwhile.

They brought in the trainer with a lot of experience in iterative development. It began with three days of intensive training for people from all over the organization, mainly on the software development side—designers, developers, quality assurance, project managers, product owners. They brought everyone into a big room and broke them into small teams. The trainer explained the approach, and the group went into practical, hands-on sessions, managing in two-week iterations with note cards and writing out stories and creating a prioritized list of tasks for the projects.

After the training, everyone went back to their small teams and started working that way. At first, this different way of working was difficult. The terminology was unfamiliar. Some people thought it was childish to be writing stories on note cards and being forced to estimate how long the stories would take to execute and then break things down again into smaller stories. The whole idea was foreign, and abandoning the effort was tempting. But a couple of team members had done this before and reassured their teammates: "I've seen this work!"

So they went through a month of it and got a lot of bumps and bruises. The trainer came back and did another day of training. He explored the problems they were encountering and helped find solutions.

Then they went through another month of it, and after about forty-five days or so, really interesting things started happening. Although not all of the staff were trained, whiteboards started appearing in other departments.

The first one that Scanlan noticed was in the accounting office. He walked by and noticed a whiteboard with note cards taped on it. His eyes went wide, and he walked in and took a look at it. He saw that accounting had created a thirty-day cycle for sending out invoices, paying bills, closing financial statements, and so on. They had created stories for the activities for the entire month. The stories were shown in cards taped to a whiteboard, showing "to be done," "in progress," and "done." They had retrofitted the process for the accounting department and were having daily stand-up meetings.

In answer to Scanlan's questions, the staff said they loved the morning huddle and being able to look up on the board and see everything that was going on. There was something very tactile that people liked about having note cards taped to a wall in front of them.

Next Scanlan noticed that the recruiting department had put all of its open requisites on the wall.

The general counsel's office dealt with all the internal legal issues, and the many regulations affecting the work. Scanlan found that they too had created a whiteboard for their work with note cards showing all the things they were working on. There was room to bring on things that came up, like a contract that needed to be executed and so on. They had retrofitted it for legal work.

The movement had taken on a life of its own.

The Journey of Standard & Poor's

In a much larger organization, Standard & Poor's (S&P), the change began with someone in the upper-middle part of the organization. Jora Gill, the vice president responsible for software development in international business systems, is based in London and oversees software development teams in London, Tokyo, and Melbourne. He is also responsible for global resource management, which is all of the offshore work, with teams in India, Russia, and Latvia.

ADAPTING THE PRACTICES FOR VIRTUAL TEAMS

The rule of thumb of conventional wisdom is that colocating a team that was previously physically dispersed normally doubles productivity. Face-to-face communication encourages frankness. Equally important is the elimination of queuing of work and phantom work jams.

The problems of geographically dispersed teams can be mitigated by strong personal rapport, continuous voice over Internet protocol communication among team members, and daily virtual stand-up meetings. Examples in this book of virtual teams working within a radical management framework are Sam Bayer's b2b2dot0, where the team members are scattered around the world but have a strong personal bond (Chapter Six), and Jora Gill at Standard & Poor's, which has an extended network of teams around the globe. Establishing strong personal bonds before attempting geographical dispersion of the team is a prerequisite to achieving any kind of productivity.

Despite the advantages of colocated teams, organizations sometimes see strong reasons for dispersing teams. It may be important to locate team members closer to their clients to facilitate client intimacy and understanding. Allowing employees to work where they want to may be important for quality of work life. The firm may also be seeking cost savings from salary differentials, although these savings are often illusory unless the geographically dispersed teams are managed skillfully.

Although colocation is generally preferable, an alternative view is that distributed teams may sometimes be more productive than colocated teams. For instance, Xebia in the Netherlands has successfully explored the possibility of hyperproductive teams that are geographically distributed.[10] The teams, some in the Netherlands and some in India, are set up in a counterintuitive way: instead of having complete teams in each country, each team is split between the two places, with half its members in the Netherlands and half in India. The dispersed teams were at least as productive as colocated teams and sometimes more productive than the teams located wholly in the Netherlands. The reason is thought to be that splitting the teams geographically forced more conversations among the team about what the client really wanted. When the team was located wholly in the Netherlands, developers tended to assume that everyone knew what the client wanted. Being forced to explain to the developers in India each day what the client wanted helped everyone get clearer and so the teams as a whole tended to become more productive.

Xebia manages the process of dispersion carefully. It grooms the entire team in the Netherlands first. It is only when the team is working well that they send half the team back to India. Achieving high productivity in such circumstances requires sophisticated team management.

Gill became aware of iterative approaches to software development when he was working at an investment bank, where the practices had been imposed from the top and there was no buy-in. Management there didn't realize that it wasn't just a process that was being introduced. Without the buy-in of both the technology people and the businesspeople, top management pushed too hard, and the approach didn't work.

When Gill joined S&P in September 2006, he found it to be a very open organization. Almost right away the businesspeople were telling him what the problems were and what should be done. He spent his first few weeks interviewing people and listening rather than coming up with ideas himself. He talked to both the information technology group and the businesspeople. He found that the two groups liked and respected each other. He saw this as a good opportunity to introduce change.

Gill didn't want to do it in a "let's get this done in three months!" approach. He wanted to introduce it and then step back, watch what happened, collate the metrics, step back again and see what was and wasn't working, and allow people to take ownership of it. Rather than their thinking, "This is something that Jora is doing to us," they could own it themselves. Rather than their thinking that Jora was some kind of guru, he wanted them to be the ones who were seen as gurus.

It took him about a year to get the approach fully adopted. He was constantly questioning people and asking: What's working well, and what's not working well? He inspected and adapted continuously. He started off with a very small proof of concept, then continued to build on that and gradually move on to larger and larger projects.

One of the problems that he faced was how he could introduce this into a large enterprise such as S&P with its stage gates requiring successive management approvals. It's even more difficult when people aren't co-located. You can't just walk across to somebody's desk or office. So Gill developed a framework around the approach that allowed a number of stage gates.[11] "In the beginning," Gill says,

> when you start a process, you need broad agreement that the idea is feasible. So I did a quick feasibility study. This wasn't a large set of written requirements, where you compile a hundred-page document and at the end of it, you find out that you've spent most of your money and you're still at the beginning of the project. I carried out a feasibility study in a streamlined way. I did just enough. It was a quick-start process of brainstorming with our IT people and our businesspeople. We quickly developed estimates. Once we had the feasibility established, and we could see that it would work, then we asked: what's the business opportunity here? Is there business value? Is there going to be enough return on the investment?

There's a need to step back and have a strategic look at: Why are we building this? Where do we see this market heading? Where do we see this product going? What will it win us either as a return on investment or from an operational efficiency perspective? And once we had looked at the opportunity and if we could see that there was a genuine opportunity, then we start building something but in a streamlined way. We do our iterations for two or three releases. Then we say "Now we have reached a velocity that we're all comfortable with. Now we can give you dates with some degree of reliability."

Then after the initial releases, we would go back to the businesspeople and ask, "Are you realizing the value that you thought you would have?"

That has helped with teams that work across the globe in different time zones and make sure that the management was on board. When you're working in a large organization, people have to sign off. Everybody needs to have a certain comfort factor.

One problem Gill encountered was the assumption that the business users would always be available. But they had their jobs to deal with. The projects were important to them, but they weren't organized to do work in iterations. So Gill appointed proxy client representatives, who talked to the business users and worked to understand their requirements.

Then representatives came to the managers who had responsibility within the businesses to deliver and manage those products. Again, he did a small proof of concept. When that was successful, he used it as a reference for the other groups. This wasn't just Gill telling them how good this was going to be. He would say, "We've already done this with another group. Why don't you listen to them and use them as a reference?" It was better when they heard it from some other part of the business. So that's how it mushroomed out and came to be adopted across all the business areas.

How did the software developers respond to the change? Initially, Gill says, the reaction was mixed. That's why he introduced it slowly. Some of them took to it on day one. They loved it and ran with it. But other developers struggled.

"You're there in a daily stand-up," Gill says, "and you're having to say what you did yesterday and admit, 'Well, I said I'd do this, but I didn't quite manage to get it done.' It can be uncomfortable to have to stand up in front of everyone and say that. In the management group we had to reassure people: 'This isn't a test. We're not judging you by this. If you're late and your velocity has slowed, that's fine. That's what we want to hear and need to hear.'"

So it took a while for some of our people to come around. "We've been at it for almost two years now," says Gill. "The feedback is very positive. They're into it and enjoying it. It took a while to get everyone on board. I wouldn't say there was universal success on day one. It just took time."

The Journey of Systematic Software

When radical management is introduced in only part of the organization, eventually the tensions between traditional management and radical management arise and have to be dealt with.

Systematic Software in Denmark is one such example. In 2006, Mikkel Harbo, director of business development and operations, and Carsten Jakobsen, senior project manager, went to see their CEO, Michael Holm, with what they knew he would see as an unusual proposal. Systematic Software, established in 1985, employs around five hundred people in Denmark, Finland, the United States, and the United Kingdom. It focuses on complex and critical information technology systems, with high demands on reliability, safety, accuracy, and usability in the defense, health care, manufacturing, and service industries. It was already a strong performer. The previous year, it had been certified as level 5—the top rating—in the Capability Maturity Model Integration, which is widely used to assess the capabilities of software firms.[12]

Harbo and Jakobsen knew that Holm was looking for ways for Systematic to do even better. So they proposed a radically different way of managing work. In the future, they said, Systematic should develop software with self-organizing teams that would themselves decide how to do the work and even how much work to do. Harbo noted that the approach had been tried successfully in many companies, beginning in 1993 with the Easel Corporation.

Holm found it counterintuitive to hand over control of the work to the staff, but he was an entrepreneur. He liked the fact that Harbo and Jakobsen were willing to take a risk and do something different. So he gave his okay.

Harbo and Jakobsen trained one team and tried it out. Harbo recalls, "In that first go, we fell flat on our bellies. The approach looked simple, but it turned out to be very hard to implement. There were lots of preconditions that we hadn't thought of. But the team was very fond of the method. So we persevered."

Once more, intensive training undertaken by all the staff and managers yielded excellent results. Costs were cut in half, and defects, already very low by industry standards, were reduced by 40 percent.

Staff were happy, as measured by Systematic's "pizza index." Harbo explains: "Pizza is what you order when you are doing overtime. The pizza index is close to zero now, because no overtime, no pizzas."

Even more important, clients were delighted because they could see what was being worked on and how it was evolving, and they could redirect effort to areas of high priority. They also perceived a higher-quality product. Harbo says, "The approach has become a key selling parameter for us."

Now, three years later, Systematic does all its software development in this way and continues to see significant productivity gains. In addition, the approach is spreading to other parts of the organization.

Looking back on the experience in software development, Harbo says, "Once you introduce this, it affects everything in the organization—the way you plan, the way you manage, the way you work. Everything is different. It changes the game fundamentally."

When I talked with the CEO, Holm, in December 2009, he was feeling the tensions between the teams that were agile and fast moving and the top of the organization. He could see the huge impact that the iterative approach had in software development, but as he looked around the organization, he could see that the software development part of the company was very fast moving and agile, while upper management was still moving like a bureaucracy. The way decisions were being taken was too slow. There was too much reporting and too much paper.

The developers had gone beyond that. They were making decisions in fast cycles with minimal report writing, whereas top management was making decisions based on written reports: a sales report, a human resource report, a report on customer relationship management, a financial report. When new reports arrived, Holm felt he already knew most of what would be in them: they had been produced the previous week and were already partly out of date. Why were people spending time writing about information that would be out of date by the time it was read and telling them mainly what they already knew?

Holm decided that the top management team had to become more agile and work like the software development teams, using real-time information and making decisions in real time. So he told the vice presidents, who all had their own offices, "Out of your offices! We are going to have a common office and work together in a different way."

Once they were in the common office, Holm put whiteboards on all the walls so that people could write on them and post notes. "It's a situation room for the whole corporation," says Holm:

> All the ongoing projects are shown on the charts on the walls. All sales cases are on one board. All projects are on another board. All staffing on another board. We have customer relationship management. We have our financial system. We don't write numbers there that are already in the computer. That's a waste of time.
>
> The whole idea is that when the top management meets every two weeks with the teams, we meet with the vice president and the project or program manager, to find out what they think is important, whether it's on schedule or behind schedule or whatever. And then we see the key issues: customer satisfaction, delivery on time or behind schedule, or whatever. We put a yellow, green, or red paper on the board. So at one glance at the wall, we can see how everything is working, what's going well and where the problems are.

> The idea is that if you need to write a report on the business, you go in there and write it from what's on the wall. There's no reason to write another report because it's already on the wall. And everything is in real time in that room. So when we discuss a project, we have the meeting in that room. During the meeting, we write the decision on the wall. We leave it there. So we can always go in there and have a picture of what the status is.
>
> It gives us tremendous transparency. This isn't about finding out who screwed up. It's about finding out what's really going on and making good decisions in real time. It's also a way of building understanding of the business.

Holm has also been having a fifteen-minute stand-up meeting with the top managers every morning. This enables everyone to find out what's going on. "We have all the vice presidents meet for fifteen minutes in the morning, standing up, and answering the standard questions," he says. "'What did you do yesterday? What are you going to do today? Do you need any help? What's your plan?' It's a quick thing. It's a way to get some focus on common themes. We don't talk about all the financial stuff or whatever if it's not interesting. We take the issues that are the most important on that day. Fifteen minutes every day. We tell each other how it is. It's like soldiers appearing for the morning parade."

The other element that Holm sees the need to develop is more interaction with customers:

> I'd like to see the customer involved in the daily stand-up meetings with the developers. Not every day maybe, but when it's important. Right now, they come here every month, and we go to them every fortnight. So there's already a lot of interaction. But there should be a way to link the customer to the daily stand-ups. It would give them some assurance that we're not just sitting on our hands, that we are really working hard to solve the problems. It would give them the confidence that inside the firm, we are taking them seriously. If they don't know what we are doing for a few weeks or even a month, they may start wondering: What are we doing? If they always know what we are doing, it would be a more confident, trusting relationship. It would be more of a dialogue. That's the direction we want to go.

The Journey of OpenView Venture Partners

OpenView Venture Partners is a Boston-based venture capital fund that got started in September 2006.[13] It invests in small to medium-sized software development firms and provides operational assistance to those firms.

Initially, founding managing director Scott Maxwell introduced iterative methods of developing software—known as Scrum—as a way of improving the performance of its portfolio companies. Once he saw the benefits there, he decided to adopt the approach for OpenView's own activities.

The approach helped deal with the issue of span of control. At the outset, when the firm was tiny, it was natural that everyone reported to the managing director. But as the firm grew, having everyone report to the managing director soon became a problem. Yet Maxwell didn't want to create a hierarchy with departments and divisions.

Maxwell found that working through self-managed and self-accountable teams not only reduced the management overhead on himself; it rapidly increased the quality of the work that the people were doing.

It also dramatically increased the quantity of work that got done, with less stress on each individual. Suddenly people weren't overloaded anymore. They were getting more done but spending less time doing it. Instead of putting in sixty-hour workweeks, staff were home in the evenings and on weekends.

Maxwell combined the work cycles of self-organizing teams with a balanced scorecard approach. At the highest level, the firm's mission, vision, and values are translated into strategic themes and goals for a year. Inside that is a quarterly cycle. And within that, the goals are broken down into initiatives, which can be spelled out in specific user stories to be implemented by the teams in weekly iterations. Maxwell calls it "extraordinary execution" and is introducing it to OpenView's portfolio companies.

Maxwell says the approach works well for software development, because it helps deal with the reality that you can't predict what's going to happen. The traditional management of software development assumes perfect predictability in which the entire project can be laid out from beginning to end, with a beautiful product coming out at the end of it.

"Software development just doesn't work that way," says Maxwell. "To deal with unpredictability, you need to say: 'Hey, let's start with the vision of where we want to go. Then let's figure out what our first release is going to be. How do we get a quick win that we can step back from and reflect on, and incorporate the new information that we have learned, such as the customers having changed their minds, or new insights that have come from the development process itself? Then we ask ourselves, based on where we are today, as well as on our vision of where we want to take this: How do we deal with the next most important set of things to take us in the right direction?"

Maxwell sees the issue of growing the company in the same way. The world next month, or next quarter, is going to look very different from today, because the firm has had an impact on the world and because the world will have changed of its own accord. So drawing up a detailed plan about how exactly it is going to get to where Maxwell wants to be three years from now is a waste of effort.

"Instead," Maxwell says, "we need to put a stake in the ground as to where we want to be in three years and then break that down. If we want to be there in three years, where ideally would we need to be in a year? And then let's break that down further. If we want to be there in a year, what would we have to do? And so on. That then flows into the user stories to be implemented by the teams in weekly iterations."

OpenView has institutionalized the operational assistance to its portfolio firms in a subsidiary called OpenView Labs. It helps the portfolio companies get better than they already are, and helps OpenView do its own work better, similar to continuous improvement at Toyota and Honda.

In mid-2009, I talked with Igor Altman, the leader of one of three such teams in OpenView Labs. Altman told me:

> In terms of working with portfolio companies, we do everything from generating a marketing lead list for salespeople to call on; structuring

a marketing campaign; helping redesign the lead qualification process; redesigning the sales process; analyzing why customers are dropping off at a certain point—whatever is needed.

In my team, we work in one-week cycles, with prioritized lists of tasks to be done, spelled out as stories. I host that meeting every week. We come together, and we help each other with the team's issues. We figure out the priorities among the things to be done. We do the iterative planning. We size the tasks. We have daily stand-ups for fifteen minutes. There are the usual three questions. What did you do yesterday? What are you going to do today? What are your impediments?

And at the end of every iteration, we have a retrospective. What went well? What could have been done better? How do we improve? What are the impediments to doing better?

The biggest issue is in learning to be a real team. I had been in groups called ''teams''' before. I thought I knew what ''team'' meant. But it was here that I found out the fundamental difference in going from individual work to being on a real team.

In this way of managing, you have to be a real team, not a pseudo-team. It's very hard to have a bunch of high-performers, who've been top of their class, and to say to them, ''It isn't your project or his project: it's our project.'' That's a huge shift.

It's very tough. There's a huge amount of face-to-face communication, transparency, and accountability of the team. If you're insecure, this is the worst possible environment for you.

All the rocks are visible. Suddenly everyone is holding you accountable. It's your peers, even people who maybe you feel are junior to you. That can be a problem if you are hierarchically minded, and particularly if you are insecure. Suddenly everyone knows what you are doing and you have to answer to everyone. Even if you are an introvert, you have to speak to everyone, every day.

You can't have your own private ways of doing things anymore. It's not your own project anymore. Now it's the team's project. The question becomes: What's the best way for the team to get this done? That takes a lot of discipline. We're dealing here with a start-up, not a big old bureaucracy. Even so, it's still very easy to do this in a mediocre way.

This way of managing surfaces core issues. Suddenly a lot of problems are visible. People may say: ''These issues weren't a problem before. Now they are a problem. So this way of managing has caused this problem." In reality, the team always had the problem. They just never had to deal with it before. Now it's brought to the surface. Now they have to deal with it.

Some organizations aren't ready to handle that. If there is no trust and people can't communicate openly with each other, this way of managing is a disaster. If the organization isn't ready to deal with those issues, it may be better for the organization to stay as it is. Creating an environment that exposes these issues will actually prevent the organization from getting anything done.

But when you pull it off, it really works, and it turns into a snowball effect. Once the team really starts working as a team, it's no longer the management driving things. The team just starts getting better and better and better. It's the team that's driving itself.

It's not just that we get a lot more done and with higher quality. Since we introduced this, the quality of life at work has also gotten better and better. No more all-nighters or any of that stuff. It's been tremendous fun. It's made me a better person. It's made me to grow in ways that otherwise I wouldn't have grown.

The Outsider as Change Agent: Björn Granvik

Sometimes the agent of change is an outsider. Björn Granvik, whom we met in Chapter Six, is a consultant who helps firms implement the principles of radical management in Java programming in Sweden and neighboring countries. Often he finds himself working with people who don't understand how to self-organize. "They sit there, and they talk about it," says Granvik. "But they haven't got the faintest idea what they're talking about or how it's done. How could they know? Until you have done it and experienced it, how can you decide what are good team practices and what aren't? So the team makes very simple mistakes."

For these kinds of teams, he invokes *Nanny McPhee*, a movie set in nineteenth-century England about a family where the father is often absent and the children are badly behaved. They scare away any nanny who comes along. But one night, Nanny McPhee arrives. She promises that she will teach them five lessons. Initially, when they don't want her, she stays. But when she has done that and they want her to stay, she leaves. He sees his role as similar.

Granvik approaches these teams as Nanny McPhee did the children. At the start, there are no options, and they hate him. But then they see how it works and they get it. They want him to stay. But Granvik says, "No, now I will leave. You don't need me anymore." He applies the same approach to managers, who also make simple mistakes. In many cases, management hasn't seen any basis for trust. How could they trust a team that has never delivered on time? It requires a leap of faith. Granvik finds that if he can get them to go along for a couple of iterations and see the team deliver, management can see for itself that it works. Both management and the team agree to suspend judgment and do what he says for a couple of iterations.

Granvik deals with two types of situations. The bottom-up approach is where the programmers have heard about the new methods and want to adopt them. The top-down approach occurs when management has heard that the team can go twice as fast or do things in half the time and they want to have that for their firm.

Granvik prefers the bottom-up situation because the people who are to do the work are ready to move, and it's not too difficult to persuade the management to go along. Top-down is more difficult. That's where he needs to be Nanny McPhee and become a sideways force to counteract whatever comes down from the top as a dogma.

The Journey of Salesforce.com

When radical management is introduced in one part of the organization, there is always some tension at the interface between the part of the company still doing traditional management and the part doing radical management. The two parts are operating in different ways and at different speeds. One way of solving the problem is to go all out on radical management right across the whole organization.

This is what happened in 2007 at Salesforce.com, a billion-dollar company in Silicon Valley. It astonished the world of software development by successfully completing a transformation from traditional management to the practices of radical management in three months.[14]

The conventional wisdom is that implementation requires staff buy-in, and so a gradualist approach is needed. Salesforce.com did the opposite. Contrary to all the experts' expectations, it was successful.

Developer Mike Cohn reports: "During the first year of making the switch, Salesforce.com released 94 percent more features, delivered 38 percent more features per developer, and delivered over 500 percent more value to their customers compared to the previous year. . . . Fifteen months after adopting Scrum, Salesforce.com surveyed its employees and found that 86 percent were having a 'good time' or the 'best time' working at the company. Prior to adopting Scrum, only 40 percent said the same thing. Further, 92 percent of employees said they would recommend an agile approach to others."[15]

How did this come to pass? Salesforce.com provides on-demand services for customer-relationship management. It routinely processes over 100 million transactions a day and has over 900,000 subscribers. The services technology group is responsible for all product development inside the firm and has grown 50 percent per year since its inception eight years ago. In its early years, the group was delivering an average of four major releases each year. By 2006, the pace had slowed to one major release a year.

The problems were the familiar ones of software development. The work was being done in a conventional sequential fashion. Software was late. Schedules were never met. Bugs were accumulating. Management couldn't figure out exactly what was happening. The features that the teams needed to be working on weren't clear until late in the production cycle. As the size of the teams grew, productivity declined.

One of the company founders, the head of the R&D technology group, saw the need for change. He created a cross-functional team to address the problems of slowing velocity, decreased predictability, and product stability. This team rebuilt the development process from the ground up using key values from the company's founding: keeping things simple, iterating quickly, and listening to customers. These values were a natural match for radical management practices.

The leadership saw the transformation not so much as a wholly new approach, but rather a return to the firm's core values. Three other elements helped the transition. First, the firm's on-demand software model was a natural fit for iterative methods. Second, an extensive automated test system was already in place to provide the backbone of the new methodology. And third, a majority of the R&D organization was working at the same location.

A document was prepared describing the new process, its benefits, and why the firm was moving away from the old process. The team held forty-five one-hour meetings with key people from all levels in the organization. Feedback from these meetings was incorporated into the document after each meeting, molding the design of the new process and creating broad organizational support for change. This open communication feedback loop allowed a large number of people to participate in the design of the new process and engage actively in the solution.

One team in the organization had already successfully run a high-visibility project using iterative methods. This experience helped when they introduced it to all the other teams.

At this point, the conventional wisdom would have been to pursue an incremental approach using pilot projects and a slow rollout. The management instead opted for a "big-bang rollout," moving all teams to the new process at the same time. It was a difficult decision. The key factor driving it was a wish to avoid organizational dissonance and a desire for decisive action. Everyone would be doing the same thing at the same time.

The process started by sending a large group of people (initially program and functional managers) to training and buying training books for all staff. Three key members from the cross-functional team developed a consolidated presentation and training deck that included concepts from the current methodology. Two-hour training sessions were held for every team. In addition, training was given to the proxy client representatives who would be setting priorities as "product owners." They also created an internal, wiki-based Web site as a reference for team members as they made the transition to the new methodology and for information about the change process.

The cross-functional team did its work in an iterative fashion and focused daily on whatever was needed to make the implementation successful. It created a global schedule for the entire process, provided coaching and guidance, identified and removed systemic impediments to change, monitored success, and evangelized the new way of working throughout the organization.

Key features of the change included a focus on team output rather than individual productivity and cross-functional teams that met daily. All teams used a simple iterative process with a common vocabulary, with prioritized work programs for each iteration. They planned the work with user stories, estimated tasks with planning poker, and defined organizational roles using the common Scrum terminology for all teams. The result was a new release of software every thirty days.

In their own review of the lessons learned from the experience, managers Chris Fry and Steve Greene included several factors:[16]

- *Strong executive support.* At several points in the transition, boundaries were tested, and without strong executive support, the transition might have failed. For example, a key executive decision was to stick to the release date regardless of the content of the release. Although many teams argued for more time to add more features, the executive management team stuck to the release date. Their ability to hold firm reinforced the principles of delivering early and often, reducing waste, and sticking to the deadline no matter what.
- *A strong nucleus to lead the charge.* Having a dedicated, fully empowered leadership team built from a cross-section of the organization also helped. This team was empowered to make decisions, used the new methodology for its own work, and held meetings in a public space where everyone could see what was going on. This enhanced accessibility, transparency, and shared ownership of the transition.

It also brought in industry experts and other companies that had adopted similar techniques.

- *Principles ahead of mechanics.* Focusing on the principles rather than the mechanics also helped people understand why the firm was moving to a new way of working. When teams ran into a problem, they could refer back to the principles and adjust anything they thought did not correlate with the principles.
- *Total openness.* During the introduction, radical transparency was a key to success. All of the daily meetings were held in a public place so that everyone could see how things were progressing. A task board was displayed on the public lunchroom wall so that everyone had access to what was going on. The willingness to share information with everyone enabled people to adapt on a daily basis to what was happening.

The Journey of Thogus Products

Where a company is young like Salesforce.com or Total Attorneys, the transition may be a relatively straightforward return to its recent roots as a start-up. When a company is fifty years old and with no history of innovation, the transition may be more disruptive.

For example, Thogus Products Company was founded in 1950 and is headquartered in the heart of the rust belt, near Cleveland, Ohio. Under CEO Matt Hlavin, Thogus is now in its third generation of family ownership.

In 1997, when Hlavin joined the company's sales staff, Thogus had about $8.5 million in sales and around 120 employees. It was a traditionally managed company with little innovation and no investment in capital equipment or technology. The goal was to produce goods with the cheapest labor possible and run as many parts as possible, principally for the large auto companies.

At that time, management saw that the firm wouldn't be able to sustain itself on commodity work in high volumes. As a result, it decided to get out of the commodity business and instead focus on developing innovative solutions for metal-to-plastic conversion, working closely with large chemical companies, and specializing in highly engineered materials, with custom solutions in small volumes. It used rapid prototyping and tooling technologies to take the cost out of the development cycle and expedite development.

Initially the transition went at a measured pace. The firm had plenty of cash and could afford to proceed in two- to five-year development cycles. It steadily developed new customer and market segments. It moved away from a principal focus on long production runs for the auto companies to customized products for a diverse mix of customers in the medical, electronics, automotive, lawn and garden, heating and air-conditioning, aerospace, and food and beverage sectors. In an industry where many molders were struggling or going out of business, Thogus was growing.

When Hlavin took over as CEO in 2008, he decided that the time was ripe to go all-out with the new strategy. The problem was that many of the staff had yet to make the transition. This was the result of poor hiring practices over the years, so that many people were in positions for which they weren't really suited.

In February 2009, after a careful evaluation of the employees, their work ethic, and their ability to change, Thogus went from 110 employees to 53. It made new investments to automate the facility with rapid prototyping and manufacturing technology. Hlavin hired 9 new engineers, some still in college and others who had been in the field for fifteen years.

Today Thogus has 61 staff. After halving the staff, the output is up 67 percent.

Hlavin sees the company as an incubator of manufacturing ideas. The focus is on the next greatest invention, the next greatest idea. Hlavin says, "We are creating an environment where anyone can come in and sit down with our people and together develop the concept and manufacture a part for them in a day or two for a minimal fee."

The focus on teams, the next-generation manufacturing facility, and the strong innovation culture have made Thogus a fun place to work for those who are willing to learn. Hlavin's proudest day will be when an employee comes to him and says: "I'm going to start my own company, and the genesis was from Thogus." He believes that if he can help create new companies, new products, new ideas, it not only spurs the economy. It spurs the creative spirit.

What We Can Learn from These Stories

Here are some pointers.

Radical Management Happens Organically or Not at All

Radical management changes everything in the organization. A significant effort is needed to make it happen, even when there is no long history of being managed in a traditional fashion. Radical management is a different way of thinking, acting, and speaking—a different way of seeing and interacting with the world. It embodies certain values, principles, and practices. As a result, it will happen in an organic fashion or not at all.

Everyone Can Be a Radical Manager

Anyone who adopts the values, principles, and practices of radical management can be a radical manager. No hierarchical decision is required for anyone to start focusing on delighting clients and collaborating with others in iterations, acting in total openness, and engaging in interactive conversations.

Whereas traditional management can happen only when someone is appointed as a manager, radical management can break out whenever people start espousing its values, principles, and practices. It is in this sense that radical management is not only disruptive of the status quo because of its productivity gains. It is also deeply subversive: it changes people's attitudes toward management. Everyone can contribute.

Top management has a special responsibility for creating the setting where radical management becomes possible. An external coach may be well positioned to share the experience of prior examples of radical management and help the team avoid pitfalls that others have fallen into.

The line manager has particular responsibilities for setting priorities and clarifying direction.

Some aspects are best done by the team members themselves. In fact, it is the rank-and-file members of the team who may be best able to provide the kind of peer coaching that will refocus and refine the implementation of the practices of radical management.

Thus, even those with no hierarchical power have a contribution to make toward implementing radical management. Those who espouse radical management who are working in an organization—even one run by traditional managers—can share the philosophy with others and can spread the word. They can educate others as to how work should be organized and what management should be like. They can start focusing their own work on delighting clients. They can start self-organizing with others who share their views. They can start arranging their own work in client-driven iterations, even if it isn't formally set up this way. They can engage in interactive conversations. In effect, they can start practicing radical management even though the hierarchy has not given them a license to do so.

The question then, to paraphrase Richard Hackman, is not who provides radical management but rather how much radical management the work space is getting.[17]

The Distinction Between Leadership and Management Dissolves

In traditional management, leadership is about promoting change, while management is about keeping the organization running smoothly—that is, bureaucracy. In radical management, the distinction between leadership and management dissolves. There is no difference between leadership and management. Managers are committed to change, and leaders also manage. Radical management is about making continuous innovation happen.

Outsiders Can Help Momentum

Responsibility for making radical management happen extends beyond the organization. Job applicants who have espoused the principles of radical management can look for organizations that are run by radical managers and create pressure in the job market for radical management.

Similarly, customers who embrace radical management can demand it from the organizations they do business with. They can expect to be delighted. If they are not, they can make their voices heard. They can shift their business to organizations that listen, respond, and are doing their best to delight them. They can accelerate market pressures for the change towards radical management.

WHAT WILL BE YOUR STORY?

What will implementation mean for you?

Close your eyes for a moment and think about what would happen in your organization if you were to implement radical management. What would your story look like? It will be different from the experiences that I have been recounting here.

In your journey of creation, you will find it useful to know how other managers have developed their methods, solved their problems, or found solutions that you might otherwise have missed. From them, you can learn the stones to step on, the stones to avoid. But there is no road map. The routes that they have followed may have been right for them. In the end, you have to make your own way. It is your own mindfulness and intuition that will enable you to step into the future.

In this effort, it's important to remember that your ability to connect with other human beings is simple and deep. Human beings are all born with mirror neurons that enable even babies to read their parents' minds, creating the foundation for communication, interaction, and collaboration. You have the innate ability to create extraordinary groups at this very moment, just as you are.

Whatever you create, it will be a story that you believe in because you have created it. Even better, because it is your own story, you may persuade others that it holds promise and induce them to pursue it in their context.

The future will thus come about not only from the story that you are reading here, but also from the story that you are beginning to create. It is your story that will make the difference between a mere transmittal of information and a fruitful new future.

So from here on, it's up to you. You have a chance to remake your workplace. It will be difficult, thrilling, frightening, and exciting, all at once. Your story will come from an understanding gathered from learning about the experiences of others and recreating the idea in your own environment, trying it out, experimenting, learning from failure, discussing and exploring it, not as a spectator but as a participant.

There will be times when nothing works, the task seems hopeless, and everyone is tempted to abandon the effort and retreat back to the old practices. But with persistence, courage, and humility, you can overcome the problems as you make your way.

Finally, when you are done and you have a workplace that is humming, vibrant, full of life, and highly productive, it will be time to look at what you have accomplished with a fresh, unprejudiced eye and see how it can be made even better.

How can you delight the clients more and sooner? Are people being open with each other? Are the root causes of problems being identified and resolved? Are the values of radical management intact and practiced? Do you see the human spirit alive and glowing? Do you see smiling faces and shining eyes?

PRACTICES TO SUPPORT IMPLEMENTATION OF RADICAL MANAGEMENT

Many of the practices here are described in more detail in my books, *The Leader's Guide to Storytelling* and *The Secret Language of Leadership*, and in Seth Kahan's book, *Getting Change Right*.[18]

Practice #1: ***Adapt Radical Management to Your Context***

Just as in the military, no plan of battle survives the first contact with the enemy, so no organizational change plan survives the first involvement with the people who are involved in execution. The process of adaptation never ends.

Practice #2: ***Form a Strong Nucleus to Lead the Charge***

A high-performance team will be needed to inspire and guide implementation. Dutiful or representative performance won't get the job done. This will be a group that is creative and energized, trusts one another, and is willing to do whatever it takes.

Practice #3: ***Proceed Through Conversations***

As explained in Chapter Ten, communications are interactive and based on social norms. The change needs to happen organically. One person starts talking to and inspiring other people, who in turn have the courage, determination, and communication skills to fire up fresh groups of people to imagine and implement a different future. In turn, they become champions and inspire others.

Practice #4: ***Establish a Beachhead***

Establishing a beachhead is important. All of the apparently successfully large-scale implementations that I have encountered have had at least some people on hand who had seen it and done it before and could say, "I've seen this work!" Creating a beachhead of such people is thus an important early step.

Practice #5: ***Begin in a Safe Space***

In the first few iterations, bumps and bruises are to be expected. Until people get the hang of it, some missteps are likely. It is therefore prudent to try it out in the first instance in a relatively safe and low-profile space.

Practice #6: *Agree on a Common Terminology*

When fundamentally different ideas are being introduced, confusions and misunderstandings are inevitable. To the extent that a common terminology can be defined, made easily accessible, and consistently used, the transition will be easier.

Practice #7: *Let the Idea Evolve*

This is not a matter of crafting a vision and then rolling it out unchanged across the organization. It's about continuously adapting the idea to the evolving circumstances of the organization. As the people in the organization adapt the story of change to their own contexts, it becomes their own story. A sense of ownership grows.

Practice #8: *Get Outside Help, But Don't Depend on It*

Learn from others who have gone on this journey before. Their journey will be different from yours, but they can alert you to pitfalls and accelerate your search for solutions to problems.

Use outside help. Intellectual energy is generated by cognitive diversity and interactions among people with different backgrounds and different ways of looking at the world. But don't depend on this help: it is dangerous to follow external advice slavishly and let others dictate the change. Evaluate the advice, and adapt it to the local needs. In the process of adapting it, the idea becomes owned. Things are not done simply because outsiders say so. They are done because they make sense in this context.

Practice #9: *Communicate the Idea Through Stories*

Springboard stories communicate the spirit of an idea and generate new stories in the minds of the listeners, which drive them into action and spark more stories that are told to others. Learn from *The Leader's Guide to Storytelling* and *The Secret Language of Leadership*. Rehearse your story before you start making a presentation to senior management. Be ready when the opportunity calls.[19]

Practice #10: *Get the Support of the Hierarchy, But Don't Depend on It*

The heart of radical management is based on social norms, not command and control. This is about inspiring people's hearts and minds, not telling them what to do. Although implementation of radical management cannot be accomplished by top-down directives or rollout programs, the support of the very top of the organization is key to creating the mandate for change. In a large organization, the top needs the support of many others to help communicate the idea throughout the organization.

Practice #11: ***Energize Your Most Influential Players***

People are at the heart of change. Take the time to engage them, and give them exciting ways to be part of the action.

Practice #12: ***Understand the Territory of Change***

Take steps to understand the territory of change, figuring out the culture and how to go forward. Listen in order to create a map of the change territory.

Practice #13: ***Form Groups of Enthusiasts Who Share the Passion***

Form groups of people who share passion for the idea and put this passion into practice. These groups advance the cause, creating systemic pull.

Practice #14: ***Generate Dramatic Surges in Progress***

Create special face-to-face events that accelerate the program. Create gatherings that bring players together in high-value, high-leverage experiences designed to push things forward in leaps and bounds.

Practice #15: ***Anticipate Logjams, and Break Through Them***

Break through logjams with a SWAT team mentality. Expect trouble. By confronting it early, you will find ways to fix it quickly.

Practice #16: ***Work Sustainable Hours***

Although occasional crises may require extended working periods, regularly working long hours is highly unproductive and leads to low-quality output. Long working hours are a sign of serious management malfunction.

12

EPILOGUE

> In our time, what is at issue is the very nature of man, the image we have of his limits and possibilities as man.
>
> **C. Wright Mills[1]**

Laughter is one thing that struck me about people practicing radical management. I don't know whether it's a truly universal characteristic, but it certainly is pervasive. Of course, I also saw periods of intense concentration and moments of dismay and alarm. But laughter was never far away. It could not be suppressed for long. It would break out in quips and cracks, a bond between those joined together in pursuing something worthwhile. Sometimes it was dark humor, even gallows humor in the face of impending disaster, but the laughter was always close to the surface, ready to explode at any moment.

If you're not hearing laughter, it's a sign you're still in the land of traditional management. The laughter of radical management is not laughter at the misfortunes of others or at those who have offended a powerful patron. Laughter in radical management is laughter with others—those with whom we have discovered that the end it seemed we were coming to has unexpectedly opened up. New possibilities are now obvious.

By contrast, my encounters with traditional management were always deadly serious. Jokes about the hierarchy were not tolerated. That's because laughing at the hierarchy puts the power structure in question. In traditional management, the power structure is no laughing matter. In radical management, jokes about the hierarchy are possible. People are doing what they are doing because they believe in it, not because of the power structure.

Once you understand radical management and the idea of delighting clients, many of the practices of traditional bureaucracy appear comical or pointless. There is an acute danger that you will pause and see no reason to continue them.

SIMPLE TO UNDERSTAND, DIFFICULT TO IMPLEMENT

The principles of radical management are simple to understand. People do best what they do for themselves in the service of delighting others. When they are in charge of their own behavior, they take responsibility for it. When they are able to work on something worthwhile with others who enjoy doing the same thing, the group tends to get better. By working in short cycles, everyone can see the impact of what is being done. When people are open about what is going on, problems get solved. Innovation occurs. Clients are surprised to find that even their unexpressed desires are being met. Work becomes, as Noel Coward suggested, more fun than fun.

The principles are less easy to implement. That's partly because radical management is very different from traditional management. It's a different way of thinking, speaking, and acting in the workplace. It has different goals. It involves different ways of looking at things, different ways of organizing, and different ways of interacting with people. Everything, in fact, is different.

Managerial habits change slowly. Traditional practices linger in people's minds as the default mental model of how to behave. The intent to do things differently is present, but entrenched policies, procedures, and structures act as a drag. Deep-seated values and worldviews that shape people's lives help preserve the status quo. Business schools and textbooks continue to teach outdated methodologies.

Yet even mediocre implementation generates benefits. And when execution is fully successful, the gains for all parties—organization, managers, workers, and clients—can be extraordinary.

Accountants will dwell on the measurable benefits, and certainly these are important. Recognizing their presence will generate support for the approach and drive it forward. Yet if we focus only on what is measurable, we may miss how the gains have been made. We may overlook the fact that any group practicing radical management has a certain lively quality. Once we understand this quality, we have a way of understanding what is happening at a deeper level.

Radical management is more than a process, more than a system, more than a methodology, and more than a way of organizing. It's an invitation into a world where things happen differently. It's a set of values, principles, and practices that spark the passion, excitement, and insights of the people who work in the organization. It ignites delight in those for whom the work is done. It also happens to be much more productive than traditional management. And it means having serious fun.

Many different types of human groups have achieved and sustained this high level of energy, excitement, and productivity. It has occurred in different industries, countries, and cultures. Once you see how and why these groups operate as they do, it becomes possible to understand what makes them alive and vibrant, as well as what makes traditional management so stagnant.

Once we see what these groups have in common, we can understand and master what's involved in generating and sustaining them for ourselves. There are no templates, no ready-made answers. We have the capacity to create them as we go, constantly taking stock of where we are and thinking through where we need to head next.

THE SPIRIT OF RADICAL MANAGEMENT

In taking the steps necessary to implement the principles of radical management, it's easy to get lost in the nuts and bolts of process: the details of setting up teams, the practices, the artifacts, the terminologies, the gatherings and their agendas. It's easy to focus on the paraphernalia and lose sight of the point: to create groups with a certain quality. It's easy to fall into a mechanical, dutiful performance of certain predetermined steps without putting our hearts into it. If we do that, we will fail.

For over a century, we have been using systems of things to get work done. That's why it's so easy for those who seek to control us to play on our fears. They will try to persuade us that we must have more systems in case we reveal and ignite the emotions that energize and inspire.

These inanimate systems were a good fit for much of the twentieth century, but that era is over. A new era is upon us.

MAKING FRIENDS WITH SURPRISE

The attitude toward surprise is another of the great divides between the traditional and radical management. Traditional managers live in dread of the unpredictable. Surprise brings traditional management to a halt, and the world no longer corresponds to the plan. The plan must be revised so that the future can be a copy of the plan!

In radical management, surprise is welcomed as the source of future growth. Surprise generates delight. With each surprise, the past reveals new beginnings that were previously hidden. New possibilities open up.

Surprise is why, in the short term, the stock market will constitute a constraint. The stock market hates surprises. It loves companies that project a facade of predictability. "The management forecast a certain level of revenue and profit, and it did slightly better. Bravo! Let's buy!"

Do none of these smart people detect anything fishy in projecting regularity in a world that is highly irregular? Do none of them wonder about the means by which a company hits its numbers?

Is it possible to imagine the stock market seeing the ephemeral gains of bad profits for what they are and paying more attention to the real source of long-term growth: client delight? In the short term, perhaps not. But these are clever people. In the financial world, the edge goes to those who can ascertain root causes rather than risk money on funny numbers.[2]

A time is thus coming in the not-too-distant future when the main topic of discussion at the analyst's phone-in with the chief financial officer will be a review of the firm's audited net promoter scores rather than its fudged quarterly financial numbers.

MEANING IN WORK AND AT WORK IS PART OF BEING HUMAN

Is radical management realistic?

Social critic Alain de Botton writes:

> The strangest thing about the world of work is the widespread expectation that our work should make us happy. For thousands of years, work was viewed as something to be done with as rapidly as possible and escaped in the imagination through alcohol or religion. Aristotle was the first of many philosophers to state that no one could be both free and obliged to earn a living. A more optimistic assessment of work had to wait until the eighteenth century and men like Jean-Jacques Rousseau and Benjamin Franklin, who for the first time argued that one's working life could be at the centre of any desire for happiness. It was during this century that our modern ideas about work were formed.[3]

Thus emerged what would have seemed to Aristotle a very odd idea: that we might both work for money and realize our dreams. This idea has replaced the previous assumption that our work put food on the table. Anything more ambitious was a question for our leisure hours.

We are the heirs of the ambitious goal of Rousseau and Franklin: we dare to believe that we can both do work and experience deep satisfaction from doing it. It is now as impossible for us to think that we could do no work and be happy as it was impossible for Aristotle to think that we could be both employed and free. Finding meaning in work and at work has become part of what it means to be human.

RADICAL MANAGEMENT IS PART OF A LARGER STORY

I spent the first four decades of my life gazing at the vast and somber edifice of the Soviet Union. Grim, impregnable, and despotic, it seemed destined to last forever. Yet economically it was rotting from within. When the Berlin Wall came down, the edifice abruptly collapsed.

Now dictatorships are an endangered species around the world. Those few that do remain feel obliged to put on a semblance of democracy with rigged elections and phony votes. Even they know that the world has changed. Human beings are no longer willing to live under tyranny.

The vast and somber edifices of the traditional corporation still stand. Grim and impregnable, they also seem destined to last forever. Yet they are also rotting from within: the return on their assets is only a quarter of what it was just a few decades ago. Their life expectancy is already startlingly brief—no more than two decades on average, even based on past experience. The despotic management practices that are causing the decline are anachronisms from a former era. It is only a matter of time before they come to be seen as uneconomic and intolerable as despotism in the political sphere.

Radical management is thus part of a larger story, an emerging process of societal change, in which the structures that we build are adjusted to enhance rather than strangle the living part of our lives.

At its best, radical management clarifies and magnifies human capacity. By opening those pathways by which human beings become productive, it brings an increase in existence for those doing work and those for whom the work is done. Through creating the space where we can live mindfully and wholeheartedly, it enlarges what may be known, what may be felt, what may be done.

APPENDIX: SUMMARY OF RADICAL MANAGEMENT PRACTICES

Delighting Clients (Chapter Four)

Practice #1: Identify your primary clients.

Practice #2: Delight primary clients by meeting their unrecognized desires.

Practice #3: Aim for the simplest possible thing that will delight.

Practice #4: Explore the possibility of delighting more by offering less.

Practice #5: Explore more alternatives.

Practice #6: Defer decisions until the last responsible moment.

Practice #7: Avoid mechanistic approaches.

Practice #8: Focus on people, not things.

Practice #9: Give the people doing the work a clear line of sight to the people for whom the work is being done.

Self-Organizing Teams (Chapter Five)

Practice #1: Articulate a compelling purpose in terms of delighting clients.

Practice #2: Consistently communicate a passionate belief in the worth of the purpose.

Practice #3: Transfer power to the team.

Practice #4: Make the transfer of power conditional on the team's accepting responsibility to deliver.

Practice #5: Recognize the contributions of the people doing the work.

Practice #6: Make sure that remuneration is perceived as fair.

Practice #7: Consistently use tools and techniques that create and sustain self-organizing teams.

Client-Driven Iterations (Chapter Six)

Practice #1: Focus on stakeholders and what is of value for them.

Practice #2: Identify the principal performance objective for the primary stakeholders.

Practice #3: Consider how to deliver more value sooner or cheaper.

Practice #4: Decide as late as responsibly possible what work is to be included in the iteration.

Practice #5: Have the client or client proxy participate in deciding priorities for the iteration.

Practice #6: Ensure that the team doing the work knows who speaks for the client.

Practice #7: Spell out the goals of each iteration before the iteration begins.

Practice #8: Define the goal of the iteration in the form of user stories.

Practice #9: Treat the user story as the beginning, not the end, of a conversation.

Practice #10: Keep the user stories simple and record them informally.

Practice #11: Display the user stories in the workplace.

Practice #12: Be ready to discuss the stories with the client or client proxy.

Practice #13: Find out more about the client's world.

Practice #14: In the user story, include a test to determine when the story has been fully executed.

Practice #15: Provide coaching to encourage good team practices.

Delivering Value to Clients (Chapter Seven)

Practice #1: Focus on finishing the most important work first.

Practice #2: Ensure that user stories are ready to be worked on.

Practice #3: Have the team itself estimate how much time work will take.

Practice #4: Give the team the responsibility for deciding how much work it can do in an iteration.

Practice #5: Let the team decide how to do the work in the iteration.

Practice #6: Encourage open communication within the team.

Practice #7: Systematically identify and remove impediments to getting work done.

Practice #8: Don't interrupt the team in the course of an iteration.

Practice #9: Have the team work sustainable hours.

Practice #10: Fix problems as soon as they are identified.

Practice #11: Measure progress in terms of value delivered to clients.

Practice #12: At the end of the iteration, get feedback from the client or the client proxy.

Practice #13: Calculate the velocity of the team.

Practice #14: Conduct a retrospective review of what has been learned in the iteration and how the next iteration can be improved.

Radical Transparency (Chapter Eight)

Radical Transparency Within the Team

Practice #1: Have the team estimate how much time work will take.

Practice #2: Let the team decide how much work to undertake.

Practice #3: Calculate the team's velocity after each iteration.

Practice #4: Have the team members stay in contact with each other on a daily basis.

Practice #5: Conduct retrospective reviews at the end of each iteration.

Practice #6: Use informal visual displays of progress.

Transparency of the Team in Relation to Management

Practice #7: Deliver value to clients at the end of each iteration.

Practice #8: Systematically identify impediments in the daily stand-up meetings.

Transparency of Management in Relation to the Team

Practice #9: Set priorities for work at the beginning of each iteration.

Practice #10: Go and see what is happening in the workplace and in the marketplace.

Practice #11: Establish a clear line of sight from the team to the client.

Practice #12: Systematically help remove impediments.

Practice #13: Accept two-sided accountability.

Continuous Self-Improvement (Chapter Nine)

Practice #1: Give the team a clear line of sight to the client.

Practice #2: Give the team the opportunity to excel.

Practice #3: Align the team's interests with those of the organization.

Practice #4: Calculate the team's velocity.

Practice #5: Get to the root causes of problems.

Practice #6: Systematically remove impediments from the team's work.

Practice #7: Share rather than enforce improved practices.

Practice #8: Foster the formation of horizontal communities of practice.

Practice #9: Remain systematically open to outside ideas.

Practice #10: Embrace the need for continuous improvement.

Interactive Communication (Chapter Ten)

Practice #1: Use authentic storytelling to inspire a passion for delighting clients.

Practice #2: Focus the goals of the team on user stories.

Practice #3: Deploy user stories as catalysts for conversation.

Practice #4: Use stories to focus teams on achieving high performance.

Practice #5: Use stories to help team members understand who they are.

Practice #6: Use stories to inspire group *philia.*

Practice #7: Stimulate the muscle memory of high-performance teams.

Practice #8: Tell springboard stories of other high-performance teams.

Practice #9: Practice deeply listening to each other's story.

Practice #10: Give recognition for identifying impediments.

Implementation of Radical Change Management (Chapter Eleven)

Practice #1: Adapt radical management to your context.

Practice #2: Form a strong nucleus to lead the charge.

Practice #3: Proceed through conversations.

Practice #4: Establish a beachhead.

Practice #5: Begin in a safe space.

Practice #6: Agree on a common terminology.

Practice #7: Let the idea evolve.

Practice #8: Get outside help, but don't depend on it.

Practice #9: Communicate the idea through stories.

Practice #10: Get the support of the hierarchy, but don't depend on it.

Practice #11: Energize your most influential players.

Practice #12: Understand the territory of change.

Practice #13: Form groups of enthusiasts who share the passion.

Practice #14: Generate dramatic surges in progress.

Practice #15: Anticipate logjams, and break through them.

Practice #16: Work sustainable hours.

NOTES

PREFACE

1. Deloitte Center for the Edge. *Measuring the Forces of Long-Term Change: The 2009 Shift Index*. 2009. http://www.edgeperspectives.com/shiftindex.pdf.
2. Deloitte Center for the Edge. *Measuring the Forces of Long-Term Change: The 2009 Shift Index*. Friedman, T. "Start-Ups, Not Bailouts." *New York Times*, Apr. 3, 2010. http://www.nytimes.com/2010/04/04/opinion/04friedman.html?hp.
3. I am indebted to Hans Samios, a manager at Intergraph Corporation in Alabama, who contacted me and suggested that I check out what was happening in software development firms.
4. The term was also used in Culbert, S. A., and McDonough, J. J. *Radical Management: Power Politics and the Pursuit of Trust.* New York: Free Press, 1985.

INTRODUCTION

1. Pirsig, R. *Zen and the Art of Motorcycle Maintenance.* New York: Morrow, 1974, p. 94.
2. As explained in Chapter Four, much of the thinking behind client delight as a goal builds on the work of Fred Reichheld: *The Ultimate Question: Driving Good Profits and True Growth.* Boston: Harvard Business School Press, 2006. See also: "Wow?" Net Promoter Blogs, Sept. 23, 2008. http://netpromoter.typepad.com/fred_reichheld/2008/09/wow.html.
3. Rust, R. T., Moorman, C., and Bhalia, G. "Rethinking Marketing." *Harvard Business Review,* Jan.-Feb. 2010, pp. 94–101.
4. Hamel, G. "Moonshots for Management." *Harvard Business Review*, Feb. 2009, pp. 91–98 at 92.
5. "Towers Perrin Global Workforce Study." 2007–2008. http://www.towersperrin.com/tp/getwebcachedoc?webc=HRS/USA/2008/200802/

GWS_handout_web.pdf. Conference Board. "U.S. Job Satisfaction at Lowest Level in Two Decades." Jan. 5, 2010. http://www.conference-board.org/utilities/pressDetail.cfm?press_ID=3820. See also the Deloitte Shift Index: "75 to 80 percent of the workforce lacks passion for the work they perform on a daily basis. This is particularly significant given the strong correlation between Worker Passion and more active participation in knowledge flows. If companies are serious about more effective participation in knowledge flows, they must find ways to draw out greater passion from their workers." Deloitte Center for the Edge. *Measuring the Forces of Long-Term Change: The 2009 Shift Index*. 2009. http://www.deloitte.com/us/shiftindex. Similar results, with country variations, are reported in a European Working Conditions Survey, "Eurofound," discussed in Bolton, S. C., and Houlihan, M. (eds.). *Work Matters: Cultural Reflections on Contemporary Work*. New York: Palgrave Macmillan, 2009.

6. Cohn, M. *Succeeding with Agile: Software Developing Using Scrum*. Upper Saddle River, N.J.: Addison-Wesley, 2009, p. 101.

CHAPTER ONE

1. Hamel, G. "Moonshots for Management." *Harvard Business Review*, Feb. 2009, pp. 91–98.

2. *Falling return on assets:* The return on assets for U.S. public companies had declined by 75 percent since 1965: Deloitte Center for the Edge. *Measuring the Forces of Long-Term Change: The Shift Index*. 2009. http://www.edgeperspectives.com/shiftindex.pdf.

   Declining innovation: The proportion of truly innovative products in corporate portfolios decreased by more than 30 percent between 1990 and 2004: Smith, P. G. *Flexible Product Development*. San Francisco: Jossey-Bass, 2007.

   Declining trust in brands: The percentage of trustworthy brands has declined from 52 percent to 22 percent in just eleven years. Gerzema, J., and Lebar, E. "The Trouble with Brands." *Strategy and Business*, May 25, 2009. http://www.strategy-business.com/article/09205.

   High-performance teams are rare: Only 2 percent of teams could be considered high-performance teams. Logan, L., King, J., and Fischer-Wright, H. *Tribal Leadership: Leveraging Natural Groups to Build a Thriving Organization*. New York: HarperBusiness, 2008.

Outsourcing has diminished the capacity to compete: Pisano, G. P., and Shih, W. C. "Restoring American Competitiveness." *Harvard Business Review,* July-Aug. 2009, pp. 114–125.

New entrants to the workplace are less willing to accept traditional management practices: Tulgan, B. *Not Everyone Gets a Trophy: How to Manage Generation Y.* San Francisco: Jossey-Bass, 2009.

3. Paul's tale is fictional and does not portray any actual company or individual. It is inspired in part by Crawford, M. *Shop Class as Soulcraft: An Inquiry into the Value of Work.* New York: Penguin, 2009.
4. Alan's tale is fictional and does not portray any actual company or individual. It is inspired in part by de Botton, A. *The Pleasures and Sorrows of Work.* New York: Penguin, 2009, chap. 8.
5. Nathalie's tale is fictional and does not portray any actual company or individual.
6. Ben's tale is fictional and does not portray any actual company or individual. It is inspired in part by Crawford, *Shop Class as Soulcraft;* Gladwell, M. "The Sure Thing." *New Yorker,* Jan. 18, 2010, pp. 24–29.
7. Connie's tale is fictional and does not portray any actual company or individual.
8. Drucker, P. *Post-Capitalist Society.* New York: HarperBusiness, 1993.

CHAPTER TWO

1. Berlin, I. *The Crooked Timber of Humanity: Chapters in the History of Ideas.* New York: Random House, 1959, p. 2.
2. Drucker, P. *Post-Capitalist Society.* New York: HarperBusiness, 1993, p. 65.
3. De Botton, A. *The Pleasures and Sorrows of Work.* New York: Penguin, 2009, p. 244.
4. "2007–2008 Towers Perrin Global Workforce Study." http://www.towersperrin.com/tp/getwebcachedoc?webc=HRS/USA/2008/200802/GWS_handout_web.pdf.
5. This paragraph draws heavily on Fred Reichheld's blog and the subsequent discussion, posted Sept. 23, 2008, at http://netpromoter.typepad.com/fred_reichheld/2008/09/wow.html.

6. Where the firm has the good fortune to find itself in a quasi-monopoly position, like Microsoft between 1990 and 2010, the milking of the cash cow may go on for some time in extraordinary quantities. But an inability to innovate will eventually catch up with any organization. For instance, Microsoft has had difficulty in competing with Google on search and in competing with Apple on mp3 players. Now cloud computing poses a threat to its Windows quasi-monopoly.
7. Martin, R. "The Age of Customer Capitalism." *Harvard Business Review*, Jan. 2010, pp. 58–65.
8. Drucker, P. *Post-Capitalist Society*. New York: HarperBusiness, 1993, p. 43.
9. Scholtes, P. *The Leader's Handbook: A Guide to Inspiring Your People and Managing the Daily Work Flow*. New York: McGraw-Hill, 1997. Chandler, A. *The Visible Hand: The Managerial Revolution in American Business*. Cambridge, Mass.: Harvard University Press, 1977.
10. U.S. Department of the Army. *Mission Command: Command Control of Army Forces*. Aug. 2003. www.dtic.mil/dticasd/sbir/sbir043/a30a.pdf.
11. Scholtes. *The Leader's Handbook*. Although it has been suggested that *manager* was a new term at the time, the term was in use in England as early as 1705 to mean someone who manages a business. *The Compact Edition of the Oxford English Dictionary*. New York: Oxford University Press, 1971.
12. Beaman, K. V. "Boundaryless HR: Human Capital Management in the Global Economy: An Interview with Christopher Bartlett." June 2002. http://www.jeitosa.com/resources/karen_beaman/Bartlett-Interview.pdf.
13. Stewart, P. "The Management Myth." *Atlantic Monthly*, June 2006, pp. 80–89 at 81.
14. Taylor, F. W. *The Principles of Scientific Management*. Charleston, S.C.: Forgotten Books, 2008, p. 2. (Originally published 1911.)
15. Quoted in Crawford, M. *Shop Class as Soulcraft: An Inquiry into the Value of Work*. New York: Penguin, 2009, p. 105.
16. Between October 1912 and October 1913, the Ford Motor Company had to hire fifty-four thousand men to maintain an average workforce of

around thirteen thousand. Ciulla, J. B. *The Working Life: The Promise and Betrayal of Modern Work.* New York: Three Rivers Press, 2001.

17. Hammer, M., and Champy, J. *Reengineering the Corporation.* New York: HarperBusiness, 1993.
18. Hammer and Champy. *Reengineering the Corporation,* p. 7.
19. Davenport, T. H. *Process Innovation: Reengineering Work Through Information Technology.* Boston: Harvard Business School Press, 1992.
20. Hammer and Champy. *Reengineering the Corporation,* p. 30.
21. Hammer and Champy. *Reengineering the Corporation,* p. 103.
22. Hammer, M. *Beyond Reengineering: How the Process-Centered Organization Is Changing Our Work and Our Lives.* New York: HarperCollins, 1997. An NFL football game has another curious analogy to the traditional U.S. corporation: although the typical NFL game lasts more than three hours, only 6 percent of the total—eleven minutes—is actually spent playing with the ball and attempting to move it forward. The other 94 percent of the time is spent sitting, standing around, and talking about playing rather than actually playing. Biderman, D. "Eleven Minutes of Action." *Wall Street Journal,* Jan. 15, 2010. http://online.wsj.com/article/SB10001424052748704281204575002852055561406.html?mod=djemMTIPOFFh.
23. Pisano, G. P., and Shih, W. C. "Restoring American Competitiveness." *Harvard Business Review,* July-Aug. 2009, pp. 114–125.
24. Department of the U.S. Army. *Mission Command.*
25. Deloitte Center for the Edge. *Measuring the Forces of Long-Term Change: The Shift Index.* 2009. http://www.edgeperspectives.com/shiftindex.pdf.
26. Friedman, T. "Start-Ups, Not Bailouts." *New York Times,* Apr. 3, 2010. http://www.nytimes.com/2010/04/04/opinion/04friedman.html?hp.
27. Kotter, J. *A Sense of Urgency.* Boston: Harvard Business School Press, 2009.
28. Pink, D. *Drive: The Surprising Truth About What Motivates Us.* New York: Riverhead Books, 2010.

CHAPTER THREE

1. Hamel, G. "Moonshots for Management." *Harvard Business Review,* Feb. 2009, p. 91.
2. Reichheld, F. *The Ultimate Question: Driving Good Profits and True Growth.* Boston: Harvard Business School Press, 2006.
3. Ohno, T. *Taiichi Ohno's Workplace Management,* trans. Jon Miller. Milketo, Wash.: Gemba Press, 2007.
4. Whether the product is actually shipped is a marketing question. Overly frequent releases and updates can be an annoyance to clients in some situations, particularly when new releases entail additional training for users.
5. Reichheld, F. *The Ultimate Question: Driving Good Profits and True Growth.* Boston: Harvard Business School Press, 2006. See also Jones, T. O., and Sasser, W. E. "Why Satisfied Customers Defect." *Harvard Business Review,* Nov.-Dec. 1995, pp. 88–99.
6. Takeuchi, H., and Nonaka, I. "The New Product Development Game." *Harvard Business Review,* 1986, *64*(1), 137–146.
7. The early history of iterative approaches in software development is described in detail by Craig Larman and Victor Basili in "Iterative and Incremental Development: A Brief History." *Computer,* 2003, *36*(6), 47–56. Iterative approaches to work build on the 1930s work of Walter Shewhart, a quality expert at Bell Labs who proposed a series of short "plan-do-study-act" (PDSA) cycles for quality improvement: Shewhart, W. *Statistical Method from the Viewpoint of Quality Control.* New York: Dover, 1986. (Originally published 1939.) Starting in the 1940s, quality guru W. Edwards Deming began vigorously promoting PDSA, which he later described in *Out of the Crisis.* Cambridge, Mass.: MIT Press, 1982. Tom Gilb also explored PDSA application to software development in later works in *Software Metrics.* New York: Little, Brown, 1976.
8. Ohno, T. *Toyota Production System: Beyond Large-Scale Production.* New York: Productivity Press, 1988.

9. Deming. *Out of the Crisis.*
10. See, for example, Denning, S. *The Springboard: How Storytelling Ignites Action in Knowledge-Era Organizations.* Burlington, Mass.: Butterworth Heinemann, 2000. Simmons, A. *The Story Factor.* San Francisco: Perseus Books, 2001. Denning, S. *The Leader's Guide to Storytelling: Mastering the Art and Discipline of Business Narrative.* San Francisco: Jossey-Bass, 2005. Denning, S. *The Secret Language of Leadership: How Leaders Inspire Action Through Narrative.* San Francisco: Jossey-Bass, 2007.
11. Takeuchi and Nonaka, "The New Product Development Game."
12. In 1986, in "The New Product Development Game," Takeuchi and Nonaka had compared a new holistic approach to innovation to the sport of rugby, where the whole team "tries to go to the distance as a unit, passing the ball back and forth." In 1991, DeGrace and Stahl, in *Wicked Problems, Righteous Solutions* (Upper Saddle River, N.J.: Prentice Hall, 1990), referred to this approach as *Scrum.* In the early 1990s, Ken Schwaber used an approach similar to Scrum at his company, Advanced Development Methods. At the same time, Jeff Sutherland, John Scumniotales, and Jeff McKenna developed Scrum at the Easel Corporation. In 1995, Sutherland and Schwaber jointly presented a paper, "The SCRUM Development Process," at the Object-Oriented Programming, Systems, Languages & Applications (OOPSLA) Conference '95 in Austin, Texas, its first public appearance. Schwaber and Sutherland collaborated during the following years to merge their writings, their experiences, and industry best practices into what is now known as Scrum. Continuously updated information about the hundreds of companies implementing Scrum are available at "Firms Using Scrum." http://scrumcommunity.pbworks.com/Firms-Using-Scrum.
13. "The Agile Manifesto." 2001. http://agilemanifesto.org/. For the twelve principles behind the manifesto: http://agilemanifesto.org/principles.html. The Agile Manifesto was a conceptual breakthrough. But nine years later, some aspects could do with some review, particularly more emphasis on delighting clients as the goal of all work, satisfying customers versus working software, providing a rationale for the use of self-organizing teams, enhanced emphasis on transparency, and more explicit emphasis on interactive communication.

14. Examples of such gains can be seen at Systematic Software, Salesforce.com, OpenView Venture Partners, and Xebia, as discussed in Chapter Eleven.
15. Liker, J. K., and Hoseus, M. *Toyota Culture: The Heart and Soul of the Toyota Way*. New York: McGraw-Hill, 2008, p. 106.
16. Some "big-bang" implementations are reported to have been successful, for example, at Salesforce.com, as reported by Mike Cohn's *Succeeding with Agile: Software Development Using Scrum*. Upper Saddle River, N.J.: Addison-Wesley, 2009, and discussed in Chapter Eleven.
17. Tomasello, M. *Why We Cooperate*. Cambridge, Mass.: MIT Press, 2009. De Waal, F. *The Age of Empathy: Nature's Lessons for a Kinder Society*. New York: Crown, 2009.

CHAPTER FOUR

1. Reichheld, F. *The Ultimate Question: Driving Good Profits and True Growth*. Boston: Harvard Business School Press, 2006, p. 118.
2. For example, Rothman, J. *Manage It! Your Guide to Modern, Pragmatic Project Management*. N.p.: Pragmatic Bookshelf, 2007.
3. Sennett, R. *The Craftsman*. New Haven, Conn.: Yale University Press, 2008.
4. McKibben, B. *Deep Economy: The Wealth of Communities and the Durable Future*. New York: Holt, 2008.
5. Pollan, M. *In Defense of Food: An Eater's Manifesto*. New York: Penguin, 2009.
6. Crawford, M. *Shopcraft as Soul Class: An Inquiry into the Value of Work*. New York: Penguin, 2009.
7. Cited in Thomas, K. (ed.). *The Oxford Book of Work*. New York: Oxford University Press, 2001, p. 168.
8. Collins, J., and Porras, J. I. *Built to Last: Successful Habits of Visionary Companies*. New York: HarperCollins, 1994.
9. Kotter, J. *Leading Change*. Boston: Harvard Business School Press, 1996, p. 81.
10. Hamel, G. *The Future of Management*. Boston: Harvard Business School Press, 2007, p. 63.

11. Hamel, *The Future of Management,* pp. 107–108.
12. General Motors Company. "Our Mission: 'Re: Invention: See How We Are Reinventing the Automobile and Our Company.'" Accessed Jan. 20, 2010, at http://www.gmreinvention.com/?brandId=gm&src=gm_com&evar24=gm_com_topnavigation.
13. Pink, D. *Drive: The Surprising Truth About What Motivates Us.* New York: Riverhead Books, 2010.
14. Hamel, *The Future of Management*, p. 64.
15. Toyota articulated the principal goal of its North American subsidiary as follows: "As an American company, contribute to the economic growth of the community and the United States." Liker, J. *The Toyota Way: Fourteen Management Principles from the World's Greatest Manufacturer.* New York: McGraw-Hill, 2003, p. 80. When Toyota decided to close its Fremont plant in 2009 because of financial pressures bearing down on the company, it became apparent that economic growth of the community is not Toyota's principal goal after all. See the discussion of Toyota in Chapter Nine.
16. Drucker, P. *Management: Tasks, Responsibilities, Practices.* New York: HarperCollins, 1973, p. 61.
17. Drucker, *Management,* p. 62.
18. For instance, a public sector organization like the World Bank has many stakeholders, including the governments of developing countries, the population of developing countries, the governments of developed countries, the contractors that bid for contracts, the nongovernmental agencies that have an interest in development, and interest groups pursuing specific issues in which the World Bank plays a role, as well as academics and interested citizens. If the World Bank tries to satisfy all of these stakeholders equally, it will end up satisfying none of them, and it will lose sight of its principal mission of reducing or eliminating global poverty. Assigning priorities among the stakeholders is key to accomplishing its mission.
19. May, M. *The Elegant Solution: Toyota's Formula for Mastering Innovation.* New York: Free Press, 2006, p. xi.
20. Crawford, *Shopcraft as Soul Class,* p. 186.

21. Schwaber, K., and Beedle, M. *Agile Software Development with Scrum.* Upper Saddle River, N.J.: Prentice Hall, 2001.
22. Martin. "The Age of Customer Capitalism."
23. Berle, A., and Means, G. *The Modern Corporation and Private Property.* New York: Macmillan, 1932.
24. Jensen, M. C., and Menckling, W. H. "Theory of the Firm: Managerial Behavior, Agency Costs, and Ownership Structure." *Journal of Financial Economics,* 1976, *3*(4), 305–360.
25. Andrews, F. "A Man of Words Is Still Partial to One: Loyalty." *New York Times,* Dec. 29, 1999.
26. Reichheld. *The Ultimate Question.* Furlong, C. G. "12 Rules for Customer Retention." *Bank Marketing,* Jan. 5, 1993, p. 14.
27. The missions of these organizations also reflect in varying degrees a focus on customer delight. For example, for Philips: "Royal Philips Electronics of the Netherlands is a diversified Health and Well-being company, focused on improving people's lives through timely innovations" (http://www.usa.philips.com/about/company/index.page). For Zappos: "We've aligned the entire organization around one mission: to provide the best customer service possible. Internally, we call this our WOW philosophy" (http://about.zappos.com/). Intuit: "Intuit: Going Beyond Innovation: As the world evolves, so do we. Yet we remain driven by our passion for inventing solutions to solve important problems, perfecting those solutions and delighting our customers" (http://about.intuit.com/about_intuit/).
28. Reichheld. *The Ultimate Question,* p. 7.
29. "A Comcast Technician Sleeping on My Couch." http://www.youtube.com/watch?v=CvVp7b5gzqU.
30. Negroni, C. "With Video, a Traveler Fights Back." *International Herald Tribune,* Oct. 29, 2009. The video is available at "United Breaks Guitars" (http://www.youtube.com/watch?v=5YGc4zOqozo).
31. Reichheld. *The Ultimate Question,* p. 4.
32. ExxonMobil: Guiding Principles. http://www.exxonmobil.com/corporate/about_operations_sbc_principles.aspx.

33. Walmart: What We Do. http://walmartstores.com/AboutUs/8123.aspx.
34. The Chevron Way. http://www.chevron.com/about/chevronway/.
35. ConocoPhilips: Who We Are. http://www.conocophillips.com/EN/about/who_we_are/Pages/index.aspx.
36. GE: Citizenship. http://www.ge.com/company/citizenship/index.html.
37. GM: Our Mission. http://www.gmreinvention.com/?brandId=gm&src=gm_com&evar24=gm_com_expleftnav_ourmission.
38. One Ford Mission. http://www.ford.com/about-ford/company-information/one-ford.
39. AT&T: Corporate Profile. http://www.att.com/gen/investor-relations?pid=5711.
40. HP: About Us. http://www.hp.com/hpinfo/abouthp/.
41. Valero: Our Business. http://www.valero.com/OurBusiness/Pages/Home.aspx.
42. Bank of America: Helping Us All Move Ahead. http://ahead.bankofamerica.com/?cm_mmc=EBZ-CorpRep-_-vanity-_-EE01VN0004_ahead-_-NA.
43. Citibank: What Citizenship Means at Citi. http://www.citigroup.com/citi/citizen/data/citizen09b.pdf.
44. Berkshire Hathaway. The Berkshire Hathaway Web site has no explicit goal. It can be inferred from the site that the firm's goal is to make money for its shareholders. www.berkshirehathaway.com.
45. IBM: IBM Basics. http://www.ibm.com/ibm/responsibility/basics.shtml.
46. McKesson: About Us. http://www.mckesson.com/en_us/McKesson.com/About%2BUs/About%2BUs.html.
47. JP Morgan Chase: Business Principles. http://www.jpmorganchase.com/corporate/About-JPMC/business-principles.htm.
48. Verizon: Commitment and Values. http://responsibility.verizon.com/home/approach/commitment-and-values/.
49. Cardinal Health: Our Promise. http://www.cardinal.com/us/en/aboutus/promise/index.asp.

50. CVS Caremark: Our Company. http://info.cvscaremark.com/our-company.

51. Procter & Gamble: Our Purpose. http://www.pg.com/company/who_we_are/ppv.shtml.

52. Command-and-control bureaucracy is the logical way to structure and manage a firm whose only goal is making money or producing goods and services. Thus, if the goal of the firm is merely to produce 1 million widgets, then you build a widget factory that will need as little labor as possible in a country where the labor is cheapest and most compliant and can be told what to do. Your firm will achieve significant economies of scale and have the lowest labor costs. The only problem: Are there buyers for your 1 million widgets? There's the rub.

53. Downsizing and outsourcing are sometimes the right choice. In some circumstances, usually due to prior bad management, a firm has no option but to downsize or outsource. However, these solutions tend to tear apart the social fabric of an organization. After it happens, management may be able to reweave the social fabric of the organization and eventually get back to self-organizing teams, but the staff will probably be bracing for the next downsizing or outsourcing rather than giving their all to the work. Even when reweaving the social fabric of an organization is successful, the process is lengthy and costly.

54. "The man who chases two rabbits," Confucius said, "catches neither." As Al Ries and Laura Ries point out in their book, *War in the Board Room,* the goal of traditional managers is typically growth to achieve economies of scale, and that leads to trying to please everyone. Instead of chasing one rabbit, they often start chasing two or even more. Ries, A., and Ries, L. *War in the Boardroom: Why Left-Brain Management and Right-Brain Marketing Don't See Eye-to-Eye—and What to Do About It*. New York: CollinsBusiness, 2009.

55. The World Bank, for instance, faces a bewildering array of people and institutions, each wanting different things from it. The governments of developing countries want cheap, hassle-free money. People in developing countries want their lives to be better. The governments of the developed

countries want various policies to be pursued by developing countries and try to use the World Bank as a lever to attain their goals. The shareholder governments want to put less money into the organization but have more control over its activities. Contractors want lucrative procurement deals to come their way. Nongovernmental organizations and public interest groups want the World Bank to give priority attention to "their" particular issue. Faced with these divergent claims on its attention, the management of the World Bank was unable for over fifty years even to come to closure on a mission statement for the organization. It was only in 1998 that the organization finally agreed that its mission was "to fight poverty with passion and professionalism for lasting results." More than a decade later, the World Bank is still working through the implications of that decision. But at least it has made a start toward identifying its primary stakeholders: people who live in poverty.

56. See the discussion of the Kano model in Scholtes, P. *The Leader's Handbook: A Guide to Inspiring Your People and Managing the Daily Work Flow.* New York: McGraw-Hill, 1997. See also "Kano Model." http://en.wikipedia.org/wiki/Kano_model.
57. Conley, C. *Peak: How Great Companies Get Their Mojo from Maslow*. San Francisco: Jossey-Bass, 2007, p. 144.
58. Conley. *Peak.*
59. Conley. *Peak.*
60. O'Connell, P. "Taking the Measure of Mood." *Harvard Business Review*, Mar. 2006.

CHAPTER FIVE

1. Arnold, K. "You Can Never Go Back!" Sept. 18, 2009. http://maketeamworkhappen.com/2009/09/18/you-can-never-go-back/.
2. Gladwell, M. "Open Secrets." *New Yorker,* Jan. 8, 2007.
3. Gladwell. "Open Secrets."
4. Gervase of Canterbury. *The Historical Works of Gervase of Canterbury.* London: Longman, 1879–1880.
5. "Assize of Clarendon." N.d. http://www.economicexpert.com/a/Assize:of:Clarendon.htm.

6. In 997, Aethelred, king of the English, published a code of laws at Wantage, which became known as the Wantage Code. It required "twelve senior thegns" (that is, knights) to publish the names of notorious or wicked men in their districts. Wormald, P. *The Making of English Law: King Alfred to the Twelfth Century*. Oxford: Blackwell, 1999, 1:8.
7. Huscroft, R. *Ruling England, 1042–1217*. Harlow, U.K.: Pearson, 2006, p. 182.
8. Page, S. *The Difference: How the Power of Diversity Creates Better Groups, Firms, Schools*. Princeton, N.J.: Princeton University Press, 2007.
9. Because both the law and the facts were unclear, the question that the jury was being asked to address was a mystery. In civil cases, where the law is clear and the issue is a simple question of fact, the issue may become a puzzle.
10. Takeuchi, H., and Nonaka, I. "The New Product Development Game." *Harvard Business Review*, 1986, *64*(1), 137–146.
11. Takeuchi and Nonaka. "The New Product Development Game," p. 141.
12. Csikszentmihalyi, M. *Flow: The Psychology of Optimal Experience*. New York: Harper Perennial, 2008, p. 3. (Originally published 1990.)
13. The task force's recommendations were approved in their entirety with one exception. We had come up with an ingenious simplification of the procedures that pleased everyone. However, we also realized that the organizational culture that had created the morass of paperwork would reassert itself unless something was done. So to get to the root cause of the problem, we recommended continuing our work and resolving the problem of procedures in a more fundamental way. Our recommendation was not accepted, and the team was disbanded. This was a minor disappointment compared to the exhilaration that we all felt at having apparently resolved a problem that had stymied the management for fifteen years. But several years later, the kudzu was back.
14. Orsburn, J., and others. *Self-Directed Work Teams: The New American Challenge*. New York: Irwin, 1990, pp. 5–6.
15. Katzenbach, J., and Smith, D. *The Wisdom of Teams, Creating High-Performance Organizations*. Boston: Harvard Business School Press, 1993, p. 3.

16. Follett, M. P. *Dynamic Administration: The Collected Papers of Mary Parker Follett: Early Sociology of Management and Organizations.* New York: Routledge, 2003.
17. Mayo, E. *The Social Problems of an Industrial Civilization.* Boston: Harvard Business School, 1945, p. 72. Cited in Stewart, M. *The Management Myth: Why the Experts Keep Getting It Wrong.* New York: Norton, 2009.
18. Barnard, C. I. *The Functions of the Executive.* Boston: Harvard College, 1938.
19. Maslow, A. H. "A Theory of Human Motivation." *Psychological Review,* 1943, *50,* 370–396.
20. McGregor, D. *The Human Side of Enterprise.* New York: McGraw-Hill/Irwin, 1960.
21. *Work in America: Report of a Special Task Force to the Secretary of Health, Education and Welfare.* Cambridge, Mass.: MIT Press, 1971.
22. Peters, T., and Waterman, R. *In Search of Excellence: Lessons from America's Best-Run Companies.* New York: HarperCollins, 1982.
23. Amazon.com video. "Gary Hamel on Building Organizations for the Future." N.d. http://www.amazon.com/Future-Management-Bill-Breen/dp/1422102505/ref=sr_1_1?ie=UTF8&s=books&qid=1252325341&sr=1-1.
24. Pseudo-teams were so abundant by the 1950s that William Whyte devoted a large part of his book, *The Organization Man,* to attacking the managerial practices of manipulating people in groups. Whyte, W. *The Organization Man*. New York: Simon & Schuster, 1955.
25. Bryant, A. "All for One, One of All, and Every Man for Himself." *New York Times,* Feb. 22, 1998. Ciulla, J. B. *The Working Life: The Promise and Betrayal of Modern Work.* New York: Three Rivers Press, 2001.
26. Hackman, J. R. *Leading Teams: Setting the Stage for Great Performances.* Boston: Harvard Business School Press, 2002.
27. Survivor bias is a statistical error in which studies on the remaining population of entities are fallaciously compared with the historic average despite the fact that the survivors have unusual properties. The phenomenon is common in finance in comparing mutual funds, and

it is pervasive in management writing. Thus, the management analyst examines a population of firms that are implementing the idea being discussed: eventually one or more firms applying the idea are found that have done consistently well. The analyst, who may or may not be aware of all the failed efforts, writes an enthusiastic paper and sends it to a business magazine, which publishes it. Readers are greatly impressed with the idea but are puzzled as to why their own efforts to replicate the successful firms are less successful. See "Survivor Bias." N.d. http://en.wikipedia.org/wiki/Survivorship_bias.

28. Buffett, M., and Clark, D. *Warren Buffett's Management Secrets: Proven Tools for Personal and Business Success*. New York: Scribner, 2009.
29. The discussion of intrinsic and extrinsic motivation draws on Dan Pink's presentation at TED on the surprising science of motivation: http://www.youtube.com/watch?v=rrkrvAUbU9Y; and his book, *Drive* (2010). Tom Coens and Mary Jenkins propose replacing traditional performance reviews with individual responsibility for the employee's own development: *Abolishing Performance Appraisals: Why They Backfire and What to Do Instead*. San Francisco: Berrett-Koehler, 2002. Jeff Sutherland offers an interesting approach to handling performance evaluation: "Agile Performance Reviews." http://jeffsutherland.com/2006/11/agile-performance-reviews.html.
30. When the CEO's salary is more than three hundred times that of a production worker, it will be hard for them to have a collaborative working relationship. Paumgarten, N. "Food Fighter." *New Yorker*, Jan. 4, 2010. Even *Barron's* magazine accepts that Wall Street compensation is excessive: Bary, A. "Diet Time!" *Barron's*, Jan. 25, 2010. http://online.barrons.com/article/SB126420745187633649.html?mod=djembwr_t.
31. A team of twelve is good for diversity, but it's not optimal for problem solving. If the team is diverse, seven plus or minus two is a better rule.

CHAPTER SIX

1. Lao Tzu. *Tao Teh King Interpreted as Nature and Intelligence* (A. J. Bahm, trans.). New York: Unger, 1958, #64.
2. McCourt, F. *Angela's Ashes*. New York: Touchstone, 1996.

3. The company has just a handful of staff, geographically dispersed, who are highly qualified. They are masters of their craft and deeply committed to the goal, and they trusted each other implicitly. With technology, software services, and an Internet-based product that they are selling, it's scalable in the sense that thousands of users can log in from all over the world, ordering millions of dollars of product a month through a Web site that is run by a couple of people.

4. Ohno, T. *Taiichi Ohno's Workplace Management* (J. Miller, trans.). Milketo, Wash.: Gemba Press, 2007, p. 53.

5. Ohno. *Taiichi Ohno's Workplace Management,* p. 53.

6. Ohno. *Taiichi Ohno's Workplace Management,* p. 53.

7. Ohno. *Taiichi Ohno's Workplace Management,* pp. 56–57.

8. Ohno. *Taiichi Ohno's Workplace Management*.

9. Larman, C., and Vodde, B. *Scaling Lean and Agile Development: Thinking and Organizational Tools for Large-Scale Scrum.* Upper Saddle River, N.J.: Addison-Wesley, 2008.

10. Poppendieck, M., and Poppendieck, T. *Implementing Lean Software Development*. Upper Saddle River, N.J.: Addison-Wesley, 2007.

11. Womack, J. P., Jones, D. T., and Roos, D. *The Machine That Changed the World*. New York: Rawson Associates, 1990.

12. Reinertsen, D. G. *Managing the Design Factory: A Product Developer's Toolkit.* New York: Simon & Schuster, 1997, p. 1.

13. Poppendieck and Poppendieck. *Implementing Lean Software Development*, pp. 133–134.

14. Takeuchi, H., Osono, E., and Shimizu, N. "The Contradictions That Drive Toyota's Success." *Harvard Business Review,* June 2008, pp. 96–104.

15. May, M. *The Elegant Solution: Toyota's Formula for Mastering Innovation.* New York: Free Press, 2006.

16. Quadrant Homes. *Annual Report.* 2008. http://quadranthomes.com/pdf/reports/QHannualReport2008_full.pdf.

17. Conley, C. *Peak: How Great Companies Get Their Mojo from Maslow*. San Francisco: Jossey-Bass, 2007, p. 89.

18. Catmull, E. "How Pixar Fosters Collective Creativity." *Harvard Business Review,* Sept. 2008, pp. 64–72.

19. Kelley, T. *The Ten Faces of Innovation: IDEO's Strategies for Defeating the Devil's Advocate and Driving Creativity Throughout Your Organization.* New York: Broadway Business, 2005.

20. Shewhart, W. *Statistical Method from the Viewpoint of Quality Control.* New York: Dover, 1986. (Originally published 1939.)

21. Deming, W. E. *Out of the Crisis.* Cambridge, Mass.: MIT Press, 1982.

22. In *Out of the Crisis,* Deming makes occasional references to the centrality of the customer, but the main thrust of the book is internally driven quality improvement. Deming's famous fourteen points for management, for instance, make no mention of the customer or client. Some writers, however, suggest that the customer was central to Deming's thinking. See, for example, Kilian, C. *The World of W. Edwards Deming.* Knoxville, Tenn.: SPC Press, 1992; Poppendieck and Poppendieck. *Implementing Lean Software.*

23. Larman and Vodde. *Scaling Lean and Agile Development.*

24. Jones, C. *Applied Software Measurement: Global Analysis of Productivity and Quality* (3rd ed.). New York: McGraw-Hill, 2008.

25. Woodward, E., Surdek, S., and Ganis, M. *A Practical Guide to Distributed Scrum.* Armonk, N.Y.: IBM Press, 2010.

26. Stalk, G. "Time—The Next Source of Competitive Advantage." *Harvard Business Review,* July-Aug. 1988, pp. 41–51.

27. Kniberg, H., and Skarin, M. "Kanban and Scrum—Making the Most of Both." http://www.infoq.com/resource/minibooks/kanban-scrum-minibook/en/pdf/KanbanAndScrumInfoQVersionFINAL.pdf. See also "Kanban and Scrum—Making the Most of Both." http://www.infoq.com/minibooks/kanban-scrum-minibook. And also Henrik Kniberg's blog: "Kanban vs Scrum," Apr. 3, 2008. http://blog.crisp.se/henrikkniberg/2009/04/03/1238795520000.html.

28. The iterative work method does have the additional transaction cost at the end of each iteration. Theoretically the iterations could become so short and frequent that the savings from iterative work patterns

would be outweighed by increased transaction costs. Steps can be taken, however, to lower the transaction cost of a process cycle or not reduce the iteration cycle beyond the point where transaction costs outweigh the gains. See Larman and Vodde, *Scaling Lean*. See also Ohno. *Taiichi Ohno's Workplace Management*.

29. Beck, K. *Extreme Programming Explained: Embrace Change*. Upper Saddle River, N.J.: Pearson, 2004, p. 136.
30. Gilb, T. *Competitive Engineering: A Handbook for Systems Engineering, Requirements Engineering, and Software Engineering Using Planguage*. Burlington, Mass.: Butterworth Heinemann, 2005.
31. The description of the Polaris program draws on Poppendieck and Poppendieck. *Implementing Lean Software Development*; and Sapolsky, H. *The Polaris System Development: Bureaucratic and Programmatic Success in Government.* Cambridge, Mass.: Harvard University Press, 1972.
32. Ironically, the Polaris experience came to symbolize working in accordance with a plan. That was because Smith had used Program Evaluation and Review (PERT) charts to persuade Congress to give him the Polaris funding. Smith explained to Congress that the money wouldn't be wasted because he would be using an innovative new scheduling system: the PERT chart—a dramatic improvement over the Gantt chart. Rather than presenting work in orderly bars, a PERT chart connects events with arrows so that multiple dependencies can be reflected. The lesson that the U.S. Congress derived from the experience was that PERT charts work. PERT was so successful as a public relations device that in due course, Congress required the U.S. Navy to use the PERT system.

    A subsequent independent review by military expert Harvey Sapolsky showed that the use of PERT charts had little to do with the success of Polaris. What the PERT system was good at was persuading the Congress to keep funding the program. It was a brilliant public relations facade by which Smith ensured continued funding of the program by progress.

    Sapolsky attributed the success of the Polaris program not to PERT but to Smith's technical leadership, his laser-like focus on synchronizing increments of technical progress, the emphasis on testing, a deep sense of mission among all participants, and the iterative approach to developing components. This iterative approach resulted in significantly more capability, faster delivery, and lower cost than the traditional way of doing work sequentially, and implementing the ultimate plan in one go. Sapolsky. *The Polaris System Development.*

33. Kelley, T. *Ten Faces of Innovation: IDEO's Strategies for Beating the Devil's Advocate and Driving Creativity Throughout Your Organization.* New York: Doubleday, 2005. If developing prototypes is costly, using a pay-as-you-use contract may be an option.
34. Larman and Vodde. *Scaling Lean and Agile Development.*
35. Cohn, M. *User Stories Applied: For Agile Software Development.* Upper Saddle River, N.J.: Addison-Wesley, 2004.
36. Mike Cohn's blog: "Advantages of the Story Template: 'As a user, I want . . .'" Apr. 26, 2008. http://blog.mountaingoatsoftware.com/advantages-of-the-as-a-user-i-want-user-story-template.
37. Cohn, M. *Succeeding with Agile: Software Development Using Scrum.* Upper Saddle River, N.J.: Addison-Wesley, 2004.
38. Shook, J. *Managing to Learn: Using the A3 Management Process to Solve Problems, Gain Agreement, Mentor, and Lead.* Cambridge, Mass.: Lean Enterprise Institute, 2008.
39. Cohn. *Succeeding with Agile.*
40. May, M. E. *The Elegant Solution: Toyota's Formula for Mastering Innovation.* New York: Free Press, 2006.
41. As an example, Columbia University's College of Physicians and Surgeons offers The Program in Narrative Medicine. http://www.narrativemedicine.org/.
42. Benefield, G. "Rolling Out Agile in a Large Enterprise (Yahoo)." In *Proceedings of the 41st Hawaii International Conference on System Sciences.* 2008. http://www2.computer.org/portal/web/csdl/doi/10.1109/HICSS.2008.382.

CHAPTER SEVEN

1. Stalk, G. "Time—The Next Source of Competitive Advantage." *Harvard Business Review,* July-Aug. 1988, p. 41.
2. For an excellent discussion of the counterintuitive nature of queues, see Larman, C., and Vodde, B. *Scaling Lean and Agile Development: Thinking*

and Organizational Tools for Large-Scale Scrum.* Upper Saddle River, N.J.: Addison-Wesley, 2008, chap. 4.

3. The reason for having lists is that a flow system (*kanban*) was better in this context than iterations. Granvik says: "You've got football. You've got school. You've got dinner. You've got laundry. God knows what else. So adding any extra burden is difficult to plan ahead. So that's why we have the system with the lists. It's more a flow style of work."
4. Sutherland, S., Jakobsen, C., and Johnson, K. "Scrum and CMMI Level 5: The Magic Potion for Code Warriors." In *Proceedings of the 41st Hawaii International Conference on System Sciences—2008.* 2008. http://jeffsutherland.com/scrum/Sutherland-ScrumCMMI6pages.pdf.
5. Graban, M. *Lean Hospitals: Improving Quality, Patient Safety and Employee Satisfaction.* Boca Raton, Fla.: CRC Press, 2009, pp. 156–157.
6. The goal is to delight the ultimate customer—in this case, the patient. The doctor is the intermediate customer. As part of its thinking about the ultimate customer, the team should be thinking how to do work in a way that enables intermediate clients like the doctor to deliver more value to ultimate customers sooner. It is not enough that the intermediate client's needs have been met. The question is whether the intermediate client has been enabled to delight the ultimate client.
7. By focusing on long production runs, traditional management is slow in identifying quality problems. Stopping a long production run is psychologically difficult. Long production runs tend to distract management from preventing problems rather than fixing them after they have occurred. It also tends to make fixing problems more expensive. In long production runs, generic problems may be building up that may be found only when everything is done. Once the problem is identified, the scale of the problem to fix is much bigger because it affects a large volume of inventory. Long production runs lead to large inventory buffers and delays. Management gets used to shelving problems rather than solving them on the spot. Long production runs almost guarantee the waste of overproduction. They are less flexible in the marketplace, hampering the organization in adjusting to unexpected fluctuations in demand. This situation leads to inventory that has to be gotten rid of, which means price reductions and rebates to move it.

From the perspective of the whole organization, not just the production process, long production runs tend to increase costs. This is the startling finding from Toyota. Once the turnaround of short production runs is mastered and all the costs to the total organization are included, the apparent economies of scale from long production runs tend to dissolve.

8. Although value stream mapping is often associated with manufacturing, it is also used in logistics, supply chain, service industries, health care, software development, and new product development.

9. For a good discussion of value stream mapping, see Poppendieck, M., and Poppendieck, T. *Implementing Lean Software Development*. Upper Saddle River, N.J.: Addison-Wesley, 2007. The originator of value stream mapping in Toyota, Shigeo Shingo, suggested drawing the value-adding steps horizontally across the map and the non-value-adding steps in vertical lines at right angles to the value stream. The vertical line is the "story" of a person or work station, and the horizontal line represents the "story" of the product being created. The object is to accelerate the horizontal story of delivering value to the customer by reducing or eliminating the steps represented by vertical lines. In most large hierarchies, much of the activity is represented by vertical lines because it doesn't add value to the ultimate customer. A value stream map dramatically draws attention to this fact.

10. Stalk, G. "Time."

11. Williams, C. *MGMT.* Mason, Ohio: Thomson South-Western, 2009. Financial Times. *Mastering Strategy: The Complete MBA Companion to Strategy.* Upper Saddle River, N.J.: Prentice Hall, 2000. *A Guide to the Project Management Body of Knowledge (PMBOK Guide)* (4th ed.). Newtown Square, Pa.: Project Management Institute, 2008. Rothman, J. *Manage It! Your Guide to Modern Pragmatic Project Management*. Raleigh, N.C.: Pragmatic Bookshelf, 2007.

12. Ohno, T. *Taiichi Ohno's Workplace Management* (J. Miller, trans.). Milketo, Wash.: Gemba Press, 2007.

13. For example, in 2008, management at Systematic Software noticed that several of its software teams were much more productive than the others. One of the successful practices they used was making sure that work was

ready. The other was finishing tasks quickly. The projects had improved "flow of implementation of story" from 32 percent at the start of 2008 to 59 percent by the end of the year. Jakobsen, C., and Sutherland, J. "Scrum and CMMI—Going from Good to Great: Are You Ready-Ready to Be Done-Done?" 2009. http://agile2009.agilealliance.com/files/WHI0001%20ScrumCMMI%20from%20Good%20to%20Great%201_11.PDF.

14. When Systematic Software investigated why several of its teams were more productive than the norm, they found a principal reason was that the team had paid particular attention to ensuring that the work introduced into an iteration was ready to be worked on. A checklist is now used to ensure that the things to be worked on are properly prepared for implementation in the iteration. By thinking systematically about what is to be addressed before work begins, the formal planning meetings became more efficient because the team knew what the features and the stories were about. Jakobsen and Sutherland. "Scrum and CMMI—Going from Good to Great."

15. Cohn, M. *Agile Estimating and Planning.* Upper Saddle River, N.J.: Prentice Hall, 2005.

16. Planning poker is a variation of the Delphi method. It is commonly used in Agile software development. The method was described by James Grenning in 2002 (http://renaissancesoftware.net/papers/14-papers/44-planing-poker.html) and later popularized by Cohn. *Agile Estimating and Planning.*

17. A strict Fibonacci series would be: 1, 2, 3, 5, 8, 13, 21, 34, 55, 89. The modified series is better suited as a tool to reflect broad orders of magnitude. See FAQs. http://store.mountaingoatsoftware.com/pages/faqs. Also see "Planning Poker." Wikipedia. http://en.wikipedia.org/wiki/Planning_poker.

18. Poppendieck and Poppendieck. *Implementing Lean Software Development.*

19. Ressler, C., and Thompson, J. *Why Work Sucks and How to Fix It: No Schedules, No Meetings, No Joke—the Simple Change That Can Make Your Job Terrific.* New York: Portfolio, 2008.

20. Just as the phantom traffic jam can be caused by having cars moving at different speeds, so management requests to expedite specific items cause the overall speed of the team to slow down. The managers may miss the fact that the overall flow is slower because their specific request was handled promptly.
21. A "flow" or *kanban* approach is illustrated by the example of Björn Granvik at the start of this chapter. For a discussion of the implications, see "Kanban and Scrum—Making the Most of Both." http://www.infoq.com/minibooks/kanban-scrum-minibook. See also Henrik Kniberg's blog: "Kanban vs Scrum," Apr. 3, 2008. http://blog.crisp.se/henrikkniberg/2009/04/03/1238795520000.html.
22. Cross, R., and Thomas, R. J. *Driving Results Through Social Networks: How Top Organizations Leverage Networks for Performance and Growth.* San Francisco: Jossey-Bass, 2009, p. 80.
23. Radical management practices enabled OpenView Venture Partners to initiate a culture of working fewer hours and no weekends while getting much more done. Sutherland, J., and Altman, I. "Take No Prisoners: How a Venture Capital Group Does Scrum." Aug. 2009. http://jeffsutherland.com/SutherlandTakeNoPrisonersAgile2009.pdf.
24. Liker, J. K., and Hoseus, M. *Toyota Culture: The Heart and Soul of the Toyota Way.* New York: McGraw-Hill, 2008, pp. 27–28.
25. At PatientKeeper, a software development firm in Boston deploying radical management practices throughout its operations, several years of hard work were needed before work was routinely completed at the end of an iteration, where the software was fully tested, deployed, and operational and the clients were satisfied with what had been deployed. When that was accomplished, client delight and revenues grew exponentially. Poppendieck and Poppendieck. *Implementing Lean Software Development*, pp. 95–98.

CHAPTER EIGHT

1. Gloria Steinem has used this quote in speeches. FreedomForum.org.http://www.freedomforum.org/templates/document.asp?documentID=15030. Compare it with: "You will know the truth, and the truth will set you free" John 8:32.

2. World Bank commitments increased from an annual level of about $1 billion in 1968 to over $13 billion in fiscal 1981. http://web.worldbank.org/WBSITE/EXTERNAL/EXTABOUTUS/EXTARCHIVES/0,,contentMDK:20502974~pagePK:36726~piPK:437378~theSitePK:29506,00.html.

3. These paragraphs draw on John Blaxall's reminiscences: "Remembering Robert S. McNamara: Seizing the Reins." Sept. 15, 2009. http://1818members.wordpress.com/2009/07/09/remembering-robert-s-mcnamara/#comments.

4. As a young division chief at the time, I encountered McNamara only occasionally. When I did see him in action, I was bowled over by his energy and his eloquence. McNamara dazzled me, as he did everyone else, with his intelligence, articulateness, and grasp of numbers. His ability to absorb information and put it in a meaningful context was extraordinary. He could sit for hours while a score of executive directors of the World Bank's board spoke and then summarize the disjointed discussion simply, clearly, and logically, and explaining some viewpoints more convincingly than the original speakers.

5. An internal review of the bank's loan portfolio, "Portfolio Management: Next Steps—A Program of Actions" (Washington, D.C.: World Bank, 1992), also known as the Wapenhans report, was leaked to the public. It reviewed the quality of the bank's portfolio and found that the bank was not enforcing 78 percent of the financial conditions in the loan agreements. Using the bank's own criteria, the reviewers discovered that 37.5 percent of recently evaluated projects were unsatisfactory, up from 15 percent in 1981. The report linked the decline in project quality to a "pervasive" "culture of approval" for loans, whereby bank staff members perceived the appraisal process as merely a "marketing device for securing loan approval," and "pressure to lend overwhelms all other considerations." Hunter, D., and Uall, L. "The World Bank's New Inspection Panel: Will It Increase the Bank's Accountability?" 1993. http://www.ciel.org/Publications/issue1.html.

6. The pressure to lend was a widely perceived phenomenon. Senior World Bank vice president Warren Baum, recalls: "My biggest problem with McNamara came from his relentless pressure on the staff to do more

and faster lending. One couldn't argue with him, since he wouldn't admit that he did it, or that there was any friction between lending more or lending better (one of my responsibilities). Not in the long run, but in daily operations, staff felt continuing pressure to reach or exceed lending targets that could lead to cutting corners or making mistakes." Baum, W. "The Maplewood Messenger: The Robert McNamara That I Knew." http://1818members.files.wordpress.com/2009/07/warren_c-_baum_about_robert_mcnamara.pdf.

7. Crawford, M. *Shop Class as Soulcraft: An Inquiry into the Value of Work.* New York: Penguin, 2009.

8. Frankfurt, H. *On Bullshit.* Princeton, N.J.: Princeton University Press, 2005.

9. In McNamara's case at the World Bank, it wasn't his first experience of trusting too much in the numbers. It had happened to him during the disastrous Bay of Pigs invasion of Cuba in 1961, for which he was responsible as secretary of defense. It had happened to him in Vietnam, where his visits were legendary. He would scurry around "looking for what he wanted to see; and he never saw nor smelled nor felt what was really there, right in front of him." Halberstam, D. *The Best and the Brightest.* New York: Random House, 1972.

10. "In those times, the universities were teaching the wrong things. Neither Galileo nor Descartes, for example, was able to pick up the mathematical skills he so desperately needed during the course of his university education. Galileo had initially studied medicine at Pisa but left before completing his degree, and in 1583 started learning mathematics at his father's house from the Florentine court instructor Ostilio Ricci, who taught military fortification, mechanics, architecture, and perspective. Descartes similarly learned his mathematics in a practical context: having studied law at Poitiers, he picked up and refined his mathematical skills in the armies of Prince Maurice of Nassau and Maximilian I, to which he was attached from 1618 to 1620." Gaukroger, S. *The Emergence of a Scientific Culture.* Oxford: Clarendon Press, 2006.

11. Even in science, the march toward truth proceeds not in straight lines but through a series of peaceful interludes punctuated by intellectually violent

revolutions. Kuhn, T. S. *The Structure of Scientific Revolutions.* Chicago: University of Chicago Press, 1996. The truth in science may also be diverted by political or financial pressures: Greenberg, D. *Science, Money, and Politics: Political Triumph and Ethical Erosion.* Chicago: University of Chicago Press, 2003.

12. Campbell, J. *The Liar's Tale.* New York: Norton, 2001.
13. Larman, C., and Vodde, B. *Scaling Lean and Agile Development: Thinking and Organizational Tools for Large-Scale Scrum.* Upper Saddle River, N.J.: Addison-Wesley, 2008.
14. Mann, D. *Creating a Lean Culture.* New York: Productivity Press, 2005, pp. 62, 65.
15. Ohno, T. *Workplace Management* (J. Miller, trans.). Milketo, Wash.: Gemba Press, 2007.
16. Culbert, S. A. *Beyond Bullsh*t: Straight-Talk at Work.* Stanford, Calif.: Stanford Business Press, 2008, pp. 76–77.

CHAPTER NINE

1. Ohno, T. *Taiichi Ohno's Workplace Management* (J. Miller, trans.). Milketo, Wash.: Gemba Press, 2007, p. 15.
2. Bremner, B., and Dawson, D. "Can Anything Stop Toyota?" *Business-Week,* Nov. 17, 2003. http://www.businessweek.com/magazine/content/03_46/b3858001_mz001.htm.
3. Liker, J., and Hoseus, M. *Toyota Culture: The Heart and Soul of the Toyota Way*, New York: McGraw-Hill, 2009, pp. 27–28.
4. Senge, P. *The Fifth Discipline: The Art and Practice of the Learning Organization*. New York: Doubleday, 1994. Garvin, D. A., Edmondson, A. C., and Gino, F. "Is Yours a Learning Organization?" *Harvard Business Review*, Mar. 2008, pp. 109–116.
5. O'Reilly, C., and Pfeffer, J. *Hidden Value.* Boston: Harvard Business School Press, 2000, p. 82.
6. Womack, J. P., Jones, D. T., and Roos, D. *The Machine That Changed the World*. New York: Rawson Associates, 1990.
7. The model for the Ford production initiatives at Hermosillo was Mazda. Starting in 1979 with a 7 percent financial stake, Ford began a partnership

that resulted in a variety of joint projects. During the 1980s, Ford increased its stake by another 20 percent. According to John Cotter, president of John J. Cotter & Associates, who worked with Ford for many years as a start-up consultant, the strong results at Hermosillo were emulated with the UAW at the Romeo engine plant in Michigan. However, internal bickering prevented learnings from either experience from being adopted elsewhere in the company. Success in a large political company like Ford makes a small number of people look good and a large number of others look not so good. So the people who end up looking less good have every incentive to deny the success of the offending initiative.

At Romeo, there was also a career issue for the directors at engine division headquarters who didn't like the decentralization of control that came with the new design: engineering and production were now colocated and worked on everything together. So they eventually forced the successful start-up plant manager to resign and replaced him with a succession of more conservative appointments.

8. Liker, J. *The Toyota Way*. New York: McGraw-Hill, 2003, p. 10. See also Vasilash, G. S. "Oh, What a Company!" *Automotive Design and Production*, Jan. 12, 2005. http://www.autofieldguide.com/articles/030501.html.
9. Sutherland, J. "Hyperproductive Distributed Scrum Teams." July 21, 2008. www.youtube.com/watch?v=Ht2xcIJrAXo.
10. Ohno, T. *Toyota Production System: Beyond Large-Scale Production*. New York: Productivity Press, 1988. (Originally published 1978.)
11. Ohno, *Toyota Production System*, pp. 4, 77.
12. Toyota. "Human Resources Development." In *Environmental and Social Report 2003*. 2003. http://www.toyota.co.jp/en/environmental_rep/03/jyugyoin03.html. Liker and Hoseus. *Toyota Culture*.
13. O'Reilly and Pfeffer. *Hidden Value*, p. 187.
14. O'Reilly and Pfeffer. *Hidden Value*, p. 192.
15. O'Reilly and Pfeffer. *Hidden Value*, p. 196.
16. Womack, Jones, and Roos. *The Machine That Changed the World*, p. 87.
17. See, for instance, "Lean Manufacturing." http://en.wikipedia.org/wiki/Lean_manufacturing.

18. At the time of the Audi cases, acceleration was handled by mechanical controls. Electronic throttle controls (ETC), which began to be introduced in 2003, sever the mechanical link between the accelerator pedal and the throttle. ETC facilitates the integration of features such as cruise control, traction control, stability control, and precrash systems. Much of the engineering involved with ETC deals with fault management and the detection of possible errors.
19. Whoriskey, P. "NHTSA Chief Says Rate of Toyota Complaints Was 'Unremarkable.'" *Washington Post*, Mar. 11, 2010. http://www.washingtonpost.com/wp-dyn/content/article/2010/03/10/AR2010031003876.html.
20. "Toyota, Lexus Slip in Key Dependability Study." *ABC News*, Mar. 18, 2010. http://abcnews.go.com/Business/wirestory?id=10135349&page=1.
21. "Toyota Chief Says Training Lapsed amid Fast Growth." *Forbes*, Mar. 17, 2010. http://www.forbes.com/feeds/ap/2010/03/17/business-as-japan-toyota_7444913.html.
22. On October 4, 2009, Brian Lyons, the spokesperson for Toyota, said: "It is conceivable we could develop software so that if the gas pedal and brake pedal were hit at the same time, the brake pedal wins. We have several ideas in mind." Jensen, C. "Toyota Seeks Solution on Mats." *New York Times*, Oct. 4, 2009. http://query.nytimes.com/gst/fullpage.html?res=9907E6DD163DF937A35753C1A96F9C8B63&scp=60&sq=toyota&st=nyt.
23. In an interesting interview, Alan Mulally explained how he introduced continuous improvement into the traditional management culture at Ford: "On Leadership: Ford CEO Alan Mulally on Catching Mistakes." *Washington Post*, Mar. 17, 2010. http://www.washingtonpost.com/wp-dyn/content/video/2010/03/17/VI2010031700340.html.
24. "Toyota President Urges Workers, Dealers to Work Toward New Start." *Japan Today*, Mar. 5, 2010. http://www.japantoday.com/category/business/view/toyota-president-urges-workers-dealers-to-work-toward-new-start.
25. Larman, C., and Vodde, B. *Scaling Lean and Agile Development: Thinking and Organizational Tools for Large-Scale Scrum*. Upper Saddle River, N.J.: Addison-Wesley, 2008. It is striking that at Toyota, no incremental

improvement is too small to be worth looking at. The result is around a million improvements proposed and implemented each year. See May, M. *The Elegant Solution: Toyota's Formula for Mastering Innovation.* New York: Free Press, 2006, p. xi.

26. Dennis, P., and Womack, J. *Getting the Right Things Done: A Leader's Guide to Planning and Execution.* Cambridge, Mass.: Lean Enterprise Institute, 2007.
27. Ohno. *Toyota Production System.* See also "5 Whys." http://en.wikipedia.org/wiki/5_Whys.
28. Larman and Vodde. *Scaling Lean.*
29. One of the characteristics of Jeff Sutherland's initial Scrum team back in 1993 involved systematically exposing the team to outside views from neighboring companies, universities, and consultants within the firm. In this way, the team was continually prodded to do better. Similarly, Procter & Gamble has drawn on outside ideas to improve the company's innovation productivity by 60 percent. The strategy presumed that for every scientist at P&G, there were at least two hundred outside the company who could do similar work. Lafley, A. G., and Charan, R. *The Game-Changer: How You Can Drive Revenue and Profit Growth with Innovation.* New York: Crown, 2008.
30. Even radical management is not "the best practice" of management. It is simply the best management practice I know of at this time. Even if it is adopted in every organization in the world today and yields the benefits I am suggesting, people will in due course discover an even better way to manage.

CHAPTER TEN

1. Drucker, P. *Post-Capitalist Society.* New York: HarperBusiness, 1993, p. 56.
2. Ariely, D. *Predictably Irrational: The Hidden Forces That Shape Our Decisions.* New York: HarperCollins, 2008, p. 68.
3. Superiors appropriate or preempt what they want or receive tribute from subordinates. Conversely, in healthy authority ranking relationships, superiors demonstrate noblesse oblige: they provide for subordinates who are in need and protect them. Fiske, A. "The Four Elementary

Forms of Sociality: Framework for a Unified Theory of Social Relations." *Psychological Review,* 1992, *99,* 689–723. One reason that the modern workplace has become so toxic is that organizations felt compelled by market forces to scrap noblesse oblige. Repeated downsizings showed that they were not able or willing to look after their workers in a time of need. Authority became the pure exercise of power without reciprocity.

4. Fiske. "The Four Elementary Forms of Sociality."
5. Ariely, *Predictability Irrational.*
6. See Todd, R. *The Thing Itself: On the Search for Authenticity.* New York: Riverhead Books, 2008.
7. Stalk, G., Lachenauer, R., and Butman, J. *Hardball: Are You Playing to Play or Playing to Win?* Boston: Harvard Business School Press, 2004.
8. See Sutherland, J. "Hyperproductive Distributed Scrum Teams." July 21, 2008. http://www.youtube.com/watch?v=Ht2xcIJrAXo. Schwaber, K. "Scrum et al." Sept. 5, 2006. http://www.youtube.com/watch?v=IyNPeTn8fpo&feature=PlayList&p=DE357C4045F1038F&playnext=1&playnext_from=PL&index=17. Poppendieck, M. "The Role of Leadership in Software Development." May 6, 2008. http://www.youtube.com/watch?v=ypEMdjslEOI&feature=PlayList&p=3A5E1DE6E9C76D0A&index=0&playnext=1.
9. Denning, S. *The Leader's Guide to Storytelling.* San Francisco: Jossey-Bass, 2007. Denning, S. *The Secret Language of Leadership.* San Francisco: Jossey-Bass, 2007.
10. Williams, C. *MGMT.* Mason, Ohio: South-Western, 2008, pp. 279–280.
11. Denning. *The Secret Language of Leadership.*
12. Denning. *The Leader's Guide to Storytelling.*
13. For detailed accounts of such adversarial encounters, see Pollan, S., and Levine, M. *Lifescripts: What to Say to Get What You Want in Life's Toughest Situations.* Hoboken, N.J.: Wiley, 2004. In most of the more than one hundred scenarios laid out in this revealing book, the end result is an apparent "victory" for the speaker. But a careful reading of the interactions suggests that the outcome generally remains full of tension, with an aftermath of bitterness at the exercise of power. In each case, the speaker "wins" the battle but is at risk of losing the war.

14. Handy, C. *Gods of Management: The Changing Work of Organizations.* New York: Oxford University Press, 1978.
15. Avery, C. M. *Teamwork Is an Individual Skill: Getting Your Work Done When Sharing Responsibility*. San Francisco: Berrett-Koehler, 2001.
16. For instance, when David Axelrod spoke on *60 Minutes* on November 4, 2008, election night, he described the mood within the Obama campaign team: "We believed in the candidate and we believed in the cause, and we believed in each other. And by the end of this thing, over two years, you forge relationships and we're like a family. The hardest thing about this is that it's ended now. It's like the end of the movie, *M*A*S*H*. The war is over. We're all going home. And we want to go home. But on the other hand, it's sort of a bit of melancholy, because we've come to love each other, and we believe in each other and we know that this will never be the same. We went through this experience and it was a singular experience and it will never be the same." *60 Minutes,* Nov. 4, 2009.
17. See, for example, "Pericles Funeral Oration." In Thucydides. *History of the Peloponnesian War*. New York: Penguin Books, 1954.

CHAPTER ELEVEN

1. Alexander, C. *The Timeless Way of Building*. New York: Oxford University Press, 1979, p. 13.
2. For example, contriving to create crises, canceling luxurious perks, using consultants to force more open discussion, banning senior management "happy talk" or bombarding workers with information about opportunities. Kotter, J. *Leading Change.* Boston: Harvard Business School Press, 1995; Kotter, J. *A Sense of Urgency.* Boston: Harvard Business School Press, 2009.
3. Quinn, R. E. *Building the Bridge as You Walk on It: A Guide for Leading Change.* San Francisco: Jossey-Bass, 2004.
4. For example, Kotter. *Leading Change.*
5. The organization was the World Bank, and the idea was knowledge management. My idea was to complement the World Bank's traditional role of lending money to developing countries to relieve poverty with a major effort to share our knowledge with the millions of people who make decisions about poverty. A detailed account of the change

process is contained in two of my books: *The Springboard* (Burlington, Mass.: Butterworth-Heinemann, 2000) and the Introduction to *The Secret Language of Leadership* (San Francisco: Jossey-Bass, 2007).

6. Two adaptations were important. First, most other organizations at the time were pursuing knowledge management as a tool to improve efficiency or win more business. In the World Bank, knowledge sharing was more important to improve organizational effectiveness. Second, most other organizations at the time were pursuing knowledge management as a way of sharing knowledge inside the organization. In the World Bank, the idea was adapted to include sharing knowledge outside the organization.
7. Kahan, S. *Getting Change Right.*
8. Could one describe the period as "happy"? It depends on what is meant by happiness. If happiness is a state of passive contentment, no: most days were filled with worry about the scale of the difficulties we faced. By contrast, psychologist Tal Ben-Shahar defines happiness as a process: "Attaining lasting happiness requires that we enjoy the journey on our way toward a destination we deem valuable. Happiness, therefore, is not about making it to the peak of the mountain, nor is it about climbing aimlessly around the mountain: happiness is the experience of climbing toward the peak." Ben-Shahar, T. http://www.talbenshahar.com/. If happiness is the experience of climbing toward the peak, then yes, we were happy.
9. Studies suggest that most successful ideas for big change enter the organization from people at the upper-middle part of management, not the top. Davenport, T., and Prusak, L. *What's the Big Idea?* Boston: Harvard Business School Press, 2003.
10. Sutherland, J. "Hyperproductive Distributed Scrum Teams." July 21, 2008. http://www.youtube.com/watch?v=Ht2xcIJrAXo. Sutherland, J., Schoonheim, G., Rustenburg, E., and Rijk, M. "Fully Distributed Scrum: The Secret Sauce for Hyperproductive Offshore Development Teams." *Agile Conference Publication.* Aug. 2008. http://ieeexplore.ieee.org/xpl/freeabs_all.jsp?arnumber=4599502.
11. Radical management doesn't mean abandoning planning, ceasing to look ahead, forgetting about budgets, neglecting customers, failing to assess

risks, or ignoring real-world constraints. At the same time, a plan, as practiced by Robert McNamara, which is simply a bunch of numbers, is a weak instrument. Tables of numbers tend to ignore critical quality issues (see Chapter Eight). A better approach is to use the concept of a business model, which is a story that explains how an organization will operate. It gives the theory of the business and is a story set in the present or near future. The narrative is tied to numbers as the elements in the business model are quantified. The business model answers questions like: Who is the customer? And what does the customer value? How do we make money in this business? What is the underlying economic logic that shows how we can deliver value to customers at an appropriate cost? Its validity depends on its narrative logic (Does the story hang together?) and the quantitative evidence (Do the numbers add up?). In an iterative approach, the story and the numbers are updated as the situation evolves. One keeps on asking: Is it still realistic, knowing what we now know? See Magretta, J. "Why Business Models Matter." *Harvard Business Review*, May 2002, pp. 87–92; Denning, S. *The Leader's Guide to Storytelling.* San Francisco: Jossey-Bass, 2005.

12. Sutherland, S., Jakobsen, C., and Johnson, K. "Scrum and CMMI Level 5: The Magic Potion for Code Warriors." In *Proceedings of the 41st Hawaii International Conference on System Sciences—2008.* 2008. http://jeffsutherland.com/scrum/Sutherland-ScrumCMMI6pages.pdf.

13. Moore, G. "Scrum Element: VC Applies Efficiency to Portfolio Firms." *Boston Business Journal,* Dec. 18, 2009. http://www.bizjournals.com/boston/stories/2009/12/21/story3.html. Moore, G. "OpenView Hopes Scrum Efficiency Will Spark Investing." *Mass High Tech: The Journal of New England Technology,* Dec. 18, 2009. http://www.masshightech.com/stories/2009/12/14/daily62-OpenView-hopes-scrum-efficiency-will-spark-investing.html.

    Sutherland, J., and Altman, I. "Take No Prisoners: How a Venture Capital Group Does Scrum." 2009. http://jeffsutherland.com/scrum/SutherlandTakeNoPrisonersAgile2009.pdf.

14. "The Year of Living Dangerously." Scrum Gathering 2008 Stockholm—Salesforce.com. http://www.slideshare.net/sgreene/scrum-gathering-2008-stockholm-salesforcecom-presentation.

15. Cohn, M. *Succeeding with Agile: Software Development Using Scrum.* Upper Saddle River, N.J.: Addison-Wesley, 2009, p. 12.
16. Fry, C., and Green, S. "Large Scale Agile Transformation in an On-Demand World." 2007. http://trailridgeconsulting.com/files/salesforce_agile_adoption_2007.pdf.
17. Hackman, J. R. *Leading Teams: Setting the Stage for Great Performances.* Boston: Harvard Business School Press, 2002.
18. Denning. *The Leader's Guide to Storytelling.* Denning. *The Secret Language of Leadership.* Kahan. *Getting Change Right.*
19. Denning. *The Leader's Guide to Storytelling.*

CHAPTER TWELVE

1. Mills, C. W. *The Sociological Imagination.* New York: Oxford University Press, 2000, p. 171. (Originally published 1959.)
2. Some will even pause long enough to ask themselves: Why did Warren Buffett focus his investments on companies where the people love what they are doing? Buffett, M., and Clark, D. *Warren Buffett's Management Secrets: Proven Tools for Personal and Business Success.* New York: Scribner, 2009.
3. De Botton, A. *The Pleasures and Sorrows of Work.* New York: Pantheon, 2009. http://www.amazon.com/Pleasures-Sorrows-Work-Alain-Botton/dp/037542444X/ref=ntt_at_ep_dpi_2.

ACKNOWLEDGMENTS

It is impossible to thank individually the huge number of people who have contributed to the creation of this book. All I can do is to signal here a few who have been particularly helpful.

This book draws on the massive literature of management and leadership. I have done my best to indicate in the text itself the sources of my thinking so that readers can immerse themselves more deeply in these vast streams of thought and practice.

I am indebted to the hundreds of people who shared their experiences of the workplace with me, including Alex Adamopoulos, Igor Altman, Sam Bayer, Lyn Dowling, Stig Efsen, Jora Gill, Christophe Gissinger, Björn Granvik, Mikkel Harbo, Matt Hlavin, Luke Hohmann, Michael Holm, Carsten Jakobsen, Joe Kinsella, Ken Krivanec, Scott Maxwell, John Ozier, Jeff Patton, Laurence Prusak, Fred Reichheld, Don Roedner, Ed Scanlan, Guido Schoonheim, John Scumniotales, and Arline Sutherland. I also received many helpful suggestions from readers of my newsletter and participants at the many workshops that I have held.

I am grateful to Hans Samios for encouraging me to look more deeply into the arcane world of software development. I am deeply grateful for the conversations with some of the leaders of the Agile/Scrum movements and of lean thinking, including Joseph Little, Matthew May, Mary Poppendieck and Tom Poppendieck, and Jeff Sutherland. I have also learned much from the books and videos of Kent Beck, Mike Cohn, Mark Graban, Craig Larman, Ken Schwaber, and Bas Vodde.

I would like to acknowledge the help of my colleagues at the World Bank, who have continued to energize and inspire me, including Seth Kahan, Lesley Shneier, Roberto Chavez, Adnan Hassan, Peter Midgley, Carol Evangelista, and Michel Pommier. I am indebted to John Blaxall for his recollections about Robert McNamara.

The global community of organization storytelling continues to inspire me toward greater authenticity in communications. I am particularly grateful to Madelyn Blair, Denise Lee, and Paul Costello, among many others.

I was fortunate to have many wonderful suggestions from several online review groups. I particularly appreciated the contributions of Dawn Anderson, Steve Barnett, Alan Bentley, Anne Bentley, Antonina Bivona, Lisa Bloom, Garry Booker, Mary Brady, Michelle Bryne, Fiona Chamberlain, Greg Cohen, John Cotter, Richard Cummins, Charles Dhewa, D. Andre Dhondt, Anthony DiMaio, Marc Dimmick, Leigh Dryden, Kathryn Dunn, Sebasten Durand, Tony Elmore, Svend-Erich Engh, Larry Forster, Matt Gelbwaks, Mark Gould, Djebar Hammouche, Petri Heiramo, Thomas Juli, Curtis Krauskopf, Theo Kukard, Nicolas Marescaux, Richard Merrick, Deborah Mills-Scofield, Bryan Murphy, Vijay Nathani, Bruce Nix, Holly Paige, Lucas Persona, Greg Petit, Christiane L. Roehler, Maurice le Rutte, Agam Sinha, Tamsin Slyce, Bruce Smith, James A. Stahley, Kathi Treiber, Nerio Vakil, Stephane Veillard, Germain Verbeemen, Cornelis Vonk, Douglas Weidner, Vic Williams, and Stanislas Yanakiev. Peter Young was always ready to help with editing suggestions and repeatedly pushed me toward greater authenticity.

Helpful editing suggestions were also received from Bruce Ross-Larsen, Amy Halladay, and Robert Randall.

Barbara Henricks was an invaluable sounding board as the book took shape.

I appreciated help from Carol Pearson in sponsoring my role as a Senior Scholar at the James McGregor Burns Academy of Leadership at the University of Maryland from 2006 to 2009.

I am especially grateful to All Souls College, Oxford University, for the Visiting Fellowship that I enjoyed in 2009. The environment was intellectually stimulating and provided an invaluable source of ideas and insights. Conversations with Jim Adams, Vincent Crawford, Christopher Hood, Noel Malcolm, Angela McLean, George Molyneux, Avner Offer,

Hew Strachan, Keith Thomas, and Benjamin Wardhaugh were particularly helpful.

I also received great help and support from Kathe Sweeney, whose courage and vision over a number of years enabled this book to happen. Other staff at Jossey-Bass/Wiley have also been very helpful, including Amy Blanchard, Rob Brandt, Mary Garrett, Adrian Morgan, Erin Moy, Amy Packard, Dani Scoville, Liane Shayer, and Erik Thrasher.

Amid all this help, the most pointed and useful management lessons have come from my own family, Irene and Stephanie, and I am deeply grateful for their support.

ABOUT THE AUTHOR

Stephen Denning is the author of eight books, including *The Secret Language of Leadership: How Leaders Inspire Action Through Narrative*, which was selected by the *Financial Times* as one of the best books of 2007. *The Leader's Guide to Storytelling: Mastering the Art and Discipline of Business Narrative* was named in 2005 by the Innovation Network as one of the twelve most important books on innovation in the past several years. *Squirrel Inc.: A Fable of Leadership Through Storytelling* was published in 2004. He has also published *Storytelling in Organizations* (2004) and *The Springboard* (2000), as well as a novel and a volume of poetry.

Denning consults with organizations in the United States, Europe, Asia, and Australia on topics of leadership, management, innovation, and business narrative. He worked at the World Bank from 1969 to 2000, where he held various management positions, including program director of knowledge management from 1996 to 2000.

In 2000, he was named as one of the world's most admired knowledge leaders (by Teleos), and in 2003, he was ranked as one of the world's top two hundred business gurus by Tom Davenport and Larry Prusak in their book, *What's the Big Idea?*

Denning studied law and psychology at Sydney University in Australia and worked as a lawyer in Sydney for several years. He then earned a postgraduate degree in law at Oxford University.

In 2009, he was a visiting fellow at All Souls College, Oxford University.

Denning's Web site (http://www.stevedenning.com) has an extensive collection of materials on radical management, leadership, innovation, knowledge management, and business narrative.

INDEX

Page references followed by *fig* indicate a figure; by *t*, a table.

N

O

P